Marketing Essentials

Student Activity Workbook

Lois Schneider Farese

Grady Kimbrell

Carl A. Woloszyk, Ph.D.

Printed in the United States of America

Send all inquiries to:
Glencoe/McGraw-Hill
4400 Easton Commons
Columbus, OH 43219

ISBN 0-07-868915-5 (Student Edition)
ISBN 0-07-868916-3 (Teacher Annotated Edition)

9 10 11 12 13   WDQ   13 12 11 10

CONTENTS

CHAPTER 1 Marketing Is All Around Us

Vocabulary Review

DIRECTIONS: *Complete each sentence with one of the terms.*

customer relationship management	market	possession utility
	marketing	products
exchange	marketing concept	target market
form utility	marketing mix	time utility
information utility	place utility	

1. _marketing_ is the process of developing, promoting, and distributing products.

2. In marketing, _products_ offered for exchange can be either goods or services.

3. The idea that a business should strive to satisfy customers' needs and wants, while generating a profit for the firm is called the _marketing consepts_.

4. The purpose of _crm_ is to identify and understand customers so that a strong long-term relationship can exist.

5. A(n) _exchange_ occurs every time legal ownership of a product changes hands.

6. The four Ps of the _marketing mix_ are product, place, price, and promotion.

7. A convenience store that is open 24 hours a day creates _____.

8. Assembling parts to build an engine is adding value through _____.

9. Cooking instructions on packaging add value to food products by providing _info utility_.

10. Credit cards and installment plans increase _possession utility_ by making products more attainable for some customers.

11. A gas station located on a heavily traveled road is an example of _____.

12. All people who share similar needs and wants and who have the ability to purchase your products are called a(n) _market_.

13. The group for which a marketing program is designed is referred to as the _target market_

CHAPTER 1 Marketing Is All Around Us

Fact and Idea Review

DIRECTIONS: *In each series of terms, circle the one that does not belong. Then explain your choice on the line below.*

1. selling   financing   pricing   communications skills

_____

2. assemble   inform   persuade   remind

_____

3. lower prices   new products   higher prices   improved products

_____

4. time   possession   sales   information

_____

5. consumer   industrial   segmented   utility

_____

6. product   market   place   price

_____

7. credit cards   promotion   personal checks   layaway plans

_____

8. understanding business   interpersonal skills   economics   research

_____

9. displays   advertising   owner's manuals   charge accounts

_____

10. product   income   ethnic background   age

_____

CHAPTER 1 Marketing Is All Around Us

Marketing Application 1

DIRECTIONS: *Functions of Marketing* *For each of the examples noted below, write the function of marketing that it describes. Select from the following seven functions of marketing: distribution, financing, marketing information management, pricing, product/service management, promotion, and selling.*

Function

Example

_____

1. A retail store employee puts a pair of shoes on a customer and asks how they feel.

_____

2. A retailer decides to mark down all swimsuits in August.

_____

3. A team of workers approach customers in a mall to ask them their opinion about the upcoming political election and the candidates running for office.

_____

4. A television commercial stresses the benefits of buying a new protein bar.

_____

5. A company uses information from its sales records to reduce its product line by eliminating the products that did not sell well in the last two years.

_____

6. A small manufacturer applies for a bank loan in order to upgrade its computer network.

_____

7. A manufacturer of apparel signs a contract with a company that specializes in trucking and warehousing of imported goods.

DIRECTIONS: *Economic Utilities* *For each of the following examples, write the economic utility that it describes. Economic utilities include: form, place, possession, time, and information.*

_____

8. Adding aloe to hand soap.

_____

9. Offering installment credit in the sale of appliances.

_____

10. Including a link on a company Web site that explains how to return used laser printer ink cartridges.

_____

11. Offering overnight delivery of candy and fresh flowers on February 13.

_____

12. A company Web site offering the sale of its products directly to consumers.

CHAPTER 1 Marketing Is All Around Us

Marketing Application 2

DIRECTIONS: *Read the following scenario, keeping in mind the following key concepts: the four Ps of the marketing mix, industrial market, consumer market, customer profile, and market share. Below, note the details of this scenario related to each concept.*

Scenario: An apparel manufacturer makes garments for sports-related activities. A major portion of its business is selling sports-related garments to high schools, colleges, and professional sports teams. The other portion of its business focuses on young males and females who buy sports-related apparel for their personal use. These young adults are between the ages of 20 and 35 with household incomes of over $50,000. They are active and fashion-conscious. The garments are designed to be comfortable. They use fabrics that are currently in fashion and are priced a little higher than most competitors. The company has 40 percent of the athletic apparel market. Some of the reasons for its popularity are the use of professional athletes to endorse this brand and the extensive advertising done in broadcast and print media. Sports-related magazines like Sports Illustrated, Golf, Tennis, and Health & Fitness are used to promote the brand. Consumers can purchase these products in specialty sports shops and major department stores.

1. Four Ps of the Marketing Mix:

_____

_____

_____

_____

_____

2. Industrial Market

_____

_____

3. Consumer Market

_____

_____

4. Customer Profile

_____

_____

5. Market Share

_____

_____

CHAPTER **1** Marketing Is All Around Us

The DECA Connection

Role Play: Marketing Consultant

Situation: You are to assume the role of a marketing consultant. A craftsman (judge) is trying to decide if he wants to expand his business and invest in marketing activities. The craftsman has little formal business experience. He has been selling his wares in local craft shows for the past five years. He has hired you to advise him on the marketing functions involved with this possible expansion. His customer base includes a few people who have hired him to make unique crafts for their homes and as gifts. He also has a small database of customers who provided their e-mail address when they bought items at local craft shows. However, he has never used that database, nor has he ever advertised his goods and services.

Activity: Use your knowledge of marketing to explain the benefits of marketing, as well as how the functions of marketing can help him grow his business. You are to create an oral presentation with accompanying examples to present to the craftsman (judge).

Evaluation: You will be evaluated on how well you meet the following performance indicators:

- Distinguish between economic goods and services.
- Determine forms of economic utility created by marketing activities.
- Describe marketing functions and related activities.
- Describe current business trends.
- Explain the concept of marketing strategies.

DIRECTIONS: *Organize your thoughts around the performance indicators noted above. Use these performance indicators to jot down your ideas during the preparation period. Time your preparation to last 15 minutes and your role play presentation to last a maximum of ten minutes. After your role play, use the performance indicators to evaluate your efforts.*

_____

_____

_____

_____

_____

_____

_____

_____

_____

Assessment: Assume each performance indicator is worth 20 points (20 × 5 = 100 points). Use the evaluation levels listed below for judging consistency.

Excellent (16–20) Participant demonstrated the performance indicator in a professional manner, exceeds business standards.

Good (10–15) Participant demonstrated the performance indicator in an acceptable manner; meets minimal business standards; there would be no need for additional formalized training at this time.

Fair (4–9) Participant demonstrated the performance indicator with limited effectiveness; performance generally fell below minimal business standards; additional training would be required to improve knowledge, attitude, and/or skills.

Poor (0–3) Participant demonstrated the performance indicator with little effectiveness or not at all; a great deal of formal training would be needed.

Distinguish between economic goods and services. Score _____

_____

_____

_____

Determine forms of economic utility created by marketing activities. Score _____

_____

_____

_____

Describe marketing functions and related activities. Score _____

_____

_____

_____

Describe current business trends. Score _____

_____

_____

_____

Explain the concept of marketing strategies. Score _____

_____

_____

_____

CHAPTER *1* Marketing Is All Around Us

Software Activity (Optional)

Spreadsheet Application

OBJECTIVE: *To determine the effect of quantity produced on the cost of a product.*

ACTIVITY: Look at the shelves of a local retail store and think about the quantity of merchandise there. For most products, the higher the quantity produced, the lower the unit cost of the item. For example, a manufacturer usually gets a quantity discount by buying a larger supply of the materials needed to make a product. This discount means a lower production cost. The cost of actually making a product usually decreases as larger quantities are produced. In most cases, a certain number of employees and equipment are needed whether 1,000 or 10,000 items are produced.

The price a manufacturer can obtain for its product is determined by the market, so the lower the production cost, the higher the manufacturer's profit. For example, if a product costs $7 per unit when 10,000 are produced and $6 per unit when 20,000 are produced, the profit will be $1 more per unit for the production quantity of 20,000.

	A	B	C	D	E	F	G	H
1	Chapter 1 Marketing Is All Around Us							
2								
3								
4	# of Units	Price	Unit Cost	Profit				
5								
6	5,000	$9.00	$6.00	$3.00				
7	10,000	$9.00						
8	15,000	$9.00						
9	20,000	$9.00						
10	25,000	$9.00						
11	30,000	$9.00						
12	35,000	$9.00						
13	40,000	$9.00						

Continued on next page

Spreadsheet Directions

1. Turn on your computer and open your spreadsheet software program.

2. Create a spreadsheet like that on page 7 using your spreadsheet software program.

3. Assume that a product costs $6 to produce in a quantity of 5,000. For each additional thousand produced, the cost decreases by $0.10 up to 30,000 units. Thereafter, the cost increases again by $0.10. In column C of the spreadsheet, input the fixed unit cost for each level of production.

4. Enter a formula in cell D7 to determine the profit for each quantity produced.

5. Save your work on a floppy disk, the hard drive, or a network file.

6. Print out a copy of your work if your teacher has instructed you to do so. Then answer the questions that follow.

Interpreting Results

1. At which level of production will the manufacturer have the highest profit per unit?

_____

_____

2. At which level of production will the manufacturer have the lowest profit per unit?

_____

_____

_____

_____

_____

Drawing Conclusions

3. Why do you think a manufacturer's fixed cost of producing a product would not just continue to decrease as a larger quantity is produced, regardless of the amount?

_____

_____

_____

_____

_____

_____

CHAPTER 2 The Marketing Plan

Vocabulary Review

DIRECTIONS: *Match each definition with the correct term.*

demographics	geographics	psychographics
discretionary income	market segmentation	situation analysis
disposable income	marketing plan	SWOT analysis
environmental scan	marketing strategy	
executive summary	mass marketing	

_____ 1. Assessment tool used by organization to determine its strengths, weaknesses, opportunities, and threats.

_____ 2. Analysis of outside influences that impact an organization.

_____ 3. Dividing the total market into smaller groups of people who share specific needs and characteristics.

_____ 4. Money left after taking out taxes.

_____ 5. Study of the internal and external factors that impact a marketing plan.

_____ 6. Statistics that describe a population in terms of personal characteristics.

_____ 7. A written document that provides direction for the marketing activities of a company for a specified period of time.

_____ 8. Marketing mix decisions that focus on selected target markets.

_____ 9. Using a single marketing strategy to reach all customers.

_____ 10. A brief overview of the entire marketing plan.

_____ 11. Refers to segmentation of a market based on where people live.

_____ 12. Involves the study of consumers based on lifestyle, and the attitudes and values that shape it.

_____ 13. Money left after paying for basic living necessities, such as food, shelter, and clothing.

CHAPTER 2 The Marketing Plan

Fact and Idea Review

DIRECTIONS: *Circle the letter of the word or phrase that best completes the sentence or answers the question.*

1. When conducting a SWOT analysis, the internal aspect of the analysis is based on

    a. sales, advertising, and promotions.

    b. the company's strengths and weakness.

    c. political, economic, socio-cultural, and technological factors.

    d. market research findings.

2. To direct the marketing activities of a company, communicate its goals, objectives, and strategies, as well as monitor its performance you would

    a. conduct a SWOT analysis.   c. write a marketing plan.

    b. conduct an environmental analysis.   d. conduct marketing research.

3. What term is used to describe people born between 1946 and 1964?

    a. the baby boom generation   c. Generation Y

    b. Generation X   d. Generation Z

4. What do geographics, demographics, psychographics, and product benefits have in common?

    a. They are methods that can be used to segment a market.

    b. They are examples of mass-marketing approaches.

    c. They are terms used frequently in sales-oriented companies.

    d. They are unrelated to one another and therefore should not be used in combination to market a product.

5. The three phases of the marketing process are

    a. directing, controlling, and evaluating.

    b. planning, implementation, and control.

    c. segmenting a market, targeting a group, and promoting a product.

    d. analyzing, performing, and evaluating.

6. Segmenting the market based on product-related behavior involves looking at

    a. benefits desired, shopping patterns, and usage rates.

    b. personality and values.

    c. mass marketing opportunities.

    d. geographics and demographics.

CHAPTER 2 The Marketing Plan

Marketing Application 1

SWOT Analysis

DIRECTIONS: *A: SWOT Analysis   Use the information in the following paragraph to prepare a SWOT analysis for Futura Fashions, Inc. Futura Fashions Inc. is a hypothetical 100-store chain that caters to a teenage market. It carries male and female clothing and accessories.*

Sales at Futura Fashions have declined in recent months and its stock shares have dropped 30 percent. An analyst that follows the stock indicated that the stock's decline is due to a loss of talent in buying and merchandising. As a result, it has lost market share to its competitors. Competitors like American Eagle and Aeropostale have had increases in sales of 14 percent and 27 percent, respectively. A recent report in Women's Wear Daily, a trade publication, indicated that a clothing manufacturer is considering opening its own retail stores that will target teens. The teenage clothing market is difficult to evaluate. Trends are important. Either you catch them or your business suffers. So, Futura Fashions has recently hired an experienced fashion buyer and merchandise manager.

The economy is strong. Consumer confidence is up and so is consumer spending. Recent reports indicated a decrease in jobless claims and an increase in employment. However, inflation is increasing slowly, so the Federal Reserve has increased interest rates a quarter of one percent, which could make consumers less inclined to spend.

SWOT Analysis for Futura Fashions

Internal Strengths	Internal Weaknesses
External Opportunities	External Threats

Continued on next page

DIRECTIONS: B: *Use the information from the SWOT analysis to develop recommendations for Futura Fashions. What should it do to get back on track?*

_____

_____

_____

_____

_____

_____

_____

_____

_____

_____

_____

_____

_____

_____

_____

_____

_____

_____

_____

_____

_____

_____

_____

_____

_____

_____

Student		Date	
Class		Teacher	

CHAPTER 2 The Marketing Plan

Marketing Application 2

Market Segmentation

The Research and Development department of a fragrance company has been given the task of developing a new product line for a more price-conscious consumer. Below is a description of its current product line and its respective target markets. Your job is to develop a customer profile for the new target market and to recommend corresponding changes in the marketing mix.

Current Product Line The current product line targets men and women in the baby boom generation with household incomes that exceed $150,000 a year. The men's and women's lines include fragrances, hair and skin care products, soaps, and shower gels. Although packaged differently, the men's and women's price ranges are similar. Prices range from $45 to $100 for individual items and from $90 to $195 for gift sets. Psychographic characteristics of this target market include an active lifestyle, as well as a desire to be considered fashionable and chic. This fragrance is currently sold in upscale department stores located in large U.S. cities and affluent suburbs.

Customer Profile for New Target Market

Demographics:

Age: _____

_____

Income: _____

_____

Gender: _____

Other: _____

_____

Geographics: _____

_____

Psychographics:

Activities: _____

_____

Attitudes: _____

_____

Personality & Values _____

Behavioral: _____

_____

Continued on next page

Marketing Mix for New Product Line

Product Decisions:

1. What design features should the product's container have?

   _____

   _____

2. What special ingredients or capabilities should the product possess and why?

   _____

   _____

3. What would you name the product?

   _____

   _____

Place Decisions:

4. Where (type of retail store, Internet, catalog, etc.) should the new product line be sold and why?

   _____

   _____

Price Decisions:

5. Suggest a retail price range for the new product line.

   _____

   _____

6. Explain your choice, given the prices of competing products and your customer profile (income level, lifestyle, etc.).

   _____

   _____

Promotion Decisions:

7. In what media should your firm advertise the new product line and why?

   _____

   _____

8. What should be the main theme or slogan of such advertising?

   _____

   _____

Student	Date
Class	Teacher

CHAPTER 2 The Marketing Plan

The DECA Connection

Role Play: Marketing Intern

Situation: You are to assume the role of an intern in the marketing department of a clothing manufacturer. This manufacturer currently makes apparel for infants and toddlers. Now that the demographics are changing and the teenage market is growing, the company wants to begin making clothes for preteens and teens. Since you are the youngest person on staff, the marketing director (judge) has asked for your input.

Activity: You are to share your ideas with the marketing director (judge). Use your knowledge of marketing planning to create a written outline of all the information you would include in a formal marketing plan for this new clothing line. Also, provide examples of your suggestions.

Evaluation: You will be evaluated on how well you meet the following performance indicators:

- Explain the role of situational analysis in the marketing planning process.
- Identify fashion trends.
- Develop a marketing plan.
- Explain the concepts of market and market identification.
- Select a target market.

DIRECTIONS: *Organize your thoughts around the performance indicators noted above. Use these performance indicators to jot down your ideas during the preparation period. Time your preparation to last 15 minutes and your role play presentation to last a maximum of ten minutes. After your role play, use the performance indicators to evaluate your efforts.*

Assessment: Assume each performance indicator is worth 20 points (20 × 5 = 100 points). Use the evaluation levels listed below for judging consistency.

Excellent (16–20) Participant demonstrated the performance indicator in a professional manner, exceeds business standards.

Good (10–15) Participant demonstrated the performance indicator in an acceptable manner; meets minimal business standards; there would be no need for additional formalized training at this time.

Fair (4–9) Participant demonstrated the performance indicator with limited effectiveness; performance generally fell below minimal business standards; additional training would be required to improve knowledge, attitude, and/or skills.

Poor (0–3) Participant demonstrated the performance indicator with little effectiveness or not at all; a great deal of formal training would be needed.

Explain the role of situational analysis in the marketing planning process. Score _____

_____

_____

_____

Identify fashion trends. Score _____

_____

_____

_____

Develop a marketing plan. Score _____

_____

_____

_____

Explain the concepts of market and market identification. Score _____

_____

_____

_____

Select a target market. Score _____

_____

_____

_____

CHAPTER 2 The Marketing Plan

Software Activity (Optional)

Database Application

OBJECTIVE: *Develop a customer profile for a business.*

ACTIVITY: In order to be successful, businesses must focus on satisfying the needs and wants of their customers. Marketers must clearly define the type of customer they want to reach. Then they need to continuously monitor their customers to determine if they are reaching their target market. For this computer activity, imagine that you own a bakery and you want to develop a customer profile. You interview your customers and collect the demographic data recorded on the printout below.

- Gender (M or F)
- Age (A = Under 21, B = 21–35, C = 36–45, D = 46–55, E = Over 55)
- Zip code
- Income range (A = Under $35,000; B = $35,000-$65,000; C = Over $66,000)
- Family size

Customer	Gender of Respondent	Age of Respondent	Zip Code	Income Range	Family Size
1	F	B	02138	A	3
2	M	A	02143	A	2
3	F	B	02138	B	4
4	F	B	02143	B	2
5	F	E	02143	B	3
6	M	C	02140	C	1
7	M	D	02138	C	3
8	F	A	02138	A	3
9	F	B	02143	B	1
10	F	B	02140	C	3
11	F	B	02138	B	4
12	M	C	02138	B	4
13	F	D	02143	C	2
14	F	B	02138	B	3
15	F	D	02138	C	5
16	F	A	02139	A	1
17	F	B	02140	C	4
18	F	E	02143	B	2
19	M	B	02143	B	1
20	M	C	02138	A	5

Continued on next page

Database Directions

1. Turn on your computer and start your database software program.

2. Create a database like that on page 17 using database software.

3. Sort the data by each of the following categories—gender, age, zip code, income range, and family size. After each sort, save your work to a different file.

4. Print out a copy of your work if your teacher has instructed you to do so.

5. Answer the following questions.

Interpreting Results

1. What is the profile of your core customer based on the data you collected?

_____

_____

_____

_____

2. What can you learn from your customers' zip codes? As a marketer, how can you use this information?

_____

_____

_____

_____

_____

3. How does developing a customer profile benefit a marketer?

_____

_____

_____

_____

_____

Drawing Conclusions

4. Why is it important for marketers to monitor their customers periodically?

_____

_____

_____

_____

_____

CHAPTER 3 Political and Economic Analysis

Vocabulary Review

DIRECTIONS: *Match each definition with the correct term.*

business cycle	consumer price index	inflation
capital	economy	infrastructure
capitalism	employee productivity	privatization
command economy	gross domestic product	scarcity

_____ 1. The way a nation makes choices about how to use its resources.

_____ 2. Money needed to start and operate a business.

_____ 3. Measure of the change in price over a set period of time of some 400 specific goods and services used by the average urban household.

_____ 4. Difference between wants and needs on one hand and available resources on the other hand.

_____ 5. In this type of economy, the government answers three basic economic questions: what, how, and for whom?

_____ 6. A measure of the goods and services produced using labor and property located in the United States.

_____ 7. Refers to rising prices.

_____ 8. Refers to a country's physical development—the state of its roads, ports, sanitation facilities, and utilities.

_____ 9. Economic system characterized by private ownership of businesses and marketplace competition.

_____ 10. Measure of output divided by input of worker hours.

_____ 11. Stages an economy goes through due to recurring slowdown and growth.

_____ 12. The process of selling government-owned businesses to private individuals.

CHAPTER 3 Political and Economic Analysis

Fact and Idea Review

DIRECTIONS: *Unless otherwise noted, circle the letter of the word or phrase that best completes each of the following sentences. In the sentences that tell you to select all that apply, you may circle more than one response.*

1. The factors of production include (circle all that apply)

   a. land   b. labor   c. capital   d. entrepreneurship

2. In socialist countries, the government (circle all that apply)

   a. tries to reduce the differences between rich and poor.

   b. provides social services to ensure a certain standard of living for everyone.

   c. provides free medical care for everyone.

   d. keeps taxes low for individuals and businesses.

3. Low unemployment, an increase in the output of goods and services, and high consumer spending best illustrates the _____ period of the business cycle.

   a. expansion   b. recession   c. trough   d. peak

4. The government answers all three economic questions in a

   a. mixed economy.   c. command economy that follows a communist model.

   b. market economy.   d. command economy that follows a socialist model.

5. When the economy is slowing down and needs a boost, the government may do the following (circle all that apply)

   a. raise taxes   b. lower taxes   c. increase interest rates   d. lower interest rates

6. A country's standard of living (circle all that apply)

   a. is a measurement of the amount of goods and services that nation's people have.

   b. is a measurement that reflects the quality of life of a nation's people.

   c. can be calculated by dividing the GDP or GNP of a country by its population.

   d. can be analyzed by reviewing free social services and number of households per 1,000 inhabitants with durable goods such as refrigerators and washing machines.

7. Productivity (output per worker hour) of a bicycle manufacturing plant with 600 employees who work 40 hours a week for 50 weeks of the year and produce 2,400,000 bicycles during the year is

   a. 1   b. 2   c. 10   d. 20

8. All of the following countries are socialist with market economies, except

   a. Canada.   b. Sweden.   c. Cuba.   d. Germany.

CHAPTER **3** Political and Economic Analysis

Marketing Application 1

DIRECTIONS: *Read the information taken from the Central Intelligence Agency's World Factbook on North Korea and South Korea. Then answer the questions that follow.*

North Korea is one of the world's most centrally planned and isolated economies. It is one of the few countries in the world with a communist political system. The nation has suffered its tenth year of food shortages because of a lack of arable land, collective farming, weather-related problems, and chronic shortages of fertilizer and fuel. Even with international food aid, the population still suffers from malnutrition and poor living conditions. Large-scale military spending eats up resources needed for investment and civilian consumption. In 2003, heightened political tensions with key donor countries and general donor fatigue threatened the flow of desperately need food aid and fuel aid as well. Since the regime relaxed restrictions on farmers' economic activities in spring 2003, there has been an expansion of market activity.

South Korea has grown into a high-tech modern world economy and has made a commitment to democracy. Its GDP per capita is 18 times that of North Korea. Its success was achieved by a system of close government/business ties, including directed credit, import restrictions, sponsorship of specific industries, and a strong labor effort. The government promoted the import of raw materials and technology at the expense of consumer goods and encouraged savings and investment over consumption. Led by consumer spending and exports, economic growth in 2002 was an impressive 6.2 percent, despite anemic global growth, followed by moderate 2.8 percent growth in 2003. In 2003 the National Assembly approved legislation reducing the six-day work week to five days.

1. How do the political systems of North Korea and South Korea differ?

_____

_____

_____

_____

_____

_____

_____

_____

_____

_____

_____

Continued on next page

2. How would you categorize North Korea's and South Korea's economic systems? Explain.

_____

_____

_____

_____

_____

_____

_____

3. Why does North Korea need food aid?

_____

_____

_____

_____

_____

_____

_____

4. Why do you think South Korea's GDP per capita is 18 times that of North Korea?

_____

_____

_____

_____

_____

_____

_____

_____

CHAPTER 3 Political and Economic Analysis

Marketing Application 2

DIRECTIONS: *Read the article below. Then answer the questions that follow.*

Despite their jitters, consumers are on track to increase their spending at an annual rate of about 3.5 percent in the third quarter. Second, companies may not be hiring in droves, but they are adding to their payrolls and going ahead with capital-spending projects. Business investment in new equipment accounted for more than a third of the growth in real gross domestic product in the second quarter. Lastly, the Fed sounded a bit more upbeat about the economy after its Sept. 21 meeting than it did in August. As expected, policymakers hiked the federal funds rate by a quarter-point, to 1.75%. In its announcement, the Fed said the economy "appears to have regained some traction" and that labor markets have improved modestly, while inflation has eased. Uncertainty has been the hallmark of this recovery. Over the past three years, demand has been buffeted by a host of unknowns, from terrorism to corporate scandals to war. One area where consumers feel no jitters is housing. Americans still see home ownership as one of the best investments around. Low interest rates also suggest that worries about consumer debt levels are overblown. What the economy needs most are the conditions in which businesses and consumers feel more secure about making the investment and spending decisions that will drive this recovery into 2005.

(*Source: From BusinessWeek, October 4, 2004, "What's Everyone So Rattled About?" by James C. Cooper and Kathleen Madigan*)

1. Which goals of an economy are addressed in this article? Explain your answer.

_____

_____

_____

_____

_____

_____

2. How are consumer spending and business investments related to growth in the gross domestic product?

_____

_____

_____

_____

_____

_____

Continued on next page

3. Analysts predicted that the Fed was going to continue to increase the federal funds by another quarter-point in the following year. Why would the Federal Reserve Board do so?

_____

_____

_____

_____

_____

_____

4. What factors suggest that the United States was in a period of economic recovery when the article was written?

_____

_____

_____

_____

_____

_____

_____

5. Why do you think home ownership was considered one of the best investments around?

_____

_____

_____

_____

_____

_____

_____

_____

_____

_____

CHAPTER 3 Political and Economic Analysis

The DECA Connection

Role Play: Drugstore Employee

Situation: You are to assume the role of an employee in a drugstore. The government recently passed legislation that involves a special prescription drug program for Medicare recipients. The program requires enrollment and selection of a discount drug card that best suits the individual. Since your pharmacy is participating in this government sponsored plan, you have been responsible for disseminating information to interested customers. In that process you have been telling potential enrollees that they may be able to save money on brand name drugs and even more money on generic drugs. However, there is a $30 annual fee for the drug discount card.

Activity. You (participant) must handle an irate customer (judge) who is upset that the government does not provide all elderly people with prescription drugs for free, as you may find in many socialist countries.

Evaluation: You will be evaluated on how well you meet the following performance indicators:

- Explain the concept of economic resources.
- Determine the relationship between government and business.
- Describe the nature of current economic problems.
- Explain the types of economic systems.
- Show empathy for others.

DIRECTIONS: *Organize your thoughts around the performance indicators noted above. Use these performance indicators to jot down your ideas during the preparation period. Time your preparation to last 15 minutes and your role play presentation to last a maximum of ten minutes. After your role play, use the performance indicators to evaluate your efforts.*

_____

_____

_____

_____

_____

_____

_____

_____

Assessment: Assume each performance indicator is worth 20 points (20 × 5 = 100 points). Use the evaluation levels listed below for judging consistency.

Excellent   (16–20)   Participant demonstrated the performance indicator in a professional manner, exceeds business standards.

Good   (10–15)   Participant demonstrated the performance indicator in an acceptable manner; meets minimal business standards; there would be no need for additional formalized training at this time.

Fair   (4–9)   Participant demonstrated the performance indicator with limited effectiveness; performance generally fell below minimal business standards; additional training would be required to improve knowledge, attitude, and/or skills.

Poor   (0–3)   Participant demonstrated the performance indicator with little effectiveness or not at all; a great deal of formal training would be needed.

Explain the concept of economic resources.   Score _____

_____

_____

_____

Determine the relationship between government and business.   Score _____

_____

_____

_____

Describe the nature of current economic problems.   Score _____

_____

_____

_____

Explain the types of economic systems.   Score _____

_____

_____

_____

Show empathy for others.   Score _____

_____

_____

_____

Student		Date
Class		Instructor

CHAPTER 3 Political and Economic Analysis

Software Activity (Optional)

Spreadsheet Application

OBJECTIVE: *To calculate worker productivity for different plants to determine plant efficiency.*

ACTIVITY: Increases in productivity help a company to maintain or increase its profit while keeping its prices competitive. The Dorris Company has three plants that make plastics used in the manufacture of other products. The company wants to know which plant has the highest productivity. The number of workers, the hours worked, and the output for each plant are shown in the printout below.

	A	B	C	D	E	F	G
1	Chapter 3 Political and Economic Analysis						
2							
3							
4					Annual	Annual	Units Produced
5	Plant	Workers	Hours	Weeks	Hours	Output	Per Hour
6							
7	A	800	40	52		2,000,000	
8	B	700	40	52		2,600,000	
9	C	900	40	52		1,800,000	

Spreadsheet Directions

1. Turn on your computer and open your spreadsheet software program.

2. Create a spreadsheet like the one above using your spreadsheet application.

3. Create a formula for cell E7 to calculate the annual productivity for each plant by multiplying the number of workers by the hours in each week and the total weeks in a year. Copy the formula to cells E8 and E9. To complete the calculation, create a formula for cell G7 to divide the annual output by the total productivity to find the average productivity per worker. Copy the formula to the remaining rows.

4. After completing your calculations, save your work. Print out a copy of your work if your teacher has instructed you to do so. Then answer the questions that follow.

Continued on next page

Interpreting Results

1. Which plant has the highest productivity? The lowest?

_____

_____

_____

_____

2. Why is worker productivity important to a manufacturing company?

_____

_____

_____

_____

_____

_____

_____

_____

Drawing Conclusions

3. Plant C is an older plant that uses old technology in its production processes, and the company is considering replacing this plant with a new, fully automated plant in a new location. Aside from the benefit of higher productivity for the company, what are the problems or benefits for the workers and the community when a company closes an old plant?

_____

_____

_____

_____

_____

_____

CHAPTER 4 Global Analysis

Vocabulary Review

DIRECTIONS: *Match each definition with the correct term.*

absolute advantage	European Union	protectionism
balance of trade	exports	quota
comparative advantage	foreign direct	tariff
contract manufacturing	investment	World Trade
customization	imports	Organization (WTO)
embargo	NAFTA	

_____ 1. Goods and services sold to other countries.

_____ 2. Establishment of a business in a foreign country.

_____ 3. A total ban on specific goods coming into and leaving a country.

_____ 4. This allows a nation to gain by selling goods it produces more efficiently than other goods.

_____ 5. Creating special products or promotions for certain countries or regions.

_____ 6. A tax on imports.

_____ 7. A global coalition of 135 governments that makes the rules governing international trade, established by the GATT.

_____ 8. Difference in value between a nation's exports and imports.

_____ 9. This lets a nation produce a given commodity at a lower cost than any other nation in the world.

_____ 10. Goods and services purchased from other countries.

_____ 11. This limits either the quantity or monetary value of a product that may be imported.

_____ 12. An international trade agreement among the United States, Canada, and Mexico.

_____ 13. Europe's trading bloc, established by the Maastricht Treaty.

_____ 14. Government policy that restricts imports to protect domestic industries.

_____ 15. Hiring a foreign manufacturer to make your products according to your specifications.

CHAPTER 4 Global Analysis

Fact and Idea Review

DIRECTIONS: *Circle the letter of the word or phrase that best completes each of the following sentences.*

1. Because different countries possess unique resources and capabilities, they
   a. practice protectionism.
   c. are self-sufficient.
   b. are independent of one another.
   d. are economically interdependent.

2. Consumers, producers, workers, and nations as a whole
   a. get hurt economically when their country takes part in international trade.
   b. benefit from international trade.
   c. do not want foreign investment in their countries.
   d. do not encourage trade with neighboring countries.

3. At present, the U.S. balance of trade can best be described as a
   a. trade equilibrium.
   c. positive balance of trade.
   b. trade surplus.
   d. negative balance of trade.

4. GATT, NAFTA, and the EU are examples of
   a. trade barriers imposed on nations.
   b. trade agreements and alliances.
   c. agencies that provide financial and advisory support to businesses that want to engage in foreign trade.
   d. free-trade zones.

5. Licensed specialists who know the applicable laws, procedures, and tariffs governing imports are called
   a. maritime brokers.
   c. freight forwarders.
   b. customs brokers.
   d. foreign importing brokers.

6. Partnerships made when direct investment in a foreign country occurs with a domestic partner are called
   a. multinationals.
   c. joint ventures.
   b. mini-nationals.
   d. cooperatives.

7. When planning a marketing strategy for the sale of a product in a foreign country, businesses that do not change anything about their product or their promotions are said to be practicing a
   a. globalization strategy.
   c. product adaptation strategy.
   b. customization strategy.
   d. promotion adaptation strategy.

CHAPTER 4 Global Analysis

Marketing Application 1

DIRECTIONS: Read the article below. Then answer the questions that follow.

It's a challenge to persuade a population to adopt novel food tastes, but this PepsiCo subsidiary [Frito-Lay] is making a go of it. Frito-Lay sells chips with such flavoring as "crispy, fragrant French chicken wings" and "fresh, crispy seafood." The goal by 2007: make Lay's the number one snack in the world's most crowded country.

Lay's potato chips didn't show up [in China] until 1997 because China bans potato imports, forcing Frito-Lay to start, quite literally, from the ground up, opening two farms to supply big, round, sturdy potatoes short on sugar (to preserve whiteness). Three years after planting its first spud in China, Lay's launched its first entry—"salty flavored"—and saw an instant hit. But in China Lay's quickly found that dishes popular in one region didn't sell as well in others. Shanghai snackers tend to like sweet tastes, southerners prefer salty, westerners go for spicy flavors and northerners prefer meaty ones, forcing Lay's to adjust its marketing.

Pepsi also had to accommodate yin and yang, the Chinese philosophy that nature and life need to balance opposing elements (like light and dark or sweet and sour). It plays out in the local palate: Chinese consider fried foods to be hot and therefore shun them in the summer because the two hots don't balance; cool would be better.

That discovery last year led to Frito-Lay's most creative effort in China so far: "cool lemon" potato chips. The yellow, strongly lemon-scented chips are dotted with greenish lime specks and mint and are sold in a package featuring images of breezy blue skies and rolling green grass. Lay's launched them with a TV ad featuring Malaysian pop star Angelica Lee, who asks fans in a stadium: "Can you eat just one?" The campaign triggered a spike in sales last summer. (China is a particularly good market for TV ads, given that it has 126 TV sets for every 100 households and still offers relatively few channels, making it harder to zap away from a barrage of commercials.)

Source: From Forbes.com, "China Is a Big Prize," May 10, 2004, by Russell Flannery.

1. What political/legal factor affected the launch of Frito Lay potato chips in China?

_____

_____

_____

2. What two cultural factors influenced the variety of Chinese Lay's potato chip flavors?

_____

_____

_____

_____

_____

Continued on next page

3. How would you classify Frito-Lay's marketing strategy of its Lay's potato chips in China—was it globalization, adaptation, or customization? Explain.

_____

_____

_____

_____

_____

_____

4. Why is China's entry into the WTO important for multinational companies, like PepsiCo?

_____

_____

_____

_____

_____

_____

_____

5. Why do you think PepsiCo's direct foreign investment was largely in joint ventures?

_____

_____

_____

_____

_____

_____

_____

6. What factor helped Frito-Lay to decide on TV as a medium for its promotional message?

_____

_____

_____

_____

_____

_____

CHAPTER 4 Global Analysis

Marketing Application 2

DIRECTIONS: *Test your cultural sensitivity by selecting the one answer that best completes the following statements or answers the questions posed in this cultural quiz.*

1. The country where you will find only beefless McDonald's hamburgers is
   a. China.
   b. Singapore.
   c. India.
   d. New Zealand.

2. You would most likely find Campbell's Watercress & Duck Gizzard Soup in
   a. China.
   b. Canada.
   c. France.
   d. Australia.

3. In which country does the law prohibit men from wearing neck jewelry?
   a. India
   b. Singapore
   c. Saudi Arabia
   d. France

4. If you give a gift in Sri Lanka, it is proper to
   a. use the right hand only.
   b. use the left hand only.
   c. use both hands.
   d. place it on their doorstep.

5. When Italians place a finger under the eye and push down slightly on the skin, it means they
   a. had a bad day.
   b. love you.
   c. need help.
   d. think someone's remarks are smart and clever.

6. Brazilians find it offensive when people speak to them in
   a. French.
   b. Italian.
   c. Portuguese.
   d. Spanish.

7. Business gift giving is important in all the following countries except:
   a. Japan
   b. South Korea
   c. Singapore
   d. Australia

8. In Mexico and Brazil, it would be considered offensive to use
   a. the American okay hand signal.
   b. the thumbs down signal.
   c. the thumbs up signal.
   d. the peace hand signal.

Continued on next page

9. In Germany, business etiquette suggests that you

   a. address business associates by their first names.

   b. shake hands with all members of a group all at once, crossing over each other.

   c. address business associates by their academic titles and surnames.

   d. conduct business meetings informally.

10. In Japan and Thailand, you do not

    a. bow when greeting business associates.

    b. sit in a way that shows the soles of your shoes.

    c. have to be on time for a business meeting.

    d. shake hands with business associates.

11. In France it is considered tacky to

    a. cross your legs when sitting down.

    b. arrive a few minutes to a social event.

    c. chew gum in public.

    d. drink wine with lunch.

12. In Portugal, pinching the ear lobe and shaking it gently while raising the eyebrows means

    a. you are angry.

    b. something is funny.

    c. something is really good.

    d. you are confused.

13. In Singapore, the Salaam, a traditional greeting is

    a. a simple handshake.

    b. palms slide together and placed on the heart.

    c. a bow.

    d. slapping hands together.

14. Which of the following numbers should not be used by marketers in Japan for product packaging, in hotel or hospital floor numbering, or even for seats on airplanes because their translations represent death and agony or suffering?

    a. 2 and 5   c. 4 and 9

    b. 3 and 6   d. 7 and 11

15. In which country should you not be offended if a business associate arrives 40 minutes late for a meeting?

    a. Argentina

    b. Germany

    c. Japan

    d. Canada

CHAPTER 4 Global Analysis

The DECA Connection

Role Play: International Trade Consultant

Situation: You are to assume the role of an international trade consultant in the marketing department of D&J Soft Drink Company. Your company would like to start selling its products in Asian countries. The United States has signed a trade agreement with Vietnam and China, as well as lifted some sanctions against North Korea. As soon as those sanctions were lifted, Coca-Cola began selling its soft drinks in North Korea, one of the few nations in the world where Coca-Cola was not being sold. Your company currently has soft drink products distributed in Europe and South America. One thing your company learned in Europe was that men would not buy diet cola because diet drinks are often perceived as feminine. Since the three nations (Vietnam, China, and North Korea) have recently opened their doors to U.S. products, your supervisor (judge) wants you to evaluate each country as a potential market for one for your company's products, then recommend a nation to be your company's first Asian market. Any economic, political, or social issues that need to be addressed should be considered along with possible solutions to any obstacles that may be apparent from your research. Cultural sensitivity is a must. Suggest marketing ideas that would help make the product launch successful in your recommended country.

Activity: Based on what you know about Asian cultures and the economies of the three nations under study, make your recommendation of which country's market to penetrate first. Prepare a memo to your supervisor (judge) that details your recommendation, rationale, and ideas for a product name, as well as marketing solutions to the competition you will face in that country from major soft drink brands, like Coca-Cola. Also address the cultural factors that must be taken into consideration when promoting, distributing, and pricing your products.

Evaluation: You will be evaluated on how well you meet the following performance indicators:

- Explain the nature of international trade.
- Identify the impact of cultural and social environments on world trade.
- Describe the nature of current economic problems.
- Evaluate influences on a nation's ability to trade.
- Develop cultural sensitivity.

DIRECTIONS: *Organize your thoughts around the performance indicators noted above. Use these performance indicators to write the memo during the preparation period. Time your preparation period to last 20 minutes and your presentation of the memo to last a maximum of five minutes, including time for follow-up questions. After your presentation, use the performance indicators to evaluate your efforts.*

_____

_____

_____

_____

Continued on next page

Assessment: Assume each performance indicator is worth 20 points (20 × 5 = 100 points). Use the evaluation levels listed below for judging consistency.

Excellent (16–20) Participant demonstrated the performance indicator in a professional manner, exceeds business standards.

Good (10–15) Participant demonstrated the performance indicator in an acceptable manner; meets minimal business standards; there would be no need for additional formalized training at this time.

Fair (4–9) Participant demonstrated the performance indicator with limited effectiveness; performance generally fell below minimal business standards; additional training would be required to improve knowledge, attitude, and/or skills.

Poor (0–3) Participant demonstrated the performance indicator with little effectiveness or not at all; a great deal of formal training would be needed.

Explain the nature of international trade. Score _____

_____

_____

_____

Identify the impact of cultural and social environments on world trade. Score _____

_____

_____

_____

Describe the nature of current economic problems. Score _____

_____

_____

_____

Evaluate influences on a nation's ability to trade. Score _____

_____

_____

_____

Develop cultural sensitivity. Score _____

_____

_____

_____

CHAPTER 4 Global Analysis

Software Activity (Optional)

Spreadsheet Application

OBJECTIVE: *To calculate the balance of trade between countries.*

ACTIVITY: In today's global marketplace, businesses must be aware of the balance of trade between countries—the difference between what a country exports and imports. A positive balance of trade occurs when a nation exports more than it imports; it has a trade surplus. A negative balance of trade occurs when a nation imports more than it exports; it has a trade deficit.

In this computer activity, you will determine whether a trade surplus or a trade deficit exists between the United States and each country listed in the spreadsheet below. To do this, you will calculate the total exports and imports and determine the balance of trade that exists between the United States and all of these countries. The spreadsheet shows the amount of exports and imports by the United States in billions of dollars for 12 countries.

	A	B	C	D	E	F	G
1	**Chapter 4 Global Analysis**						
2							
3	Country	U.S. Imports	U.S. Exports	Trade			
4	(Imports from/Exports to)	in Billions	in Billions	Surplus			
5		of Dollars	of Dollars	or Deficit			
6							
7	Austria	32.4	38.9				
8	Belgium	100.0	98.5				
9	Canada	116.2	114.0				
10	Denmark	28.0	26.6				
11	France	172.8	190.6				
12	Italy	149.2	162.3				
13	Japan	275.2	210.8				
14	Netherlands	107.8	104.2				
15	Spain	44.4	71.5				
16	Sweden	51.5	48.9				
17	Switzerland	51.5	58.2				
18	United Kingdom	152.6	197.6				
19	Totals						

Continued on next page

Spreadsheet Directions

1. Turn on your computer and open your spreadsheet software program.

2. Create a spreadsheet like the one on page 37 using your spreadsheet application.

3. Enter a formula to calculate the trade deficit or surplus between the United States and each of the selected countries. Copy the formula to appropriate cells in all remaining rows.

4. Enter formulas to calculate the total imports, exports, and balance of trade for the countries listed.

5. After completing all your calculations, save your work.

6. Print out a copy of your work if your teacher has instructed you to do so.

7. Answer the questions that follow.

Interpreting Results

1. Does the United States have a total trade surplus or a trade deficit with the countries listed? What is the amount?

_____

_____

2. List the countries with which the United States has a trade surplus.

_____

_____

_____

3. List the countries with which the United States has a trade deficit.

_____

_____

_____

Drawing Conclusions

4. What are some effects of a negative balance of trade on a nation's economy?

_____

_____

_____

_____

_____

_____

CHAPTER 5 The Free Enterprise System

Vocabulary Review

DIRECTIONS: *Match each definition with the correct term.*

business risk	global business	private sector
competition	monopoly	profit
demand	nonprice competition	public sector
domestic business	nonprofit organization	supply
equilibrium	patent	
free enterprise system	price competition	

_____ 1. In theory, this encourages individuals to start and operate their own businesses without government involvement.

_____ 2. Exclusive control over a product or the means of producing it.

_____ 3. Refers to consumer willingness and ability to buy products.

_____ 4. State that exists when the amount of product supplied is equal to the amount of product demanded.

_____ 5. Struggle between companies for customers.

_____ 6. Money earned from conducting business after all costs and expenses have been paid.

_____ 7. The property rights to an item or idea.

_____ 8. Amount of goods producers are willing to make and sell.

_____ 9. Competition that focuses on factors that are not related to price.

_____ 10. Potential for loss or failure in relation to the potential for improved earnings.

_____ 11. Competition that focuses on the sale price of a product.

_____ 12. Businesses not associated with government agencies.

_____ 13. Firm that sells its products in more than one country.

_____ 14. Functions like a business but uses the money it makes to fund the cause identified in its charter.

_____ 15. Firm that limits its scope of operation to one country.

_____ 16. Government-financed agencies.

CHAPTER **5** The Free Enterprise System

Fact and Idea Review

DIRECTIONS: *Unless otherwise noted, circle the letter of the word or phrase that best completes each of the following sentences. In the sentences that tell you to select all that apply, you may circle more than one response.*

1. Economic benefits of profitable businesses include (select all that apply)

   a. The value of a company's stock goes down.

   b. Government makes more money from taxation of the companies and their employees.

   c. Profitable companies attract competition.

   d. Profitable businesses can cut back on research and development.

2. Four main functions of an organization's operation are

   a. production, marketing, management, and finance.

   b. accounting, production, promotion, and sales.

   c. management, accounting, finance, and advertising.

   d. marketing, management, accounting, and finance.

3. The five rights of merchandising (select all that apply)

   a. are having the right goods, in the right amount, at the right price, in the right place, and at the right time.

   b. are often in a SWOT analysis for wholesalers and retailers.

   c. are used by manufacturers to determine what new products to develop.

   d. involve evaluating the rights of consumers in relation to marketing goods.

4. When evaluating the production function during a SWOT analysis, you would look for (record all that apply)

   a. innovation.   c. efficiency.

   b. speed to marketing.   d. level of success with products.

5. Demand for consumer goods and their respective consumer trends

   a. create derived demand in the industrial market.

   b. are not related to demand in the industrial market.

   c. are only useful to businesses in the consumer market.

   d. create problems with suppliers in the industrial market.

CHAPTER 5 The Free Enterprise System

Marketing Application 1

DIRECTIONS: *Read the text below. Then answer the questions that follow.*

Competition the Old Fashioned Way

An 80-year-old tool company, Snap-On Tools has succeeded because of a unique and extremely effective way of doing business.

Snap-On Tools makes and sells tools and equipment for the automotive industry. Rather than sell through traditional retail stores, Snap-On's franchisees sell out of big white trucks emblazoned with the red Snap-On logo. Each truck is fully stocked with tools and equipment, a fully mobile retail establishment. Each franchise owner drives to service stations, car dealerships, independent garages, and other places where car enthusiasts work. The franchise owner takes the store to them, building a strong relationship with his customers.

Although Snap-On's tools are generally more expensive than their competitors', Snap-On wins loyal customers by offering high-quality tools and unparalleled customer service. Besides the freedom of being able to shop at work, Snap-On customers can receive interest-free credit on many sales and interest-bearing loans for expensive equipment. In addition, the company, which prides itself on its service and vision, continues to increase its product line to meet the needs of its customers. The company has moved beyond wrenches to products such as computerized diagnostic systems.

1. How would you describe Snap-on Tools' competitive strategy—does it fit a price or nonprice model? Explain.

_____

_____

_____

2. Is there any risk for the franchised dealers who must purchase the truck, tools, and equipment from Snap-on? Explain your answer.

_____

_____

_____

3. How are the free enterprise "freedoms" of ownership and profit depicted in this article on Snap-on Tools?

_____

_____

CHAPTER 5 The Free Enterprise System

Marketing Application 2

DIRECTIONS: *Study the supply and demand schedule below. Use it to draw supply and demand curves on the grid. (Be sure to label the two curves.) Then answer the questions that follow.*

Supply and Demand Schedule for Backpacks

Price	Number Demanded	Number Supplied	Surplus or Shortage
$20	2,000	500	_____
25	1,600	1,200	_____
30	1,400	1,400	_____
35	1,200	1,600	_____
40	1,000	1,800	_____
45	750	2,000	_____

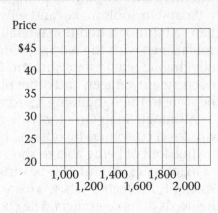

1a. At what point on the graph do the supply and demand curves meet? (Specify both price and number of units.)

_____

1b. What is the name given to this point?

_____

2. What is the significance of this point for buyers and sellers?

_____

_____

3a. What happens to demand when prices go down?

_____

3b. What happens to demand when prices go up?

_____

4. Complete the final column of the supply and demand schedule provided above. Fill in the difference between the amount supplied and the amount demanded. Indicate whether each entry is a surplus or a shortage by using a plus or minus sign, respectively.

5. Indicate on the graph which area represents surplus and which represents shortage. Code these, using different colors or patterns.

CHAPTER 5 The Free Enterprise System

The DECA Connection

Role Play: E-Commerce Security Consultant

Situation: You are to assume the role of employee of a specialty retail establishment. Your employer (judge) is the owner of the business, which sells unique gift packages of fruits, nuts, candies, coffees, teas, and cheeses. Your employer has noticed a decline in online sales. After spending a lot of money for the design and maintenance of the company's Web site, your employer is concerned. Recent newspaper reports indicated hackers were stealing credit card numbers from cyberspace. You know most browsers come with a scrambling feature, which makes it virtually impossible to intercept a credit card number. However, when hacking attempts are made, most businesses ask their customers to cancel their credit cards as a precaution. This inconvenience causes customers to reassess online shopping. Even with these problems, all your employer's competitors have Web sites for online shopping.

Activity: Since you have direct contact with online customers, your employer (judge) wants your input on whether or not to keep the online business. What risks are involved? What can be done to correct this problem?

Evaluation: You will be evaluated on how well you meet the following performance indicators:

- Explain the nature of risk management.
- Identify ways that technology impacts business.
- Explain key factors in building a clientele.
- Demonstrate problem-solving skills.
- Explain routine security precautions.

DIRECTIONS: *Organize your thoughts around the performance indicators noted above. Use these performance indicators to jot down your ideas during the preparation period. Time your preparation period to last 15 minutes and your role play presentation to last a maximum of ten minutes. After your role play, use the performance indicators to evaluate your efforts.*

_____

_____

_____

_____

_____

_____

_____

Continued on next page

Assessment: Assume each performance indicator is worth 20 points (20 × 5 = 100 points). Use the evaluation levels listed below for judging consistency.

Excellent   (16–20)   Participant demonstrated the performance indicator in a professional manner, exceeds business standards.

Good   (10–15)   Participant demonstrated the performance indicator in an acceptable manner; meets minimal business standards; there would be no need for additional formalized training at this time.

Fair   (4–9)   Participant demonstrated the performance indicator with limited effectiveness; performance generally fell below minimal business standards; additional training would be required to improve knowledge, attitude, and/or skills.

Poor   (0–3)   Participant demonstrated the performance indicator with little effectiveness or not at all; a great deal of formal training would be needed.

Explain the nature of risk management.   Score _____

_____

_____

_____

Identify ways that technology impacts business.   Score _____

_____

_____

_____

Explain key factors in building a clientele.   Score _____

_____

_____

_____

Demonstrate problem-solving skills.   Score _____

_____

_____

_____

Explain routine security precautions.   Score _____

_____

_____

_____

CHAPTER **5** The Free Enterprise System

Spreadsheet Application

OBJECTIVE: *To illustrate how supply and demand determines price.*

ACTIVITY: In a market economy, it is important for managers to understand the relationship between supply and demand. Demand refers to the amount of goods or services that consumers are willing to buy at certain prices; supply refers to the amount of goods or services that producers are willing to make and sell at certain prices. Although consumers will be willing to purchase the most at a low price, producers will be willing to supply the most at a high price. Consumers want low prices, while producers want high prices for their products.

In this computer activity, you will create a graph to illustrate the supply and demand curves for a product. Look at the printout below, which shows the supply and demand for a product at ten different retail prices. Notice that as the price increases, the quantity supplied increases, but the quantity demanded decreases.

	A	B	C
1	Chapter 5 The Free Enterprise System		
2			
3	**Retail Price**	**Quantity Supplied**	**Quantity Demanded**
4	$0.10	10	100
5	$0.20	20	80
6	$0.30	30	75
7	$0.40	50	65
8	$0.50	60	60
9	$0.60	70	50
10	$0.70	80	40
11	$0.80	90	30
12	$0.90	100	20
13	$1.00	120	5

Continued on next page

Spreadsheet Directions

1. Turn on your computer and open your spreadsheet software program.

2. Create a spreadsheet like that on page 45 using spreadsheet software program.

3. Follow the instructions for your software to create a scatter graph of the data. A graph in which two lines cross should be the result.

4. After completing your graph, save your work to a new file.

5. Print out a copy of your work if your teacher has instructed you to do so. Then answer the questions that follow.

Interpreting Results

1. On the graph that you have created, what is the equilibrium price for the product?

_____

2. Explain what the equilibrium price means to a marketer.

_____

_____

_____

_____

Drawing Conclusions

3. If the supplier established a retail price of $1.40 instead of using the equilibrium price, what would probably happen?

_____

_____

_____

_____

4. If the supplier established a retail price of 40 cents instead of using the equilibrium price, what would probably happen?

_____

_____

_____

_____

CHAPTER 6 Legal and Ethical Issues

Vocabulary Review

DEFINITIONS: *Match each definition with the correct term.*

Ad Council	ethics	Occupational Safety & Health Administration (OSHA)
Better Business Bureau (BBB)	Federal Trade Commission (FTC)	
consumerism	flextime	price gouging
Environmental Protection Agency (EPA)	Food and Drug Administration (FDA)	Securities and Exchange Commission (SEC)
Equal Employment Opportunity Commission (EEOC)	green marketing	telecommuting
		whistle-blowing

_____ 1. Regulates the labeling and safety of food, drugs, and cosmetics sold in the United States.

_____ 2. Is responsible for the fair and equitable treatment of employees with regard to hiring, firing, and promotions.

_____ 3. Provides guidelines for workplace safety and enforces those regulations.

_____ 4. Regulates the sale of stocks and bonds.

_____ 5. Monitors and seeks to reduce air, oil, and water pollution; oversees hazardous waste disposal and recycling.

_____ 6. Responsible for enforcing the principles of a free enterprise system and protecting consumers from unfair or deceptive business practices.

_____ 7. Allows workers to choose their work hours.

_____ 8. Working at home, usually on a computer.

_____ 9. A nonprofit organization that helps produce public service advertising campaigns for government agencies and other qualified sponsors.

_____ 10. Companies' efforts to produce and promote environmentally safe products.

_____ 11. Guidelines for good behavior.

_____ 12. Societal effort to protect consumer rights by putting legal, moral, and economic pressure on business.

_____ 13. A nonprofit organization established to help foster self-regulation among businesses.

_____ 14. Pricing products unreasonably high when high demand is created by a monopoly status or natural disasters.

_____ 15. Reporting an illegal action of one's employer.

CHAPTER 6   Legal and Ethical Issues

Fact and Idea Review

DIRECTIONS: *Select the letter of the word or phrase that best completes the sentence or answers the question.*

1. The branch of government responsible for interpreting, applying, and administering the laws of the United States is the

   a. executive branch.   c. judicial branch.

   b. legislative branch.   d. state government.

2. When selling goods and services to the government for use in government agencies, vendors often must do all of the following **except**

   a. follow guidelines for price bidding.

   b. show proof that they use minority suppliers.

   c. show proof that they are an equal opportunity employer.

   d. offer their products at cost.

3. The bureau under the direction of the Federal Trade Commission that has the responsibility for enforcing laws related to clothing labels, scams related to marketing practices, and truth in advertising is the Bureau of

   a. Consumer Protection.   c. Economics.

   b. Competition.   d. Finance.

4. This workplace benefit helps to reduce employee absenteeism and employee turnover.

   a. Extended family leave   c. Time off with pay when sick

   b. Health care benefits   d. On-site child care

5. Voluntary product recalls are examples of good

   a. marketing.   c. resource management.

   b. business ethics.   d. environmental safety.

6. The Sarbanes-Oxley Act of 2002 has provisions for all of the following except:

   a. protection for whistle-blowers.

   b. holding executives and their consulting firms accountable.

   c. proper reporting of a corporation's financial situation.

   d. workplace safety.

CHAPTER 6 Legal and Ethical Issues

Marketing Application 1

DIRECTIONS: *Read the article below. Then answer the questions that follow.*

Washington, DC – (June 17, 2004) – The Better Business Bureau system, Visa USA, Call For Action, and the Federal Trade Commission (FTC) today announced a joint education campaign to help consumers "cut the line on phishing scams."

During the campaign, the BBB and its partners will educate consumers on how to identify phishing scams; how to avoid becoming a victim; and how to report a suspicious e-mail. Comprehensive phishing resources will be available on the Internet for consumers by all parties involved in this campaign—BBB, Visa USA, Call For Action [a consumer-advocacy group], and FTC.

Phishing is an e-mail scam in which fraudsters attempt to convince consumers to reveal personal information—such as their credit or debit account numbers, checking account information, Social Security numbers, and banking account passwords—though official-looking fake Web sites or in a reply e-mail. According to the Anti-Phishing Working Group, phishing scams grew 178 percent from March to April of 2004.

(Source: www.bbb.org/alerts/article.asp?ID=516)

1. Which of the groups involved in this national campaign to help credit card holders and others protect their identities is

   A. a government agency? _____

   B. an organization involved in business self-regulation? _____

   C. an example of consumerism? _____

2. Why would the four organizations noted in this article want to fight against phishing?

   _____

   _____

   _____

   _____

3. If you were suspicious of an e-mail and thought it might be phishing, what would you do?

   _____

   _____

4. In addition to online support, what else could each of the organizations involved in this effort do to educate consumers about phishing scams?

   _____

   _____

   _____

   _____

CHAPTER **6** Legal and Ethical Issues

Marketing Application 2

DIRECTIONS: *Use the situations described below to clarify your views on the social responsibility of businesses. Study each situation and answer the questions that follow.*

1. You own and operate a small fast-food restaurant located on the main street of town. Both businesspeople and shoppers stop in to eat. The junior high school is also just a half-block away, so many students eat there.

    Garrick Hughes, an old friend of yours, stops in for lunch. Garrick works for a vending machine company. He wants to install a cigarette machine in your restaurant. It would give your customers a choice of 20 brands of cigarettes.

    You know that cigarette companies need about 1,000 new smokers every day to replace those who die from smoking-related illnesses. Garrick knows this too, so he offers you a special inducement—a sales promotion that will net you more than $500 every month. All you have to do is let him put in the vending machine. What will you tell Garrick? Why?

    _____

    _____

    _____

    _____

    _____

    _____

2. You are a middle-level manager of a large chemical products company. You have just learned that one of your plants is disposing of chemical waste by draining it underground into a nearby river.

    You are not sure whether top management knows about the situation. The people who live in the community do not. There has been a modest die-off of fish in the river, but no one has made the connection to your company.

    The local plant manager asks you to keep what you have discovered a secret. What will you do?

    _____

    _____

    _____

    _____

    _____

    _____

CHAPTER 6 Legal and Ethical Issues

The DECA Connection

Role Play: Volunteer Coordinator

Situation: You are to assume the role of an employee of a locally owned small business. The business owner (judge) feels strongly that his/her employees should be involved in volunteer work within the community. Your employer is uncertain, however, about the best way to implement such an activity.

Activity: As a team leader, you have been asked to meet with the members of your team to develop a proposal for employee participation in community volunteer work.

Evaluation: You will be evaluated on how well you meet the following performance indicators:

- Develop a project plan.
- Develop criteria for deciding which activities will qualify for the incentive.
- Explain the role of business in society.
- Participate as a team member.
- Demonstrate appropriate creativity.

DIRECTIONS: *Organize your thoughts around the performance indicators noted above. Use these performance indicators to jot down your ideas during the preparation period. Time your preparation period to last 15 minutes and your role play presentation to last a maximum of ten minutes. After your role play, use the performance indicators to evaluate your efforts.*

_____

_____

_____

_____

_____

_____

_____

_____

_____

_____

Continued on next page

Assessment: Assume each performance indicator is worth 20 points (20 × 5 = 100 points). Use the evaluation levels listed below for judging consistency.

Excellent   (16–20)   Participant demonstrated the performance indicator in a professional manner, exceeds business standards.

Good   (10–15)   Participant demonstrated the performance indicator in an acceptable manner; meets minimal business standards; there would be no need for additional formalized training at this time.

Fair   (4–9)   Participant demonstrated the performance indicator with limited effectiveness; performance generally fell below minimal business standards; additional training would be required to improve knowledge, attitude, and/or skills.

Poor   (0–3)   Participant demonstrated the performance indicator with little effectiveness or not at all; a great deal of formal training would be needed.

Develop a project plan.   Score _____

_____

_____

Develop criteria for deciding which activities will qualify for the incentive.   Score _____

_____

_____

Explain the role of business in society.   Score _____

_____

_____

Participate as a team member.   Score _____

_____

_____

Demonstrate appropriate creativity.   Score _____

_____

_____

CHAPTER 6 Legal and Ethical Issues

Word Processing Application

OBJECTIVE: *To develop a code of ethics for sales representatives.*

ACTIVITY: In most companies, a code of ethics is provided to managers to guide them in responding to different business situations. The principles of conduct employees are expected to follow in making decisions within the organization are outlined in the code of ethics. A code of ethics alone, however, does not prevent unethical behavior; ethical codes must be enforced if they are to be effective.

As sales manager at Beta Corporation, which produces and markets office furniture, you manage 45 salespeople. You are responsible for developing a code of ethics that addresses three specific topics. Create a handout that explains your proposed ethical codes. You will distribute the handout to all sales managers at the company's next sales meeting.

The topics you must address are listed below. You may revise the wording of the headings or add an introduction to the handout, if you wish.

Code of Ethics Topics
SALES STAFF, BETA CORPORATION

1. Salespeople's use of payments or gifts to obtain business.

2. Obtaining and using information about competitors.

3. Honest and accurate completion of expense reports.

Word Processing Directions

1. Turn on your computer and open your word processing software program.

2. Develop and write a code of ethics for the three areas listed. Proofread and edit your work to make sure that it is correct and concise.

3. Save your work. Print out a copy of your completed code of ethics if your teacher has instructed you to do so.

4. Answer the questions that follow.

Continued on next page

Interpreting Results

1. What would you include in an ethical code regarding payments of money or gifts by salespeople to obtain business?

_____

_____

_____

2. What would you include in an ethical code concerning the acquisition and use of information about competitors?

_____

_____

_____

3. What you would include in a code of ethics concerning the honest and accurate completion of expense reports?

_____

_____

_____

_____

Drawing Conclusions

4. Why might offering money or gifts to potential customers be considered unethical behavior?

_____

_____

_____

_____

5. In making the right ethical choices, what are three questions marketers should answer?

_____

_____

_____

_____

CHAPTER 7 Basic Math Skills

Vocabulary Review

DIRECTIONS: *Review your understanding of the important terms in this chapter by answering the following questions.*

1. Write the digits in our numbering system.

   _____

2. **a.** Write the number 234,056,008 in words.

   _____

   b. Which digit represents millions? _____

   tens? _____

   thousands? _____

3. What is a fraction?

   _____

4. **a.** Write a fraction with a numerator of 96 and a denominator of 30. _____ / _____

   b. Write the above fraction as a mixed number, _____, and as a decimal number, _____.

   c. Write the above decimal number in words. _____

5. **a.** What does percentage mean? _____

   b. When a percentage is written as a fraction, what number is the denominator? _____

6. What are graphs?

   _____

7. What kind of graph would most commonly be used to illustrate each of the following? Your choices are bar graph, line graph, and circle graph.

   _____ **a.** A change in a variable quantity, such as the changes in the stock market.

   _____ **b.** Relative sizes of the parts of a whole, such as the cost of football uniforms compared to the entire cost of the football program.

   _____ **c.** The relationship between two sets of information, such as the number of soft drinks purchased and the month of the year.

CHAPTER 7 Basic Math Skills

Fact and Idea Review

DIRECTIONS: *Complete the following statements by filling in the blanks.*

1. The value of a digit is determined by its _____ in a number.

2. When writing whole numbers in words, never use the word _____.

3. A fraction that describes a number greater than one can be written as a _____.

4. When writing a check, use the word *and* to indicate where the _____ is placed.

5. A fraction or mixed number whose denominator is a power of ten is called a _____.

6. When adding or subtracting decimal numbers, you should keep the decimal points _____.

7. When you multiply two numbers that each have two decimal places, the product will have _____ decimal places.

8. To convert a fraction to a decimal, divide the _____ by the _____.

9. Two-thirds of the class is equal to 66.7 _____ of the class.

10. The process of _____ a figure to the nearest whole number is useful when estimating the answer to a problem.

11. When converting a decimal number to a percent, you move the decimal point two places to the _____.

12. When using a calculator, you should check the answer you get against a(n) _____.

13. The three main types of central tendency are _____, _____, and _____.

CHAPTER 7 Basic Math Skills

Marketing Application 1

DIRECTIONS: *Fill out the checks below using the following information:*

Check No. 351 To Mr. Arnold Gowens for $324.57 (word processing services)

Check No. 352 To Windsor Auto Repair for $80.29 (car repairs)

Check No. 353 To Realty Associates for $17,500 (deposit on house)

Leslie Carmichael
4793 Ardon Drive
Houston, TX 77002

_____ 20 _____   **351**
18-24/979
1202(7)

PAY TO THE
ORDER
OF _____ $ _____

_____ DOLLARS

First State Bank
1800 Plains Avenue
Houston, TX 77002

Memo _____ _____

Leslie Carmichael
4793 Ardon Drive
Houston, TX 77002

_____ 20 _____   **352**
18-24/979
1202(7)

PAY TO THE
ORDER
OF _____ $ _____

_____ DOLLARS

First State Bank
1800 Plains Avenue
Houston, TX 77002

Memo _____ _____

Leslie Carmichael
4793 Ardon Drive
Houston, TX 77002

_____ 20 _____   **353**
18-24/979
1202(7)

PAY TO THE
ORDER
OF _____ $ _____

_____ DOLLARS

First State Bank
1800 Plains Avenue
Houston, TX 77002

Memo _____ _____

CHAPTER 7 Basic Math Skills

Marketing Application 2

DIRECTIONS: *A. Estimate the answer to each of the following problems. Then use a calculator to solve the problems. Write and compare both of your answers.*

1. 385 + 694 + 918 + 42   Estimate _____   Answer _____

2. $18,918.47 − $3,298.95   Estimate _____   Answer _____

3. 36,916 × 2.74   Estimate _____   Answer _____

4. $^{696}/_{12}$ Estimate _____   Answer _____

DIRECTIONS: *B. Line graphs are used to show trends. Use the following information and the grid below to show the trend in savings interest rates for a six month period.*

July	3½%	October	4¾%
August	3¼%	November	5%
September	3¾%	December	5%

Passbook Savings Rates by Month (20--)

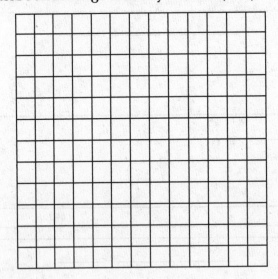

5. What was the trend for interest rates for the period? _____

6. Which month showed a down trend? _____

7. Which month showed the sharpest increase? _____

8. Which month showed no change? _____

CHAPTER 7 Basic Math Skills

The DECA Connection

Role Play: Assistant Manager

Situation: You are to assume the role of assistant manager of an interior design shop. You must often provide customers with estimates for time and materials necessary to complete a job. You have noticed that some of your fellow employees have difficulty with the concept of estimating. Their mistakes cause problems for the shop owner and the customers.

Activity: The shop owner (judge) has asked you to plan a practice session to improve the skills of the employees. You must demonstrate to the shop owner that you can teach the employees how to improve their estimating skills.

Evaluation: You will be evaluated on how well you meet the following performance indicators:

- Demonstrate problem-solving skills.
- Explain the nature of positive customer/client relations.
- Determine customer/client needs.
- Calculate miscellaneous charges.
- Give directions for completing job tasks.

DIRECTIONS: *Organize your thoughts around the performance indicators noted above. Use these performance indicators to jot down your ideas during the preparation period. Time your preparation period to last 15 minutes and your role play presentation to last a maximum of ten minutes. After your role play, use the performance indicators to evaluate your efforts.*

_____

_____

_____

_____

_____

_____

_____

_____

_____

_____

_____

Continued on next page

Assessment: Assume each performance indicator is worth 20 points (20 × 5 = 100 points). Use the evaluation levels listed below for judging consistency.

Excellent (16–20) Participant demonstrated the performance indicator in a professional manner, exceeds business standards.

Good (10–15) Participant demonstrated the performance indicator in an acceptable manner; meets minimal business standards; there would be no need for additional formalized training at this time.

Fair (4–9) Participant demonstrated the performance indicator with limited effectiveness; performance generally fell below minimal business standards; additional training would be required to improve knowledge, attitude, and/or skills.

Poor (0–3) Participant demonstrated the performance indicator with little effectiveness or not at all; a great deal of formal training would be needed.

Demonstrate problem-solving skills. Score _____

_____

_____

_____

Explain the nature of positive customer/client relations. Score _____

_____

_____

_____

Determine customer/client needs. Score _____

_____

_____

_____

Calculate miscellaneous charges. Score _____

_____

_____

_____

Give directions for completing job tasks. Score _____

_____

_____

_____

CHAPTER 7 Basic Math Skills

Software Activity (Optional)

Spreadsheet Application

OBJECTIVE: *To calculate the average number of transactions and average sales each employee had per hour.*

ACTIVITY: As the owner of the Holiday Gift Shop, you have monitored the sales output of each of your employees. The printout below shows sales information for seven employees. For each employee, it shows the number of hours worked, the number of sales transactions, and the dollar sales that resulted from those transactions. Because each employee has worked a different number of hours, averages must be calculated before any comparisons can be made.

Use your spreadsheet program to calculate the average number of transactions that each employee had per hour. Then calculate the average hourly sales that each employee generated.

	A	B	C	D	E	F
1	Chapter 7 Basic Math Skills					
2						
3						
4		Hours	Number of		Mean	Mean
5	Employee	Worked	Transactions	Dollar Sales	Transactions	Sales
6	Name	per week	per week	per week	per hour	per hour
7						
8	Pedro Garcia	35	378	$11,368.98		
9	Liz McCarthy	43	420	$13,440.43		
10	LaDonna Reese	37	356	$10,324.50		
11	Mark Abrams	37	389	$9,725.00		
12	Jerome Devers	40	502	$15,562.78		
13	Kim Lee	15	140	$3,360.00		
14	Kendall Rice	20	190	$5,890.00		
15	All Employees					

Spreadsheet Directions

1. Turn on your computer and open your spreadsheet software program.

2. Create a spreadsheet like the one above using your spreadsheet application.

3. Enter a formula to calculate the mean number of transactions per hour for Pedro Garcia. Copy the formula to appropriate cells in all remaining rows.

4. Enter a formula to calculate the mean hourly sales for Pedro Garcia. Copy the formula to appropriate cells in all remaining rows.

Continued on next page

5. Calculate the mean number of transactions per hour and the mean hourly sales for all employees.

6. After completing your calculations, save your work to a new file.

7. Print out a copy of your work if your teacher has instructed you to do so. Then answer the questions that follow.

Interpreting Results

1. What were the mean number of transactions per hour figures for each employee and for all employees?

Pedro Garcia	_____	Jerome Devers	_____
Liz McCarthy	_____	Kim Lee	_____
LaDonna Reese	_____	Kendall Rice	_____
Mark Abrams	_____	All Employees	_____

2. What were the mean hourly sales figures for each employee and for all employees?

Pedro Garcia	_____	Jerome Devers	_____
Liz McCarthy	_____	Kim Lee	_____
LaDonna Reese	_____	Kendall Rice	_____
Mark Abrams	_____	All Employees	_____

Drawing Conclusions

3. How can you use this data to help your salespeople and improve business?

_____

_____

_____

_____

_____

4. Of the two calculations, which one is more meaningful in evaluating each employee's output?

_____

_____

_____

_____

_____

CHAPTER 8 Communication Skills

Vocabulary Review

DIRECTIONS: A. *Study the lists below and the puzzle block, called a Magic Square. Notice that each lettered vocabulary term has a matching lettered cell in the square. To solve the puzzle, select a definition for each term from the numbered list. Then write each definition's number in the appropriately labeled puzzle cell. If you have correctly matched all the terms and definitions, the total of the numbers will be the same across each row and down each column.*

A. jargon

B. barriers

C. feedback

D. communication

E. distractions

F. messages

G. channels/media

H. emotional barriers

I. setting

1. Circumstances under which communication takes place.

2. The process of exchanging ideas, information, and feelings.

3. Obstacles that interfere with the understanding of a message.

4. Things that compete with the message for the listener's attention.

5. The receiver's response to the message.

6. The avenues through which messages are delivered.

7. Specialized vocabulary, used by members of a particular group.

8. Biases against the opinion expressed that prevent a listener from understanding.

9. The information, ideas, or feelings the sender wants to communicate.

A	B	C
D	E	F
G	H	I

Magic number: all rows and columns add up to _____.

DIRECTIONS: B. *On the lines below, explain the relationship between parliamentary procedure and a quorum.*

_____

_____

_____

_____

CHAPTER **8** Communication Skills

Fact and Idea Review

DIRECTIONS: A. *In each series of items, circle the one that does not belong. Then explain your choice on the line below.*

1. Body   Closing   Subject Title   Reports   Greeting

   _____

2. Feedback   Inflections   Channels   Listening   Setting

   _____

3. Biases   Focusing   Interruptions   Noises   Planning a response

   _____

4. Cause and effect   Comparison and contrast   Enumeration
   Generalization with example   Memos and reports

   _____

DIRECTIONS: B. *Circle the letter of the choice that best completes each of the following sentences.*

1. Things that get in the way of effective listening are called

   a. annoyances.   **b.** barriers.   **c.** enumerations.   **d.** feedback.

2. Skills that help you read with more understanding include focusing your mind, improving your vocabulary, and

   a. comparing and contrasting.   **c.** knowing the purpose of your reading.

   b. forming pictures.   **d.** planning a response.

3. People usually speak in order to inform, to entertain, and to

   a. draw a conclusion.   **c.** generalize.

   b. enumerate.   **d.** persuade.

4. It is important when writing that you know your purpose, your subject, and your

   a. interest.   **b.** jargon.   **c.** audience.   **d.** setting.

5. When speaking on the telephone, enunciate clearly, use your most pleasant tone, and

   a. draw on your extensive vocabulary.   **c.** shout.

   b. interrupt as necessary.   **d.** speak loudly enough to be heard.

6. The trend in business writing is toward

   a. a direct, conversational style.   **c.** heavy reliance on jargon.

   b. frequent generalization.   **d.** overuse of abbreviations.

Student	Date
Class	Teacher

CHAPTER **8** Communication Skills

Marketing Application 1

DIRECTIONS: *Many elements affect communication. Consider the situations described below and answer the questions that follow.*

1. Two major channels of communication are speaking and writing. Tell which channel you think would be most effective in each of the situations. Explain your answers.

   a. An invitation to an informal gathering after work.

   _____

   _____

   _____

   _____

   _____

   b. A new idea you would like your supervisor to consider.

   _____

   _____

   _____

   _____

   _____

   c. A progress report on an important project.

   _____

   _____

   _____

   _____

   _____

2. Describe with detail the appropriate setting for each of the following.

   a. A team meeting to celebrate reaching an important goal.

   _____

   _____

   _____

Continued on next page

b. A training session to explain new office procedures.

_____

_____

_____

_____

_____

3. Describe a situation in which each of the following barriers to listening is present.

a. Distractions

_____

_____

_____

_____

_____

_____

b. Emotional Barriers

_____

_____

_____

_____

_____

_____

_____

c. Planning a Response

_____

_____

_____

_____

_____

CHAPTER **8** Communication Skills

Marketing Application 2

DIRECTIONS: _Consider the situations described below and on the next page. Then, in the space provided, write a business e-mail appropriate to each._

1. You are a buyer for the Fun-4-U toy stores. You have just received a shipment of defective rocking horses from Schlock Rockers, Inc. It is the third time you have received defective merchandise from the company.

   Write a business e-mail advising the firm that you are returning its latest shipment and wish to cancel any pending orders. Be sure to explain why you are taking this action.

_____

_____

_____

_____

_____

_____

_____

_____

_____

_____

_____

_____

_____

_____

_____

_____

_____

_____

_____

Continued on next page

2. You are a sales representative for American Classics, a furniture company. You have decided to try marketing your company's products to a hotel chain in another part of the country. Your first step is to write a business e-mail introducing your company and its product lines.

Address your e-mail to the purchasing agent of the hotel chain. Describe the company and its merchandise in a way that will make the agent want to buy. Include that you will be sending some catalogs of your furniture, and finish by asking for an appointment to meet with the agent in person.

_____

_____

_____

_____

_____

_____

_____

_____

_____

_____

_____

_____

_____

_____

_____

_____

_____

_____

_____

_____

_____

_____

CHAPTER 8 Communication Skills

The DECA Connection

Role Play: Clerical Staff Representative

Situation: You are to assume the role of a member of a large clerical staff for a catalog company. Management has announced a very strict policy stating that employees may not use the company computers for personal business of any sort. You and your fellow employees feel that this policy is too strict. You would like to have the privilege of using the company computers during your break times and during lunch hours or after work.

Activity: You have been selected as the representative to convey these feelings to the office manager (judge).

Evaluation: You will be evaluated on how well you meet the following performance indicators:

- Persuade others.
- Demonstrate ethical work habits.
- Describe the nature of organizational conflict.
- Demonstrate responsible behavior.
- Foster positive working relationships.

DIRECTIONS: *Organize your thoughts around the performance indicators noted above. Use these performance indicators to jot down your ideas during the preparation period. Time your preparation period to last 15 minutes and your role play presentation to last a maximum of ten minutes. After your role play, use the performance indicators to evaluate your efforts.*

_____

_____

_____

_____

_____

_____

_____

_____

_____

_____

_____

_____

Continued on next page

Assessment: Assume each performance indicator is worth 20 points (20 × 5 = 100 points). Use the evaluation levels listed below for judging consistency.

Excellent (16–20) Participant demonstrated the performance indicator in a professional manner, exceeds business standards.

Good (10–15) Participant demonstrated the performance indicator in an acceptable manner; meets minimal business standards; there would be no need for additional formalized training at this time.

Fair (4–9) Participant demonstrated the performance indicator with limited effectiveness; performance generally fell below minimal business standards; additional training would be required to improve knowledge, attitude, and/or skills.

Poor (0–3) Participant demonstrated the performance indicator with little effectiveness or not at all; a great deal of formal training would be needed.

Persuade others. Score _____

_____

_____

_____

Demonstrate ethical work habits. Score _____

_____

_____

_____

Describe the nature of organizational conflict. Score _____

_____

_____

_____

Demonstrate responsible behavior. Score _____

_____

_____

_____

Foster positive working relationships. Score _____

_____

_____

_____

CHAPTER 8 Communication Skills

Presentation Application

OBJECTIVE: *Demonstrate persuasive verbal communication skills.*

ACTIVITY: Most jobs in business, especially in marketing, require good communication skills. Successful marketers constantly use verbal communication to sell their ideas and products or services. Sometimes this is done in a formal setting, like a meeting, but most of the time verbal communication is informal.

In this computer activity, you will make an oral presentation supported by a computer-aided presentation. In this presentation, you will attempt to persuade your classmates to support your viewpoint on an issue. The topic of your presentation should be approved by your instructor and be of interest to you and your classmates. Topics might include "All business should be conducted in a socially responsible manner," or "Ethics should be the number one consideration when doing business."

Prepare an outline of your presentation, listing the key points. Be sure to include examples that can be used to illustrate the important points. Think about what counterpoints might be raised by your classmates, and plan responses to opposing positions.

Use your key points, examples, and planned counterpoint rebuttals to develop an oral and slide presentation. You will develop a title slide and at least three other slides to support your viewpoint.

Presentation Directions

1. Turn on your computer and open your software program.

2. Follow the instructions for your software to create a title slide for your presentation. Save the file as **CH8PROB**.

3. Based on your ideas, develop at least four more slides to support your argument.

4. Save your work and print out a copy of your slides for your instructor.

5. Answer the following questions:

Interpreting Results

1. In what situations might verbal communications be used on the job?

_____

_____

_____

_____

_____

Continued on next page

2. Why should you consider who your audience is before planning an oral presentation?

_____

_____

_____

_____

_____

_____

Drawing Conclusions

3. After completing your presentation, survey your classmates to find out if they were swayed by your arguments. Ask for feedback from those classmates not convinced by your arguments. Why will some people oppose your viewpoint despite the strength of your arguments?

_____

_____

_____

_____

_____

_____

_____

4. Why is it necessary to follow up some verbal communication with written communication?

_____

_____

_____

_____

_____

_____

_____

_____

_____

CHAPTER 9 Technology Applications for Marketing

Vocabulary Review

DIRECTIONS: *Fill in the puzzle blanks by using key terms from the chapter. Then read down the circled letters to discover the Mystery Phrase.*

Clues

1. This links together documents on the Internet.
2. The entry point for a Web site.
3. Electronic mail.
4. Programs used to create text documents.
5. Software that lets users edit text and graphics in one document.
6. A network of computer networks, allowing the free flow of information.
7. This outlines what can be found on each page within a Web site.
8. Software for producing slide shows or multimedia presentations.
9. Programs that let computer users electronically communicate.
10. A collection of interlinked electronic documents that is a subset of the Internet.
11. This establishes a wireless Internet connection using radio frequencies.
12. Software used to organize, calculate, and analyze numerical data.
13. Checkpoint that protects information on networked computers.
14. Software that stores and organizes information.
15. Also known as the Web address, this protocol identifies and locates Web pages.
16. Software that integrates all parts of a company's business management.

1. ___ ___ ___ ___ ___ ___ ___   ___ ___ ___ ___ ___ ___ ___   ___ ___ ___ ___ Ⓞ ___ ___
2. ___ Ⓞ ___ ___   ___ ___ ___ ___
3. ___ - ___ Ⓞ ___ ___
4. ___ ___ ___ ___ Ⓞ ___ ___ ___ ___ ___ ___ ___ ___
5. ___ ___ ___ ___ ___ Ⓞ ___ ___ ___ ___ ___ ___ ___
6. ___ ___ Ⓞ ___ ___ ___ ___ ___
7. ___ ___ ___ Ⓞ ___ ___ ___ ___
8. ___ Ⓞ ___ ___ ___ ___ ___ ___ ___ ___ ___ ___
9. ___ ___ ___ ___ ___ ___ ___ ___ ___ Ⓞ
10. ___ Ⓞ ___ ___ ___ ___ ___ ___ ___ ___ ___ ___ ___
11. ___ ___ - Ⓞ ___ ___
12. ___ ___ ___ ___ ___ ___ ___ Ⓞ ___ ___ ___
13. ___ ___ ___ Ⓞ ___ ___ ___ ___
14. ___ Ⓞ ___ ___ ___ ___ ___ ___
15. ___ ___ ___ ___ Ⓞ ___ ___ ___ ___   ___ ___ ___ ___ ___ ___ ___ ___
16. Ⓞ ___ ___ ___ ___ ___ ___ ___   ___ ___ ___ ___ ___ ___ ___ ___   ___ ___ ___ ___ ___ ___ ___

Mystery Phrase: _____

CHAPTER 9 Technology Applications for Marketing

Fact and Idea Review

DIRECTIONS: A. *Marketing uses many kinds of technology. Some of it is designed for use by the customer, while some is for use by the business. Classify each of the following technologies as used by the customer (C) or used by the business (B).*

_____ point-of-sale systems

_____ customer relationship management (CRM) software

_____ interactive TV

_____ enterprise resource planning (ERP) software.

_____ interactive touch-screen computers

_____ Web sites

DIRECTIONS: B. *In each series of terms, circle the one that does not belong. Explain your choice on the line below.*

1. Hypertext transfer protocol (HTTP)   Firewall   Search engine
   Uniform resource locator (URL)   Browser

   _____

2. Word processing   Database   Desktop publishing
   Video game   Presentation

   _____

3. Site map   Wi-Fi   Digital subscriber line (DSL)
   Dial-up   Power grid

   _____

4. Videoconferencing   E-mail   Enterprise resource planning (ERP)
   Instant messaging   Telephone

   _____

5. Touch-screen computers   Interactive TV   Internet   E-mail   Database

   _____

CHAPTER 9 Technology Applications for Marketing

Marketing Application 1

DIRECTIONS: *Read the situations described below. Assume you are a salesperson for a computer software dealer. What software would you recommend to the customer in each of the situations? Explain your answers.*

1. Fred is a cartographer. He needs to scan aerial photographs and use the scans as templates over which he draws a map of the area photographed. Sometimes he uses a large number of maps to produce an atlas, which is a book of maps. What software does he need to produce the files that he gives the printer?

   _____

   _____

   _____

   _____

   _____

2. Eileen is the manager of sales and distribution for a small publisher. She deals with about 400 clients and needs to collect, organize, and continually update information about her clients, mostly small retail stores. She needs to know the following about each store: contact name, telephone number, fax number, e-mail address, address, resale number, store hours, and credit limit. She often corresponds with clients via both form letters and individualized letters. What software must she have?

   _____

   _____

3. George is a physicist. His hobby is the design of sundials. To design a sundial he needs to know the latitude and longitude of the sundial's location. With that information and a set of equations, he can calculate the angle of the sun's shadow on the sundial face given the time of day. His sundials are marked every 15 minutes. George wants to quickly calculate the angles from 6 am to 6 pm for any location and then do it again for another location. What software does he need?

   _____

4. George, Fred, and Eileen decide to form a small company that markets Fred's maps and George's sundials. Naturally they want to set up a Web site, but they also want to go on the road giving presentations, and do old-fashioned things like a mass mailing of brochures. What software will they need over and above what they already have?

   _____

   _____

   _____

CHAPTER 9 Technology Applications for Marketing

Marketing Application 2

DIRECTIONS: *Online shopping services are an important new venue for marketing. Use the following exercise to explore this market. Select a product that you would like to sell using an online marketing approach. Answer the questions to help you think about a marketing plan.*

1. Name of the product.

   _____

2. Why did you select this product?

   _____
   _____
   _____
   _____

3. How is this product currently marketed?

   _____
   _____
   _____

4. What value does online marketing add to this product?

   _____
   _____
   _____

5. What disadvantages might a consumer experience in shopping for this product through an online service as compared to the way it is primarily marketed?

   _____
   _____
   _____

6. Do you believe that online services will become a significant part of the market in the future? Explain your answer.

   _____
   _____
   _____

CHAPTER 9 Technology Applications for Marketing

The DECA Connection

Role Play: E-Commerce Consultant

Situation: You are to assume the role of an e-commerce consultant working for a map publishing business. The owner of the business (judge) has asked you to investigate ways that the company's products could be marketed online. Your research indicates that the cost of hiring a company to design and implement a Web site can cost up to $200,000, depending on the complexity of the Web site. The company you contacted has Web designers who get paid $170 to $340 per hour, and the job may take six months to a year to complete. If the business wants the ability to take orders, send confirmations, track customer preferences, and provide the necessary security for the business and its customers, the total cost could be as high as $400,000. This firm will review your client's requirements and help you decide on a strategy, as well as design, implement, test, and roll out the Web site. A simpler version of a Web site, one that is used for advertising the product and then providing a toll-free number to place orders may only take a few months and cost a lot less money.

Activity: You have been asked to make a recommendation regarding the design and implementation of a Web site for the company. After reviewing the costs and benefits of online marketing of the company's maps with the business owner (judge), suggest what you think would be the best method(s) to use.

Evaluation: You will be evaluated on how well you meet the following performance indicators:

- Analyze technology for use in the sales function.
- Identify ways that technology impacts business.
- Use communication technologies.
- Determine services to provide to customers.
- Present report findings and recommendations.

DIRECTIONS: *Organize your thoughts around the performance indicators noted above. Use these performance indicators to jot down your ideas during the preparation period. Time your preparation period to last 15 minutes and your role play presentation to last a maximum of 10 minutes. After your role play, use the performance indicators to evaluate your efforts.*

_____

_____

_____

_____

_____

_____

Continued on next page

Assessment: Assume each performance indicator is worth 20 points (20 × 5 = 100 points). Use the evaluation levels listed below for judging consistency.

Excellent   (16–20)   Participant demonstrated the performance indicator in a professional manner, exceeds business standards.

Good   (10–15)   Participant demonstrated the performance indicator in an acceptable manner; meets minimal business standards; there would be no need for additional formalized training at this time.

Fair   (4–9)   Participant demonstrated the performance indicator with limited effectiveness; performance generally fell below minimal business standards; additional training would be required to improve knowledge, attitude, and/or skills.

Poor   (0–3)   Participant demonstrated the performance indicator with little effectiveness or not at all; a great deal of formal training would be needed.

Analyze technology for use in the sales function.   Score _____

_____

_____

_____

Identify ways that technology impacts business.   Score _____

_____

_____

_____

Use communication technologies.   Score _____

_____

_____

_____

Determine services to provide to customers.   Score _____

_____

_____

_____

Present report findings and recommendations.   Score _____

_____

_____

_____

CHAPTER 9 Technology Applications for Marketing

Software Activity (Optional)

Spreadsheet Application

OBJECTIVE: *To evaluate marketing and sales costs by calculating their ratio to sales.*

ACTIVITY: The Exerfit Corporation manufactures exercise equipment that it sells to retail stores around the country. The company has seven sales regions, as shown in the computer printout below. The managers of these regions all report to the national sales manager. You are assisting the sales manager in evaluating the cost of salaries, sales, and marketing for each region. Total annual sales for each region are shown on the printout, along with salary, sales, and marketing expenses.

	A	B	C	D	E	F	G	
1	Chapter 9 Technology Applications for Marketing							
2								
3						Sales		Marketing
4						Expenses		Expenses
5				Salaries as		as		as
6			Salaries &	Percentage	Sales	Percentage	Marketing	Percentage
7	Region	Sales	Benefits	of Sales	Expenses	of Sales	Expenses	of Sales
8								
9	Northeast	$2,458,000	$148,900	6.1%	$225,000	9.2%	$250,000	10.2%
10	Southeast	$3,242,000	$132,700		$218,000		$267,400	
11	South	$2,898,000	$124,400		$197,500		$245,000	
12	Midwest	$4,012,111	$169,600		$242,400		$291,200	
13	Central	$1,950,000	$108,000		$131,600		$162,700	
14	Northwest	$3,982,000	$151,300		$232,500		$485,000	
15	Southwest	$2,624,000	$118,000		$167,000		$251,700	
16								

Continued on next page

Spreadsheet Directions

1. Turn on your computer and open your spreadsheet software program.

2. Create a spreadsheet like the one on page 79 using your spreadsheet application.

3. Write a formula to calculate salaries as a percentage of sales, rounding to the tenths place. Do the same for sales and marketing expenses. Copy these formulas to the remaining rows.

4. Save your work. Print out a copy of your work if your teacher has instructed you to do so.

5. Answer the following questions about the completed spreadsheet.

Interpreting Results

1. Which region has the highest salary cost as a percentage of sales? the lowest?

_____

_____

_____

2. Which region has the highest marketing expenses in dollar amounts? As a percentage of sales?

_____

_____

_____

3. Assume the Exerfit Corporation has a budget goal of keeping sales expenses below 6.5 percent of sales and marketing expenses below 8 percent of sales. Which regions are below budget in each category?

_____

_____

_____

Drawing Conclusions

4. Looking at the spreadsheet results, you can see that marketing costs in the Northwest region are quite a bit higher than in other regions, while salary costs are lower. Suppose the Northwest regional manager has been using part-time or freelance marketing help, which explains the higher marketing costs and lower salary costs. What are some reasons why the manager might not use full-time employees?

_____

_____

_____

_____

CHAPTER 10 Interpersonal Skills

Vocabulary Review

DIRECTIONS: *After reading each sentence below, circle the letter of the choice that comes closest in meaning to the underlined word or phrase. Then, on the lines below, write your own sentence using the selected word or phrase.*

1. Maria was <u>assertive</u> when asking her supervisor to assign her more responsibility.

   a. angry   **b.** firm   **c.** honest   **d.** understanding

   _____

   _____

2. George <u>empathized with</u> Sharon's dilemma.

   a. criticized   **c.** understood

   b. tried to resolve   **d.** was interested in

   _____

   _____

3. Carmen had <u>an agreement with</u> her supervisor to complete four computer classes.

   a. instructions from   **b.** a suggestion from   **c.** an arrangement with

   _____

   _____

4. Win's <u>ethics</u> helped her gain the trust of her co-workers.

   a. self-esteem   **b.** negotiation skills   **c.** basic values

   _____

   _____

5. Robert was skilled at getting his team to reach <u>a consensus</u>.

   a. an agreement   **b.** an understanding   **c.** its goals   **d** varied opinions

   _____

   _____

6. As a supervisor, Ramon values Dan's <u>initiative</u>.

   a. honesty   **b** responsibility   **c** creativity   **d** drive to get things done

   _____

   _____

CHAPTER **10** Interpersonal Skills

Fact and Idea Review

DIRECTIONS: *Complete each sentence using a term from the Word Bank. Use all of the words in completing this exercise. Some sentences will require more than one answer.*

listening	initiative	shared leadership
creativity	integrity	shared responsibility
enthusiasm	interest	establishing a plan
self-awareness	roles	team goals
self-esteem	equity	honesty

1. Two procedures that will help you in dealing with customer complaints are _____.

2. Ethical behavior includes the personal traits of _____.

3. Personal traits that foster a positive attitude are _____.

4. The first step to making personal changes is _____.

5. Confidence is enhanced by good _____.

6. Two important elements of teamwork are _____.

7. Consensus is an important element in setting _____.

8. Using your imagination and acting on your ideas demonstrate the personal traits of _____.

9. Establishing standards so all employees have equal rights and opportunities creates _____.

10. Cross training makes it possible for team members to be assigned many _____.

CHAPTER **10** Interpersonal Skills

Marketing Application 1

DIRECTIONS: *Use the situations described below to explore your grasp of interpersonal skills. Study each situation and then answer the questions that follow.*

1. Gail is a sales representative for an engineering services company. She has called on her customer, Tom, just a couple of times. Each time he has purchased services, but he has been very cold and abrupt with Gail. Gail is determined to break the ice with him. The next time she calls on Tom, she comments on some photos in his office of him skiing. Soon they are talking about favorite skiing locations and sharing stories. That day, Tom purchased more engineering services than usual from Gail and treated her in a much friendlier manner.

   a. What caused Tom to change his attitude?

   _____

   _____

   _____

   b. What other things could Gail have done to improve her relationship with Tom?

   _____

   _____

   _____

2. Bill performed so well in his entry-level position at a marketing firm that he was quickly promoted to a managerial position. In his new job, Bill seemed to undergo a personality change. He was no longer friendly with his coworkers; instead, he became very formal and bossy. He was very critical of the people he supervised and rarely gave praise. The members of his team soon began to complain about him.

   a. Why do you think Bill behaved the way he did?

   _____

   _____

   _____

   b. If you were his supervisor, what would you do?

   _____

   _____

   _____

   _____

CHAPTER 10 Interpersonal Skills

Marketing Application 2

DIRECTIONS: *Use the situations described below to explore your grasp of interpersonal skills. Study each situation and then answer the questions that follow.*

1. Dan is a member of a four-person sales team in a gourmet kitchen shop. All of the sales team members have been cross-trained in the daily assignments that must be completed. Their first task each day is to restock shelves, clean, and prepare the store for opening. Dan is often late to work, arriving just a few minutes before opening time. He is an excellent salesperson and loves to work with customers on the floor. He will often trade his cashiering shift with another team member so that he can work with customers. His excellent sales record helps to ensure that his team always meets their sales goal. However, some of the team members are complaining that he is not a good team player.

   a. How would you feel about working with Dan?

   _____

   _____

   _____

   b. What would you do if you were the store manager?

   _____

   _____

   _____

2. Maxine's team at the pizza parlor was working toward a bonus that their manager had offered to whichever team received the fewest customer complaints. Maxine noticed that one of her team members, Julie, often made mistakes when writing up customer orders. Maxine tried to encourage her to be more careful, but Julie seemed to resent her suggestions.

   a. What would you do if you were in Maxine's situation?

   _____

   _____

   _____

   b. What would you do if you were the manager?

   _____

   _____

   _____

CHAPTER 10 Interpersonal Skills

The DECA Connection

Role Play: Customer Service Manager

Situation: You are to assume the role of supervisor of a group of customer service representatives at a franchised auto dealership. The dealership's mission for handling customer complaints is "Do what needs to be done in order to ensure customer satisfaction." This policy is part of the franchise agreement with the auto manufacturer. A recent report from the auto manufacturer indicated that your customer service representatives are not handling customer complaints uniformly, nor are they receiving good grades in follow-up customer satisfaction surveys. This poor evaluation has led to problems among your employees, who are trying to put the blame elsewhere.

Activity: The general manager of the auto dealership (judge) wants to know how you plan to resolve this problem with your employees. He has asked you to prepare a plan for an upcoming staff meeting, where you address this issue. He wants to see an outline of your plan and hear exactly how you will conduct that staff meeting.

Evaluation: You will be evaluated on how well you meet the following performance indicators:

- Explain the nature of positive customer/client relations.
- Foster positive working relationships.
- Give directions for completing job tasks.
- Conduct staff meetings.
- Establish standards for job performance.

DIRECTIONS: *Organize your thoughts around the performance indicators noted above. Use these performance indicators to jot down your ideas during the preparation period. Time your preparation period to last 15 minutes and your role play presentation to last a maximum of ten minutes. After your role play, use the performance indicators to evaluate your efforts.*

_____

_____

_____

_____

_____

_____

_____

_____

_____

Continued on next page

Assessment: Assume each performance indicator is worth 20 points (20 × 5 = 100 points). Use the evaluation levels listed below for judging consistency.

Excellent (16–20) Participant demonstrated the performance indicator in a professional manner, exceeds business standards.

Good (10–15) Participant demonstrated the performance indicator in an acceptable manner; meets minimal business standards; there would be no need for additional formalized training at this time.

Fair (4–9) Participant demonstrated the performance indicator with limited effectiveness; performance generally fell below minimal business standards; additional training would be required to improve knowledge, attitude, and/or skills.

Poor (0–3) Participant demonstrated the performance indicator with little effectiveness or not at all; a great deal of formal training would be needed.

Explain the nature of positive customer/client relations. Score _____

_____

_____

_____

Foster positive working relationships. Score _____

_____

_____

_____

Give directions for completing job tasks. Score _____

_____

_____

_____

Conduct staff meetings. Score _____

_____

_____

_____

Establish standards for job performance. Score _____

_____

_____

_____

CHAPTER 10 Interpersonal Skills

Software Activity (Optional)

Word Processing Application

OBJECTIVE: *Write a letter in response to a customer complaint.*

ACTIVITY: You work in the customer service department for a mail-order company that sells gardening equipment and supplies. Ms. Johnetta Winter has written a letter explaining that the workbench she ordered is missing the hardware that is needed for assembly. Write a letter apologizing for the missing hardware. Tell Ms. Winter that you are enclosing the hardware in the package with your letter. The address for the letter is shown below. Remember to leave one blank line after the salutation. Also leave one blank line between paragraphs of your letter and between the last line of the last paragraph and the closing. Include an enclosure notation after the closing to indicate that the hardware is being sent with this letter. Add an appropriate closing at the end of your letter and sign your name.

Ms. Johnetta Winter
2403 Bremerton Avenue
Westerville, OH 43081

Word Processing Directions

1. Turn on your computer and open your word processing software program.

2. Write a letter to Ms. Winter in response to her complaint.

3. Save your work. Print out a copy of your work if your teacher has instructed you to do so. Then answer the questions that follow.

Evaluating Results

1. What is the purpose of your letter?

_____

_____

_____

_____

_____

_____

_____

Continued on next page

2. Reread your letter and imagine that you are the person receiving the letter. Does it make you feel that your problem has been handled efficiently? Does it leave you with a positive impression of the company?

_____

_____

_____

_____

_____

_____

_____

_____

_____

_____

Drawing Conclusions

3. What are some general guidelines that you think should be followed in writing letters responding to a customer's complaint?

_____

_____

_____

_____

_____

_____

_____

_____

_____

_____

_____

_____

_____

_____

CHAPTER 11 Management Skills

Vocabulary Review

DIRECTIONS: *Match each definition with the correct term.*

controlling	mission statement	supervisory-level
empowerment	organizing	management
horizontal organization	planning	top management
middle management		vertical organization

_____ 1. Management structure characterized by self-managing teams.

_____ 2. Coordinating efforts to reach established goals.

_____ 3. Persons with greatest responsibility, such as CEO, president, etc.

_____ 4. Description of the ultimate goals of a company or organization.

_____ 5. Traditional hierarchical management structure.

_____ 6. Process of encouraging individuals to take responsibility.

_____ 7. Link between the top and supervisory levels of management.

_____ 8. Setting goals and establishing methods to achieve them.

_____ 9. Management that interacts directly with employees on the job.

_____ 10. Setting standards, evaluating performance, and solving problems.

CHAPTER **11** Management Skills

Fact and Idea Review

DIRECTIONS: A. *In each series of terms, circle the one that does not belong. Then explain your choice on the line below.*

1. CEO   Executive   Supervisor   Top management   Vice president

   _____

2. Customer orientation   Empowerment   Functional divisions

   Organization by process   Self-managing teams

   _____

3. Evaluating performance   Setting standards   Solving problems

   Assigning duties   Suggesting changes

   _____

4. Be consistent   Be firm   Define the problem   Give clear directions

   Set a good example

   _____

DIRECTIONS: B. *Complete the following statements by filling in the blanks.*

5. The process of reaching goals through the use of human resources, technology, and material resources is called _____.

6. Flattening the organization is an expression describing

   _____ organization.

7. The practice of encouraging employees to contribute and take responsibility for the management process is called _____.

8. Providing frequent feedback, rewarding smart work, and encouraging creativity are important in _____ employees.

9. Recruiting, hiring, and providing in-service training programs are responsibilities of the

   _____ department.

CHAPTER *11* Management Skills

Marketing Application 1

DIRECTIONS: *Read the situation described below. Then write a description telling how you would organize the group to reach the goal. Tell whether your plan illustrates vertical or horizontal organization. Explain why you chose this organizational structure.*

You are the leader of an 18-member jazz band at Belmont High School. The group recently took top honors in a national competition and as a result has been invited to perform at the White House. Unfortunately, the band's travel budget for the year was used up attending the nationals. In order to accept this invitation, you and the band will have to raise $12,600 in the next two months.

_____

_____

_____

_____

_____

_____

_____

_____

_____

_____

_____

_____

_____

_____

_____

_____

_____

_____

_____

_____

CHAPTER 11 Management Skills

Marketing Application 2

DIRECTIONS: *Use the situation described below to practice your management decision-making skills. Study the situation carefully, and then answer the questions that follow.*

Jason works in the editorial department at Resorts Unlimited. A two-year veteran, he has edited three major directories. He always works more hours than anyone in the office. By working nights for several weeks, Jason was able to complete the editing on two of the three directories on schedule. The last directory, however, was late getting into production because some of Jason's calls to resorts weren't returned. The delay cost the company several thousand dollars. Now, Jason is editing a directory of tennis resorts. Since he started this project, he has been arriving at the office an hour early and always stays at least an hour after everyone else leaves. However, he mentioned that he may be delayed again because he is having difficulty contacting a few resort managers.

Derrick, who had no previous editing experience, was also hired by Resorts Unlimited two years ago. He comes to the office at 8 am and goes home at 5 pm. He worked late only one evening when he was finishing his last project, a directory of ski resorts. Twice, when he felt he could not get all the information he needed on the telephone, he visited resorts in Colorado and New Mexico. Each time, he left the office on Thursday evening, flew to the resort, spent the weekend skiing, and returned by noon Monday. On his first three projects, Derrick finished editing a few days ahead of schedule, and he appears to be on schedule for his current one.

1. How would you evaluate the performance of each man? If an opening were to occur for editorial director, which would you promote? Why?

_____

_____

_____

_____

2. Within three months of the publication of Derrick's ski directory, complaints start coming in with regularity from users and listed resorts. It seems that large blocks of information are either inaccurate or out-of-date. The result is an early reprint with heavy alteration costs and a disturbing loss of goodwill. Would these facts alter your earlier evaluations of Jason and Derrick? Explain why or why not.

_____

_____

_____

_____

_____

CHAPTER **11** Management Skills

The DECA Connection

Role Play: Assistant Manager

Situation: You are to assume the role of an assistant manager of a catalog company that specializes in high quality casual clothing for men and women. The vice president of sales (judge) has set new goals that she wants the company to achieve in the next 12 months, including increasing sales by 20 percent and generating a minimum of 15 new customers per month. She thinks the best way to achieve those objectives is through an employee incentive program that focuses on your staff of 10 full-time and 20 part-time telephone order takers. You have been given a budget of $2,500 to implement an incentive program. You think a more realistic budget would be $5,000.

Activity: The vice president of sales (judge) has asked you to report your ideas for this employee incentive program.

Evaluation: You will be evaluated on how well you meet the following performance indicators:

- Develop strategies to achieve company goals/objectives.
- Explain the concept of staff motivation.
- Explain the nature of staff communication.
- Demonstrate appropriate creativity.
- Persuade others.

DIRECTIONS: *Organize your thoughts around the performance indicators noted above. Use these performance indicators to jot down your ideas during the preparation period. Time your preparation period to last 15 minutes and your role play presentation to last a maximum of 10 minutes. After your role play, use the performance indicators to evaluate your efforts.*

_____

_____

_____

_____

_____

_____

_____

_____

_____

Continued on next page

Assessment: Assume each performance indicator is worth 20 points (20 × 5 = 100 points). Use the evaluation levels listed below for judging consistency.

Excellent (16–20) Participant demonstrated the performance indicator in a professional manner, exceeds business standards.

Good (10–15) Participant demonstrated the performance indicator in an acceptable manner; meets minimal business standards; there would be no need for additional formalized training at this time.

Fair (4–9) Participant demonstrated the performance indicator with limited effectiveness; performance generally fell below minimal business standards; additional training would be required to improve knowledge, attitude, and/or skills.

Poor (0–3) Participant demonstrated the performance indicator with little effectiveness or not at all; a great deal of formal training would be needed.

Develop strategies to achieve company goals/objectives.   Score _____

_____

_____

_____

Explain the concept of staff motivation.   Score _____

_____

_____

_____

Explain the nature of staff communication.   Score _____

_____

_____

_____

Demonstrate appropriate creativity.   Score _____

_____

_____

_____

Persuade others.   Score _____

_____

_____

_____

CHAPTER **11** Management Skills

Software Activity (Optional)

Word Processing Application

OBJECTIVE: *Identify the benefits of delegating.*

ACTIVITY: You are the general manager for Somer's Plumbing Supplies, Inc. You have observed that none of the six departmental managers you supervise use delegation to get their work done quickly and effectively.

Use your word processing software to create a memo to your departmental managers. In the memo, stress the benefits of delegating tasks and responsibilities to others.

The heading for the memo is shown below.

To: Department Managers, Somer's Plumbing Supplies, Inc.
From: Your Name
Re: Using Delegation More Effectively
Date: Today's Date

Word Processing Directions

1. Turn on your computer and open your word processing software program.

2. Write the memo. Proofread and edit your work to make sure that it is correct and concise.

3. Save your work. Print out a copy of your memo if your teacher has instructed you to do so.

4. Answer the questions that follow.

Interpreting Results

1. What primary benefits of delegating responsibility should be included in the memo?

_____

_____

_____

_____

_____

_____

_____

_____

_____

Continued on next page

2. What tips on how to delegate effectively should be included in the memo?

_____

_____

_____

_____

_____

Drawing Conclusions

3. What are some reasons managers fail to delegate authority?

_____

_____

_____

_____

_____

_____

4. What are some reasons employees might try to avoid accepting tasks that are delegated?

_____

_____

_____

_____

_____

_____

_____

_____

_____

CHAPTER 12 Preparing for the Sale

Vocabulary Review

DIRECTIONS: *Match each definition with the correct term.*

cold canvassing	extensive decision making	product features
consultative selling	feature-benefit selling	prospect or lead
customer benefits	limited decision making	rational motive
emotional motive	personal selling	routine decision making
endless chain method	pre-approach	telemarketing

_____ 1. Matching product characteristics to a customer's needs and wants.

_____ 2. Advantages or personal satisfaction a customer will get from a good or service.

_____ 3. Used when a person buys goods and services that he or she has purchased before, but not on a regular basis.

_____ 4. A feeling that a customer associates with a product.

_____ 5. Direct contact between a salesperson and a customer.

_____ 6. A potential customer.

_____ 7. Used when a person needs little information because of a high degree of prior experience with a product or low perceived risk.

_____ 8. Basic, physical, or extended attributes of a product or purchase.

_____ 9. Conscious, factual reason for a purchase.

_____ 10. Used when there has been little or no previous experience with an infrequently purchased item.

_____ 11. Getting ready for the face-to-face selling encounter.

_____ 12. Technique used when a salesperson tries to locate potential customers with little or no direct help.

_____ 13. Technique used when a salesperson asks existing customers for names of potential customers.

_____ 14. Providing solutions to customers' problems by finding products that meet their needs.

_____ 15. Process of selling over the telephone.

CHAPTER **12** Preparing for the Sale

Fact and Idea Review

DIRECTIONS: *Circle the letters of all choices that accurately complete each of the following sentences.*

1. Salespeople can get product information they need through
   a. direct experience with the product.
   b. formal training.
   c. friends, relatives, coworkers, and customers.
   d. printed resources (such as packaging, labels, user's manuals, and publications like *Consumer Reports*).

2. Extended product feature(s) for a Reebok running shoe might include the
   a. Duratech rubber sole.
   b. Reebok brand name.
   c. removable molded sock liner.
   d. limited warranty.

3. When buying an automobile, a customer may have
   a. rational reasons for making the purchase, such as monetary savings gained through gas economy.
   b. emotional motives for making the purchase, such as social approval and prestige generated by the image associated with a high-priced car.
   c. both rational and emotional reasons for the purchase based on features such as air bags and a 24-hour emergency roadside service.
   d. reasons different from those of other customers who purchased the same vehicle.

4. The two goals of selling are
   a. to persuade customers to buy something regardless of their need for the item.
   b. to help customers make satisfying buying decisions.
   c. to create an ongoing, profitable relationship with a customer.
   d. to make management's sales quotas any way you can.

5. When a salesperson researches a prospect to determine if he or she needs the product the salesperson is selling, has the financial resources to pay, and is the person who has the authority to buy, we say the salesperson is
   a. prospecting.
   b. using the endless chain method.
   c. cold canvassing.
   d. qualifying the lead.

6. Two pressures on sales staff that can lead to illegal or unethical selling practices if not handled properly by sales personnel are
   a. commission sales.
   b. sales quotas.
   c. sales training requirements.
   d. company policies that address teamwork.

CHAPTER 12 Preparing for the Sale

Marketing Application 1

DIRECTIONS: *Prepare a detailed feature-benefit chart for the Sony CFD-970 Sports Series CD/ Radio Cassette Recorder. Remember, to develop customer benefits, you need to answer the following two questions:*

1. *How does the feature help the product's performance?*
2. *How does the performance information give the customer a personal reason to buy the product?*

To help you, the cassette recorder's key features have already been listed on this and the following page. The first benefit has also been entered.

Feature-Benefit Chart
Sony CFD-970 Sports Series CD/Radio Cassette Recorder

Product Feature: High-impact plastic case with rubber gaskets, bushings, and waterproof seals.

Customer Benefits: Rugged and splash resistant to help keep out water, moisture, and dirt, which allows you to take the recorder anywhere you go.

Product Feature: Built-in compact disk player and stereo cassette deck.

Customer Benefits: _____

_____

_____

_____

Product Feature: Sony Mega Bass® sound system.

Customer Benefits: _____

_____

_____

_____

Product Feature: AM/FM stereo tuner.

Customer Benefits: _____

_____

_____

_____

Continued on next page

Product Feature: Two-way power supply (six DC 9-volt batteries or household current).

Customer Benefits: _____

_____

_____

Product Feature: Two four-inch speakers.

Customer Benefits: _____

_____

_____

Product Feature: Yellow color.

Customer Benefits: _____

_____

_____

Product Feature: Weight: 9 lbs., 4 oz. with batteries.

Customer Benefits: _____

_____

_____

What additional features would you add to the feature-benefit chart so that a retail salesperson would be fully prepared to sell this product?

_____

_____

_____

_____

_____

_____

_____

CHAPTER **12** Preparing for the Sale

Marketing Application 2

DIRECTIONS: *Assume you were just hired as a sales representative for a new start-up company that sells men's and women's fashion accessories. The line includes belts, scarves, ties, tie tacks, unique jewelry, wallets, money clips, and a host of other specialty items. The deal is that you will be paid on straight commission at a rate of eight percent. This means you will only get paid if you sell these products. So, you must begin by studying the products and industry trends, and by prospecting. You need to develop your own leads. How are you going to prepare for the sale?*

1. **Developing Product Information** –What will you do to develop the product information you need to be knowledgeable about the product line?

_____

_____

_____

_____

_____

_____

_____

_____

_____

_____

2. **Industry Trends** – How will you learn about industry trends?

_____

_____

_____

_____

_____

_____

Continued on next page

3. Prospecting – What will you do to locate potential customers (leads)?

_____

_____

_____

_____

_____

_____

4. Qualifying Leads – What will you do to qualify potential customers (leads)?

_____

_____

_____

_____

_____

_____

5. Last Step in the Pre-approach – Once you identify a qualified prospect, what will you do?

_____

_____

_____

_____

_____

_____

6. Commission Sales – If one of your leads buys $2,000 worth of products, how much will you get paid?

_____

_____

_____

_____

CHAPTER 12 Preparing for the Sale

The DECA Connection

Role Play: Prospector

Situation: You are to assume the role of volunteer in the children's ward at a local hospital. The hospital's new public relations/marketing director (judge) wants to raise money for the children's ward in order to renovate it and buy much-needed equipment. A celebrity fashion show is being planned as the fundraiser.

Activity: With your sales background and knowledge of the community, the public relations director (judge) has asked you to help. He would like you to compile a list of prospects for the sale of fashion show fundraiser tickets. The list should include individuals who would be willing to pay $75 for a ticket, as well as companies and organizations that might buy blocks of tickets (10 tickets = $750). Organizations and businesses should also be asked to provide door prizes and raffle prizes that will be given away during the fashion show. Additionally, you have been asked to write a sales letter and a telemarketing script that can be used to qualify the prospects (and identify the hopeless prospects so future sales efforts can be directed to the most promising leads).

Evaluation: You will be evaluated on how well you meet the following performance indicators:

- Differentiate between consumer and organization buying behavior.
- Prospect for customers.
- Persuade others.
- Write sales letters.
- Use proper grammar and vocabulary.

DIRECTIONS: *Organize your thoughts around the performance indicators noted above. Use these performance indicators to jot down your ideas during the preparation period. Time your preparation period to last 15 minutes and your role play presentation to last a maximum of 10 minutes. After your role play, use the performance indicators to evaluate your efforts.*

_____

_____

_____

_____

_____

_____

_____

Continued on next page

Assessment: Assume each performance indicator is worth 20 points (20 × 5 = 100 points). Use the evaluation levels listed below for judging consistency.

Excellent (16–20) Participant demonstrated the performance indicator in a professional manner, exceeds business standards.

Good (10–15) Participant demonstrated the performance indicator in an acceptable manner; meets minimal business standards; there would be no need for additional formalized training at this time.

Fair (4–9) Participant demonstrated the performance indicator with limited effectiveness; performance generally fell below minimal business standards; additional training would be required to improve knowledge, attitude, and/or skills.

Poor (0–3) Participant demonstrated the performance indicator with little effectiveness or not at all; a great deal of formal training would be needed.

Differentiate between consumer and organization buying behavior.   Score _____

_____

_____

_____

Prospect for customers.   Score _____

_____

_____

_____

Persuade others.   Score _____

_____

_____

Write sales letters.   Score _____

_____

_____

_____

Use proper grammar and vocabulary.   Score _____

_____

_____

_____

CHAPTER **12** Preparing for the Sale

Software Activity (Optional)

Spreadsheet Application

OBJECTIVE: *To evaluate the effect of customer preferences on buying decisions.*

ACTIVITY: A local car dealer has collected information about the preferences of new car buyers. The spreadsheet below lists car features and customer ratings for each feature. The list shows how many male and female customers ranked each feature as a key factor in a buying decision. The dealer will use this information to plan future advertising campaigns and sales personnel will use the information in discussing the various car models with potential customers.

	A	B	C	D	E	F	G
1	Chapter 12 Preparing for the Sale						
2							
3							
4			Percentage		Percentage		
5		Men	of	Women	of		
6	Features	(260)	Total Men	(248)	Total Women		
7							
8	Airbags	220		230			
9	Air conditioning	208		180			
10	Antilock brakes	240		215			
11	Automatic transmission	180		196			
12	CD player	170		150			
13	High performance tires	190		130			
14	Maintenance costs	198		200			
15	Power seat adjustments	150		170			
16	Repair record	210		180			
17	Standard transmission	85		68			
18	Stereo radio	88		80			
19	Variety of colors	100		90			

Continued on next page

Spreadsheet Directions

1. Turn on your computer and open your spreadsheet software program.

2. Create a spreadsheet like the one on page 105 using your spreadsheet application.

3. Write formulas to calculate the percentages of men and women who ranked each feature as a major reason for buying a car. Then copy the formulas to the remaining rows.

4. Save your work. Print out a copy of your work if your teacher has instructed you to do so. Then answer the questions that follow.

Interpreting Results

1. Which feature is rated as most important by men? by women? What is the percentage for each?

_____

_____

_____

_____

2. Which feature is the least important for men? for women? What is the percentage for each?

_____

_____

_____

_____

Drawing Conclusions

3. If you were the sales manager for this car dealer, how would you use this information in planning special sales promotions or in sales situations?

_____

_____

_____

_____

_____

_____

_____

_____

CHAPTER 13 Initiating the Sale

Vocabulary Review

DIRECTIONS: *Match each definition with the correct term.*

greeting approach method   open-ended questions
merchandise approach method   service approach method
nonverbal communication

_____ 1. Upon initial face-to-face contact with the customer, the salesperson makes a comment or asks questions about a product that the customer is looking at.

_____ 2. Upon initial face-to-face contact, the salesperson simply welcomes the customer to the store.

_____ 3. Upon initial face-to-face contact, the salesperson asks the customer if he or she needs assistance.

_____ 4. Inquiries that require more than a yes or no answer.

_____ 5. Expressing yourself through body language.

DIRECTIONS: *In the space below, write a brief scenario (story) of a selling situation that illustrates at least three terms from the Word Bank above. You may select the product of your choice. Circle the words from the Word Bank when they appear in the story. Products you might want to consider using are a computer, a copier, running shoes, a camera, luggage, or a CD player.*

_____

_____

_____

_____

_____

_____

_____

_____

CHAPTER **13** Initiating the Sale

Fact and Idea Review

DIRECTIONS: *Circle the letter of the word or phrase that best completes each of the following sentences.*

1. The three purposes of the approach include all of the following except
   a. to begin conversation.
   b. to establish rapport with the customer.
   c. to focus on the merchandise.
   d. to handle customer objections.

2. "Good morning, Mr. Escalona. How's your golf game?" This is an example of
   a. an unacceptable retail approach.
   b. the greeting approach method.
   c. the merchandise approach method.
   d. the service approach method.

3. "You are looking at the newest tennis racket in the Prince line. It has a bigger sweet spot than any of the previous models." This is an example of
   a. the greeting approach method.
   b. the merchandise approach method.
   c. the research approach method.
   d. the service approach method.

4. General concepts that industrial salespeople would use in their opening statements to prospective customers during the initial approach include all of the following except
   a. having the financial resources to pay.
   b. being a better competitor.
   c. increasing productivity.
   d. reducing costs and expenses.

5. Determining needs is an important step in the sales process because
   a. it helps you focus everything you say and do on your customer's needs and wants.
   b. it gives you an opportunity to show and tell the customer everything you know about the product.
   c. you can't handle customers' objections without having first determined their needs.
   d. it is the first contact that you have with the customer and therefore can make or break the sale.

6. A salesperson should begin determining a customer's needs
   a. after the product presentation begins.
   b. as soon as possible in the sales process.
   c. before closing the sale.
   d. when the customer introduces an objection.

7. Determining needs can best be achieved by
   a. observing, asking questions, and listening to your customers.
   b. presenting product features.
   c. asking easy, yes/no questions.
   d. asking many questions in a row to gather all the facts you need before showing a customer any products.

CHAPTER 13 Initiating the Sale

Marketing Application 1

DIRECTIONS: *Read the following scenarios and write an appropriate approach for the initial face-to-face meeting with the customer. After writing the approach, practice saying it to a classmate to check that what you wrote is how you would actually speak.*

Situation 1: You work in the sales department of The Delta Hotel, a large hotel with a conference center that includes several meeting rooms, a business center where guests can send and receive faxes, and nicely furnished guest rooms. The hotel also has two restaurants and offers catering services for special events in its ballroom. Ms. Rodriguez, a representative from a local business, is in the outside office waiting to meet with you. Since she made her appointment through your assistant, you have yet to speak with her directly. She did tell your assistant that her company was considering holding a three-day business conference in your hotel.

_____

_____

_____

_____

_____

_____

_____

Situation 2: You work as a sales associate in a camera store. You observe a woman looking at a digital camera.

_____

_____

_____

_____

_____

_____

_____

_____

Continued on next page

Situation 3: You work as an in-house sales representative in the New York showroom of a men's apparel manufacturer. John Armstrong, an out-of-town buyer whom you have known for the past five years, has an appointment with you to see the new fall line. You see him walking into the showroom 30 minutes early and you are still working with a buyer who had the first appointment of the day.

_____

_____

_____

_____

_____

_____

_____

_____

_____

_____

Situation 4: As a sales clerk in a self-service stationery store, you are often asked to work at the service desk where customers come for assistance. One such customer is now approaching the service desk.

_____

_____

_____

_____

_____

_____

_____

_____

_____

_____

_____

CHAPTER 13 Initiating the Sale

Marketing Application 2

DIRECTIONS: **A.** *Questioning Imagine that you work in a retail store that specializes in outdoor apparel and sporting goods. After you approach a customer who is looking at the Canyon Meadow jacket, you begin to determine her needs. To familiarize yourself with this product, view its Feature-Benefit Chart found in Chapter 12 of Marketing Essentials.*

1. Write one question that you could use to determine why the customer is looking at the jacket.

_____

_____

_____

_____

2. Write two questions to determine the customer's previous experience with the Columbia Sportswear Company (manufacturer of the Canyon Meadow jacket) and its products.

   a. _____

   _____

   b. _____

   _____

3. Write four questions related to specific features of the jacket that will help you decide if it is the one that will satisfy your customer's needs and wants.

   a. _____

   _____

   b. _____

   _____

   c. _____

   _____

   d. _____

   _____

Continued on next page

DIRECTIONS: B. Listening *To assess a customer's needs accurately, you must be a good listener. Based on the following statements made by different customers, determine if the Canyon Meadow jacket is suited to their needs. Explain your conclusion to the customer in each instance.*

1. *Customer:* I'm looking for a waterproof jacket for my children.

   Response:

   _____

   _____

   _____

   _____

   _____

   _____

   _____

2. *Customer:* I need a jacket for my daughter who will be going on a Girl Scouts camping trip. It cannot be bulky because she is limited to one backpack for this trip.

   Response:

   _____

   _____

   _____

   _____

   _____

   _____

   _____

   _____

   _____

CHAPTER 13 Initiating the Sale

The DECA Connection

Role Play: Sales Representative

Situation: You are to assume the role of sales representative for a manufacturer of insulated clothing and accessories for use in business-to-business situations that involve cold environments. Your primary customers are wholesalers that have large warehouses of refrigerated and frozen foods they sell to retail stores and restaurants. The warehouses vary in temperature from 40-degree rooms to freezer rooms where the temperature is a constant 20 degrees below zero. Employees who work in those rooms must have protective clothing to wear when receiving goods and picking customers' orders. Your company manufactures insulated clothing with varying levels of insulation for the different temperatures. The clothing includes jackets, pants, footwear, headwear, and gloves. The gloves come with special grips and degrees of thickness for employees' needs in handling goods and inputting information in computers.

Activity: Your sales manager (judge) wants to put together a training manual for new sales employees. She has asked you to write and present the section on approaching new customers and determining their needs at the next sales meeting. You are expected to generate a minimum of ten questions that can be used to determine the customer's needs. Tell why and when these questions should be asked. Prepare three introductions you might use when approaching a purchasing agent face-to-face for the first time.

Evaluation: You will be evaluated on how well you meet the following performance indicators:

- Establish a relationship with client/customer.
- Address the needs of individuals.
- Determine customer/client needs.
- Prepare for the sales presentation.
- Address people properly.

DIRECTIONS: *Organize your thoughts around the performance indicators noted above. Use these performance indicators to jot down your ideas during the preparation period. Time your preparation period to last 15 minutes and your role play presentation to last a maximum of ten minutes. After your role play, use the performance indicators to evaluate your efforts.*

_____

_____

_____

_____

_____

Continued on next page

Assessment: Assume each performance indicator is worth 20 points (20 × 5 = 100 points). Use the evaluation levels listed below for judging consistency.

Excellent (16–20) Participant demonstrated the performance indicator in a professional manner; exceeds business standards.

Good (10–15) Participant demonstrated the performance indicator in an acceptable and effective manner; meets at least minimal business standards; there would be no need for additional formalized training at this time.

Fair (4–9) Participant demonstrated the performance indicator with limited effectiveness; performance generally fell below minimal business standards; additional training would be required to improve knowledge, attitude, and/or skills.

Poor (0–3) Participant demonstrated the performance indicator with little effectiveness or not at all; a great deal of formal training would be needed.

Establish a relationship with client/customer. Score_____

_____

_____

_____

Address the needs of individuals. Score_____

_____

_____

_____

Determine customer/client needs. Score_____

_____

_____

_____

Prepare for the sales presentation. Score_____

_____

_____

_____

Address people properly. Score_____

_____

_____

_____

CHAPTER **13** Initiating the Sale

Software Activity (Optional)

Spreadsheet Application

OBJECTIVE: *To use population and income data to determine sales opportunities.*

ACTIVITY: The Home Supply Store is planning to build a new retail store in one of five areas of a large city. The population, total income, and number of people over 30 in each area are listed in the spreadsheet below. Home Supply has found that its stores do better in areas with a population of at least 55,000 over age 30 and average income of $28,000. About 70 percent of the store's regular customers are over 30.

A	B	C	D	E	F	G	
1	Chapter 13 Initiating the Sale						
2							
3							
4		Population	Total Income	Average	Population	Percentage	
5				Income	Over 30	Over 30	
6	North	84,600	$2,453,400,000		57,700		
7	South	78,400	$2,138,600,000		55,890		
8	East	67,600	$1,876,000,000		48,690		
9	West	82,700	$2,670,000,000		68,600		
10	Central	76,800	$1,958,000,000		49,500		

Spreadsheet Directions

1. Turn on your computer and open your spreadsheet software program.

2. Create a spreadsheet like the one above using your spreadsheet application.

3. Create a formula to calculate average income in each area, then copy it to the remaining rows. Create a formula to calculate the percentage of population over 30 in each area, then copy the formula to the remaining rows.

4. Save your work.

5. Print out a copy of your work if your teacher has instructed you to do so. Then answer the questions that follow.

Continued on next page

Interpreting Results

1. Which of the areas meets the Home Supply Store's guidelines for establishing a new store?

_____

_____

_____

_____

2. Which area offers the highest percentage of residents over 30?

_____

_____

_____

_____

3. Which area has the highest average income?

_____

_____

_____

_____

Drawing Conclusions

4. Make a recommendation for the area in which Home Supply should locate its new store. Give reasons for your recommendation.

_____

_____

_____

_____

_____

_____

_____

CHAPTER 14 Presenting the Product

Vocabulary Review

DIRECTIONS: *Match each definition with the correct term.*

boomerang method	objections
excuse	paraphrase
jargon	substitution method
layman's terms	superior point method
objection analysis sheet	third party method

_____ 1. Technical or specialized vocabulary used by members of a particular profession or industry.

_____ 2. Words the average customer can understand.

_____ 3. Sending an objection back to the customer as a selling point.

_____ 4. An insincere reason for not buying or not seeing the salesperson.

_____ 5. To restate the meaning of the customer's concern in different words.

_____ 6. Concerns, hesitations, doubts, or other honest reasons a customer has for not making a purchase.

_____ 7. Using a previous customer or another neutral person who can give a testimonial about the product.

_____ 8. This enumerates common customer objections and possible responses to those objections.

_____ 9. Handling an objection by recommending a different product that would still satisfy a customer's needs.

_____ 10. A technique that permits a salesperson to acknowledge objections as valid, yet still offset them with other product features and benefits.

CHAPTER 14 Presenting the Product

Fact and Idea Review

DIRECTIONS: *Circle the letter of the choice that best completes each of the following sentences.*

1. The goal of the product presentation is to
   a. answer all of the customer's questions.
   b. match the customer's needs with appropriate product features and benefits.
   c. persuade a customer to buy the most expensive model in the product line.
   d. show the customer as many products as time permits.

2. During the product presentation in the sale of running shoes, a salesperson should not
   a. show a video tape of Olympic runners wearing specific running shoes.
   b. use a model of a running shoe cut in half to show its construction and hidden features.
   c. have the customer try on a running shoe and walk around in it.
   d. present the customer with five or six models of running shoes to consider at one time.

3. When you do not know the customer's price range and your knowledge of the intended use is insufficient to determine a price range,
   a. begin by showing the medium-priced product in the line.
   b. begin by showing the highest-priced product in the line.
   c. begin by showing the lowest-priced product in the line.
   d. ask the customer how much he or she wants to spend.

4. You are a sales representative for a manufacturer of strep throat testing equipment and supplies. When you call on a physician who is too busy to see you, you should
   a. tell the receptionist that you will not be in the area again for a very long time.
   b. leave your business card and literature about your product.
   c. sit in the office until all the patients have been seen and the doctor has time to see you.
   d. simply leave the office and make a note to return another day.

5. You are a retail sales associate in a clothing store. After speaking with you for a few minutes, a customer explains that she is just browsing and did not plan on buying anything today. At this point, you should
   a. tell the customer how annoyed you are that she wasted your time.
   b. simply leave her alone.
   c. encourage the customer to look around and ask you any questions she may have.
   d. follow the customer around the store just in case she is a shoplifter.

6. If a customer said, "That's more than I wanted to spend on a bicycle built for two. I had no idea they were so expensive," you would use the
   a. superior point method.   c. demonstration method.
   b. direct denial method.   d. third party method.

CHAPTER 14 Presenting the Product

Marketing Application 1

DIRECTIONS: *Plan a product presentation for a Sharp Digital Viewcam. Write exactly what you would say and do to present the product features listed below.*

1. Dimensions (W×H×D Inches) 16.2 × 3.8 × 2.9 and approximate weight 1.2 pounds without tape or battery

   a. What would you say and do to demonstrate this feature?

   _____

   _____

   _____

   _____

   b. How would you involve the customer?

   _____

   _____

   c. What would you say while using an article from *Consumers Digest* as a sales aid?

   _____

   _____

   _____

2. 100 × Digital Zoom

   a. What would you say to demonstrate this feature?

   _____

   _____

   _____

   _____

   b. What would you say to get the customer involved?

   _____

   _____

   c. What would you say while using the owner's manual as a sales aid?

   _____

   _____

   _____

CHAPTER 14 Presenting the Product

Marketing Application 2

DIRECTIONS: *For each customer objection below, write a salesperson's response using the indicated method. For ideas, refer to the feature-benefit chart for the Canyon Meadows jacket found in chapter 12 of Marketing Essentials.*

1. **Objection:** "This jacket is so thin. It can't possibly keep out the rain."

    Response: (Use the boomerang method.)

    _____

    _____

    _____

    _____

    _____

2. **Objection:** "I like this jacket, but I'm not sure my daughter really needs all of its features. She just needs a jacket to wear to school."

    Response: (Use the third party method.)

    _____

    _____

    _____

    _____

    _____

3. **Nonverbal Objection:** Customer has a skeptical look on his face when you tell him how easy it is to pack up the jacket into a pouch.

    Response: (Use the demonstration method.)

    _____

    _____

    _____

    _____

    _____

CHAPTER 14 Presenting the Product

The DECA Connection

Role Play: Sales Associate

Situation: You are to assume the role of sales associate at Luggage & Bags Unlimited. You are responsible for selling a variety of luggage, attaché cases, backpacks, and related products. You know that it is important to use layman's terms, show how product features translate into consumer benefits, involve the customer in the sale, demonstrate the product features, and use sales aids. You also realize that during a product presentation it is common to handle objections that may occur. Another sales associate who started helping a customer must leave and has asked that you take over. He tells you that the consumer is a teenager who is entering high school next month but the customer (judge) is the teen's mother, who will be paying for the purchase.

Activity: You are responsible for presenting the features and benefits of a backpack and handling any objections the consumer and customer (judge) may have. Some of those objections may involve the price, durability, capacity, and ergonomic issues. Use your own backpack or bag to make your product presentation.

Evaluation: You will be evaluated on how well you meet the following performance indicators:

- Analyze product information to identify product features and benefits.
- Prescribe a solution to customer needs.
- Demonstrate the product.
- Convert customer/client objections into selling points.
- Recommend a specific product.

DIRECTIONS: *Organize your thoughts around the performance indicators noted above. Use these performance indicators to jot down your ideas during the preparation period. Time your preparation period to last 15 minutes and your role play presentation to last a maximum of ten minutes. After your role play, use the performance indicators to evaluate your efforts.*

_____

_____

_____

_____

_____

_____

_____

_____

Continued on next page

Assessment: Assume each performance indicator is worth 20 points (20 × 5 = 100 points). Use the evaluation levels listed below for judging consistency.

Excellent   (16–20)   Participant demonstrated the performance indicator in a professional manner; exceeds business standards.

Good   (10–15)   Participant demonstrated the performance indicator in an acceptable and effective manner; meets at least minimal business standards; there would be no need for additional formalized training at this time.

Fair   (4–9)   Participant demonstrated the performance indicator with limited effectiveness; performance generally fell below minimal business standards; additional training would be required to improve knowledge, attitude, and/or skills.

Poor   (0–3)   Participant demonstrated the performance indicator with little effectiveness or not at all; a great deal of formal training would be needed.

Analyze product information to identify product features and benefits.   Score ———

_____

_____

_____

Prescribe a solution to customer needs.   Score ———

_____

_____

_____

Demonstrate the product.   Score ———

_____

_____

_____

Convert customer/client objections into selling points.   Score ———

_____

_____

_____

Recommend a specific product.   Score ———

_____

_____

_____

CHAPTER **14** Presenting the Product

Spreadsheet Application

OBJECTIVE: *To analyze the percentage of sales calls resulting in sales and the average dollar value of a sale.*

ACTIVITY: You are a sales rep with a company that manufactures doors and windows for use in residential and commercial buildings. Much of your time is spent traveling from site to site presenting the company's product lines to building contractors. Your manager has asked you to analyze the amount of time you spend making sales calls and how many of those calls actually result in sales. You have collected the information shown in the spreadsheet below. This information includes the number of sales calls you have made during each of the last eight months. Also included are average times per sales call, number of sales made, and the total dollar volume in sales each month.

	A	B	C	D	E	F	G	H
1	Chapter 14 Presenting the Product							
2								
3				Number	Percentage			
4		Sales	Average	of	of Calls	Dollar	Average	
5		Calls	Time Per	Sales	Resulting	Amount	Sale Per	
6		Made	Call	Made	in Sales	of Sales	Sales Call	
7								
8	January	80	43	40		$408,000		
9	February	76	48	32		$350,000		
10	March	82	40	38		$378,000		
11	April	78	50	41		$280,000		
12	May	74	62	42		$397,800		
13	June	74	58	36		$358,600		
14	July	70	60	38		$419,400		
15	August	72	64	40		$465,000		

Continued on next page

Spreadsheet Directions

1. Turn on your computer and open your spreadsheet software program.

2. Create a spreadsheet like the one on page 123 using your spreadsheet application.

3. Create a formula to calculate the percentage of sales calls that resulted in sales. Then copy the formula to the remaining rows.

4. Create a formula to calculate the average sales dollars per sales call made during the month. Copy the formula to the remaining rows.

5. Save your work.

6. Print out a copy of your work if your teacher has instructed you to do so. Then answer the questions that follow.

Interpreting Results

1. What relationship do you see between the number of minutes spent on sales calls and the percentage of calls that result in sales?

_____

_____

_____

_____

2. What is the highest percentage of sales calls resulting in sales? the lowest?

_____

Drawing Conclusions

3. Using the information in the spreadsheet, develop a plan to increase your sales for the next several months. Explain the data on which you have based your conclusions for how to increase sales.

_____

_____

_____

_____

_____

_____

_____

_____

CHAPTER 15 Closing the Sale

Vocabulary Review

DIRECTIONS: *Match each definition with the correct term.*

buying signals	direct close	suggestion selling
closing the sale	service close	trial close
customer relationship management	standing-room-only close	which close

_____ 1. Involves finding customers and keeping them satisfied.

_____ 2. Closing method that encourages a customer to make a decision between two items.

_____ 3. Closing method in which you ask for the sale.

_____ 4. Obtaining positive agreement from the customer to buy.

_____ 5. Selling additional goods or services to the customer.

_____ 6. Closing method that explains services that overcome obstacles or problems.

_____ 7. Things a customer does or says to indicate a readiness to buy.

_____ 8. Closing method used when a product is in short supply or when the price will be going up in the near future.

_____ 9. Initial effort to close a sale.

CHAPTER 15 Closing the Sale

Fact and Idea Review

DIRECTIONS: *Circle the letter of the choice that best completes each of the following sentences.*

1. You should close the sale

    a. at the same point in each sales presentation.

    b. after a customer says, "I'll take it."

    c. only after you have finished presenting all of your product's selling points.

    d. when your customer is ready to buy.

2. When a customer is having difficulty making a buying decision,

    a. leave the customer alone.

    b. help by summarizing the major features and benefits of the product.

    c. rush the customer.

    d. show the customer additional merchandise.

3. Continuing to tell a customer about the features and benefits of a product that he or she is ready to buy

    a. is an effective sales practice.

    b. helps reduce a customer's doubts about a product.

    c. is especially important in the sale of expensive merchandise.

    d. may cause the salesperson to lose the sale.

4. A specialized closing technique that should be used only when the situation warrants is the

    a. direct close.

    b. service close.

    c. standing-room-only close.

    d. which close.

5. Suggestion selling

    a. can make the original purchase more enjoyable.

    b. hurts a firm because of increased sales-related expenses.

    c. means loading customers down with unwanted goods or services.

    d. should only be attempted when salespeople have time.

6. Customer Relationship Management suggests that

    a. the sale is the first step in developing a relationship with your customer, not the final one.

    b. taking payment or taking the order is the last step in the sales process.

    c. if you did not close the sale today, the sale is lost forever.

    d. after-sale activities are just that and, as such, not part of the formal sales process.

CHAPTER 15 Closing the Sale

Marketing Application 1

DIRECTIONS: *Write what you would say to close the sale in each situation.*

1. You work as a sales associate for Carol's Electronics.

   a. Your store is having a one-day sale to celebrate your town's bicentennial. All merchandise in the store is marked down ten percent for one day. Your customer says, "I like the Sharp Digital Viewcam, but I didn't expect to buy anything today. I'd like my wife to see it before I make a final decision." (Use the standing-room-only close in combination with an appropriate service close.)

   _____

   _____

   _____

   _____

   _____

   b. Your customer says, "I can't wait to start videotaping using the power zoom." (Use a direct close.)

   _____

   _____

   _____

2. You work as a sales representative for the Sharp Manufacturing Company.

   a. You just finished showing the buyer for JTS Electronics, a retailer, all the features and benefits of the Sharp Digital Viewcam, and you think it is time to try a close. (Use a nonthreatening question as a trial close.)

   _____

   _____

   _____

   b. A buyer for PNC Electronic Wholesalers asks, "If I order six dozen Sharp Digital Viewcams to start and they sell well, how quickly can I get a reorder?" (Use a direct close.)

   _____

   _____

   _____

CHAPTER 15 Closing the Sale

Marketing Application 2

DIRECTIONS: A. *Suggestion Selling* *Study the sales situations below. Then, in each case, tell what additional merchandise or service you would suggest and what you would say to recommend it.*

1. You work in a bicycle store and have just sold a couple a bicycle for their young daughter.

   Suggested item:

   _____

   What would you say?

   _____

   _____

2. You are a sales representative for the Sharp Manufacturing Company. The company is offering free shipping on all orders that exceed $5,000, if the order is placed within the next week. You just closed a sale with a retail store buyer who wants to place a $4,500 order.

   Suggested item:

   _____

   What would you say?

   _____

   _____

DIRECTIONS: B. *Customer Relationship Management* *Study the sales situations below. Then, in each case, tell what you would do establish a relationship with the customer.*

3. You are a sales representative for the Sharp Manufacturing Company. A retail store buyer has just placed an order with you for $100,000 with specifications regarding delivery.

   _____

   _____

4. You are a sales associate for an upscale clothing store.

   _____

   _____

   _____

   _____

CHAPTER **15** Closing the Sale

The DECA Connection

Role Play: Computer Salesperson

Situation: You are to assume the role of sales associate for Computers Etc. You have been working with a customer (judge) for the past 20 minutes. You have determined his needs, and presented the features and benefits of a computer and monitor that meets those needs. You now feel it is time to close the sale and suggest additional items that will help the customer use and enjoy the computer. The customer (judge) is interested in a 15" monitor and a computer with a high-speed modem, a CD writeable drive, and a DVD drive, at a retail price of $1,299. In addition to printers and computer software, your company offers several services that the customer (judge) may be interested in, such as leasing, extended warranty (at a cost of $49.99 for three years), home installation ($25 fee), classes on operating systems and software applications, and Internet use (free with the purchase of a computer). The company also offers a toll-free phone number for tech support and a special policy for VIP support at a fee of $19.99 for a year. To keep your customers from experiencing doubt after purchase, you are expected to check on customers to see if they are having any problems or have any questions. To ensure customer satisfaction, an independent market research company conducts a follow-up survey with your customers to check on how they were treated by store employees during and after the sale. It might be a good idea to tell your customer (judge) about the customer satisfaction survey so he will respond to it.

Activity: Close the sale with the customer (judge) and suggest appropriate goods and services to enhance the original purchase. Before the customer (judge) leaves, tell him what you are going to do as a follow-up to the sale.

Evaluation: You will be evaluated on how well you meet the following performance indicators:

- Facilitate customer-buying decisions.
- Close the sale.
- Demonstrate suggestion selling.
- Explain the role of customer service as a component of selling relationships.
- Plan follow-up strategies for use in selling.

DIRECTIONS: *Organize your thoughts around the performance indicators noted above. Use these performance indicators to jot down your ideas during the preparation period. Time your preparation period to last 15 minutes and your role play presentation to last a maximum of ten minutes. After your role play, use the performance indicators to evaluate your efforts.*

_____

_____

_____

_____

Continued on next page

Assessment: Assume each performance indicator is worth 20 points (20 × 5 = 100 points). Use the evaluation levels listed below for judging consistency.

Excellent (16–20) Participant demonstrated the performance indicator in a professional manner; exceeds business standards.

Good (10–15) Participant demonstrated the performance indicator in an acceptable and effective manner; meets at least minimal business standards; there would be no need for additional formalized training at this time.

Fair (4–9) Participant demonstrated the performance indicator with limited effectiveness; performance generally fell below minimal business standards; additional training would be required to improve knowledge, attitude, and/or skills.

Poor (0–3) Participant demonstrated the performance indicator with little effectiveness or not at all; a great deal of formal training would be needed.

Facilitate customer-buying decisions. Score _____

_____

_____

_____

Close the sale. Score _____

_____

_____

_____

Demonstrate suggestion selling. Score _____

_____

_____

_____

Explain the role of customer service as a component of selling relationships. Score _____

_____

_____

_____

Plan follow-up strategies for use in selling. Score _____

_____

_____

_____

Student _____ Date _____

Class _____ Teacher _____

CHAPTER 15 Closing the Sale

Spreadsheet Application

OBJECTIVE: *To estimate sales for a future period.*

ACTIVITY: The manager of the Pine Mountain Ski Resort is making a budget for the upcoming season. One of the first things the manager does is forecast revenue from room rentals for each of the five months of the season. Those months are December through April. The manager uses past experience to estimate the number of rooms that will be filled during each month, which is the occupancy rate. The spreadsheet below shows the price of the rooms per night and the occupancy rate for each month.

	A	B	C	D	E	F	G
1	Chapter 15 Closing the Sale						
2							
3							
4			Average				
5		Number	Room	Occupancy			
6	Month	of Rooms	Rate	Rate	Revenue		
7							
8	December	100	$128	95%			
9	January	100	$128	92%			
10	February	100	$128	89%			
11	March	100	$128	74%			
12	April	100	$128	48%			
13							
14	TOTAL REVENUE						

Continued on next page

Spreadsheet Directions

1. Turn on your computer and open your spreadsheet software program.

2. Create a spreadsheet like the one on page 131 using your spreadsheet application.

3. Input a formula to determine the estimated revenue for the month of December. Copy the formula to the remaining cells.

4. Calculate the total revenue by entering the appropriate formula to add the revenue column.

5. Save your work to a new file.

6. Print out a copy of your work if your teacher has instructed you to do so. Then answer the questions that follow.

Interpreting Results

1. What is the total revenue based on the projections of occupancy for the months of December through April?

_____

2. Which month has the highest revenue from rooms? the lowest?

_____

Drawing Conclusions

3. Why is the occupancy rate important in projecting future income from the rental of rooms? How would the occupancy rate help the manager to forecast sales for other non-room items, such as ski lift tickets and restaurant income?

_____

_____

_____

_____

_____

_____

_____

_____

_____

_____

_____

_____

CHAPTER 16 Using Math in Sales

Vocabulary Review

DIRECTIONS: Complete the crossword puzzle using terms from the chapter.

Across

3. Type of sale that permits a customer to take an item home for further consideration. (two words)

5. A trade of one item for another.

6. Partial refund (usually because of a flaw in the merchandise)

7. Acronym for a bar code.

8. Type of sale involving payment by check or currency.

11. Maximum amount that can be charged without special authorization. (two words)

14. Type of sale involving payment by Visa, MasterCard, etc.

15. Acronym for a combined cash register and computer.

Down

1. Sale, return, exchange, etc.

2. Bank card that allows automatic transfer of funds at time of sale. (two words)

3. Money in the register drawer at the beginning of the business day. (three words)

4. Also known as will-call.

9. Acronym that means to be paid for when delivered.

10. You get money or credit back with one of these.

12. Money drawer in a cash register.

13. A bill for merchandise purchased.

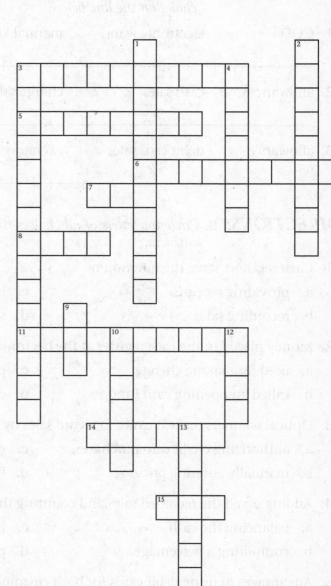

CHAPTER 16 Using Math in Sales

Fact and Idea Review

DIRECTIONS: **A.** *In each series of items, circle the one that does not belong. Then explain your choice on the line below.*

1. COD   electronic wand   manual key   optical scanner   UPC

   _____

2. allowances   cash sales   charge sales   layaway   on approval

   _____

3. allowance   debit card sale   exchange   return

   _____

DIRECTIONS: **B.** *Circle the letters of all choices that accurately complete each of the following sentences.*

1. Cash registers serve the function of
   a. providing receipts.
   b. recording sales.
   c. issuing vendor marketing codes.
   d. storing cash and sales documents.

2. Money placed in the cash register at the beginning of each day is
   a. used for making change.
   b. called an opening cash fund.
   c. part of the day's sales.
   d. deposited in the bank.

3. Optical scanners make it easier to record sales by relieving salesclerks of the responsibility for
   a. authorizing credit card purchases.
   b. manually entering prices.
   c. calling out prices.
   d. figuring discounts.

4. Adding up all the recorded sales and counting the cash at the end of a business day is called
   a. balancing the cash.
   b. computing a percentage.
   c. balancing the till.
   d. putting an item on layaway.

5. Advantages of using debit cards for both customers and businesses include
   a. immediate payment.
   b. convenience.
   c. theft protection.
   d. protection against bad checks.

6. In a business-to-business transaction, a buyer who wants to take advantage of the discount offered on a January 21 invoice that has dating terms of 2/10, net 45, could do so if he or she made payment on
   a. January 31.
   b. February 12.
   c. March 15.
   d. March 31.

CHAPTER 16 Using Math in Sales

Marketing Application 1

DIRECTIONS: **A.** *Study the illustration of a cash drawer below. Then on the appropriate line write the name of the currency or coin that is customarily placed in each compartment.*

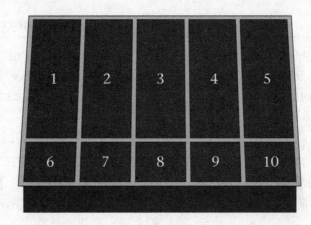

1. _____   6. _____

2. _____   7. _____

3. _____   8. _____

4. _____   9. _____

5. _____   10. _____

DIRECTIONS: **B.** *Imagine yourself in the following sales situation: Your friend Howie comes into Stepworth Audio, where you work. He buys two used CD's for a total cost of $18.37 and gives you a $20 dollar bill.*

1. Name the coins and bills you will give Howie. (Be sure to use the proper order for making change.)

_____

2. How would you verbally count the change back to Howie?.

_____

3. How would you count the change if you had a POS system?

_____

CHAPTER 16 Using Math in Sales

Marketing Application 2

DIRECTIONS: You are a salesclerk (ID. No. 38760, Dept. 6) at Old West Togs 'n Tack. Prepare sales slips for your first two customers of the day. Their purchases are described below. Use the current date, and assume the state sales tax is six percent.

Customer 1	Customer 2
3 shirts @ $29.95	2 pairs of jeans @ $34.95
2 belts @ $36.95	3 shirts @ $32.95
2 pairs of boots @ $125.00	2 saddle racks @ $28.50
3 halters @ $37.95	

OLD WEST TOGS 'N TACK
400 Mesquite Hwy., Mina, NV 89824

Sold To _____

Address _____

Date	Dept.	Clerk #

Qty	Description	Price	Amount
	Subtotal		
	Sales Tax		
	Total		

OLD WEST TOGS 'N TACK
400 Mesquite Hwy., Mina, NV 89824

Sold To _____

Address _____

Date	Dept.	Clerk #

Qty	Description	Price	Amount
	Subtotal		
	Sales Tax		
	Total		

CHAPTER *16* Using Math in Sales

The DECA Connection

Role Play: Sales Team Member

Situation: You are to assume the role of member of a sales team for a stationery store. Most of the store's business comes from custom invitation orders. When taking custom orders, many special charges must be calculated for custom inks, special printing, quality of paper, shipping and handling, etc.

Activity: Your boss (judge) has asked you to design a generic sales check that can be used to record charges for these orders. Your boss also wants you to train new employees on how to use the sales checks to record sales.

Evaluation: You will be evaluated on how well you meet the following performance indicators:

- Describe the nature of business records.
- Sell a good/service/idea to groups.
- Conduct training class/program.
- Prepare simple written reports.
- Demonstrate appropriate creativity.

DIRECTIONS: *Organize your thoughts around the performance indicators noted above. Use these performance indicators to jot down your ideas during the preparation period. Time your preparation period to last 15 minutes and your role play presentation to last a maximum of ten minutes. After your role play, use the performance indicators to evaluate your efforts.*

_____

_____

_____

_____

_____

_____

_____

_____

_____

_____

_____

Continued on next page

Assessment: Assume each performance indicator is worth 20 points (20 × 5 = 100 points). Use the evaluation levels listed below for judging consistency.

Excellent (16–20) Participant demonstrated the performance indicator in a professional manner; exceeds business standards.

Good (10–15) Participant demonstrated the performance indicator in an acceptable and effective manner; meets at least minimal business standards; there would be no need for additional formalized training at this time.

Fair (4–9) Participant demonstrated the performance indicator with limited effectiveness; performance generally fell below minimal business standards; additional training would be required to improve knowledge, attitude, and/or skills.

Poor (0–3) Participant demonstrated the performance indicator with little effectiveness or not at all; a great deal of formal training would be needed.

Describe the nature of business records. Score ———

_____

_____

_____

Sell a good/service/idea to groups. Score ———

_____

_____

_____

Conduct training class/program. Score ———

_____

_____

_____

Prepare simple written reports. Score ———

_____

_____

_____

Demonstrate appropriate creativity. Score ———

_____

_____

_____

CHAPTER 16 Using Math in Sales

Software Activity (Optional)

Spreadsheet Application

OBJECTIVE: *Calculate growth in selected business sectors.*

ACTIVITY: You want to invest in a high-growth business. You have studied market and economic factors and you have narrowed your choices to the business sectors listed below. You want to choose the sector that has the highest growth rate.

The printout below shows data that you have collected about current sales, as well as anticipated sales in five years. To calculate the growth rate for each business sector, first subtract the current sales from the anticipated sales in five years. Then divide the result by current sales totals.

	A	B	C	D
1	Chapter 16 Using Math in Sales			
2				
3				
4			Anticipated	
5	Business	Current	Sales in	Growth
6	Category	Sales	Five Years	Rate
7				
8	Restaurants	$48,926	$86,109	
9	Retailing (non-food)	$18,790	$33,530	
10	Hotels/Motels	$14,631	$22,511	
11	Convenience Stores	$12,309	$19,377	
12	Business Services	$12,076	$21,282	
13	Automotive Products and Services	$10,604	$15,944	
14	Food Retailing	$10,370	$14,544	
15	Rental Services	$5,282	$8,900	
16	Construction and Home Services	$3,720	$9,255	
17	Recreation/Entertainment/Travel	$1,840	$6,573	

Spreadsheet Directions

1. Start your spreadsheet software program.

2. Create a spreadsheet like the one above using your spreadsheet application.

3. Enter a formula to calculate growth rate for each of the business sectors listed.

4. After completing your calculations, save your work.

5. Print out a copy of your work if your teacher has instructed you to do so.

6. Answer the following questions.

Continued on next page

Interpreting Results

1. Which business sector shows the largest growth rate?

_____

_____

_____

2. Which business sector shows the smallest growth rate?

_____

_____

Drawing Conclusions

3. Based on your calculations, which business sector would be the best investment choice? Why?

_____

_____

_____

_____

_____

_____

_____

4. Based on your calculations about growth rate, which of these business sectors would be the least desirable investment opportunity? Explain.

_____

_____

_____

_____

_____

_____

_____

CHAPTER 17 Promotional Concepts and Strategies

Vocabulary Review

DIRECTIONS: *Match each definition with the correct term.*

advertising	premiums	promotional tie-ins
direct marketing	product promotion	publicity
incentives	promotion	public relations
institutional promotion	promotional mix	sales promotion
news release		

_____ 1. Paid form of nonpersonal presentation and promotion of ideas, goods, or services by an identified sponsor.

_____ 2. This creates a favorable image for a business.

_____ 3. Any form of communication used by a business to inform, persuade, or remind people about its products and improve its public image.

_____ 4. Used by a business to convince potential customers to buy products from it instead of a competitor.

_____ 5. Special kind of public relations that involves placing positive information about a business, its products, or policies in the media.

_____ 6. Low-cost items given away free to customers with a purchase.

_____ 7. Products earned and given through contests, or as sweepstakes awards.

_____ 8. All marketing activities, other than personal selling, advertising, and publicity, that are used to stimulate consumer purchasing and sales effectiveness.

_____ 9. The combination of different types of promotion.

_____ 10. This refers to any activity designed to create goodwill toward a business.

_____ 11. A prewritten story about a company that is sent to the media.

_____ 12. Advertising directed at a target group rather than a mass market.

_____ 13. Sales promotional arrangements between one or more retailers or manufacturers.

CHAPTER **17** Promotional Concepts and Strategies

Fact and Idea Review

DIRECTIONS: *Classify each of the following promotional activities as advertising (**A**), public relations (**P**), direct marketing (**D**), sales promotion (**SP**), or personal selling (**PS**).*

_____ 1. Jeep/Eagle introduces a new product on television during the NFL Super Bowl.

_____ 2. Post Cereal places CD-ROMs in some of its branded cereals.

_____ 3. The GAP provides clothes for a local DECA chapter fashion show.

_____ 4. A publishing company sends an e-mail to its current customers.

_____ 5. The *Chicago Tribune* runs a favorable review of a new play opening in the city.

_____ 6. A Prudential insurance representative gives an in-home presentation about life insurance.

_____ 7. Ocean Spray places a "$1.00 off" coupon in a freestanding insert as part of a Sunday newspaper.

_____ 8. Edward Jones sends a notice to its investors about a new municipal bond offering.

_____ 9. A local credit union buys a ½-page ad in the high school yearbook.

_____ 10. Home Depot is recognized for its sponsorship of Habitat for Humanity International.

_____ 11. AT&T develops a four-color brochure about the unique features of a facsimile machine it is selling.

_____ 12. A sales associate at J.C. Penney convinces a customer to buy a dress shirt and matching tie.

_____ 13. Northwest Airlines and Disney combine resources to sponsor a vacation package.

_____ 14. Ohio State University gives permission to an apparel manufacturer to print its logo on football caps.

_____ 15. A local theater introduces a new movie by buying a 15-second spot on the local radio station.

_____ 16. A new interior display is constructed by Neiman Marcus to feature summer apparel.

_____ 17. The counter clerk at a Taco Bell restaurant takes your order.

_____ 18. A Shade Tree Enterprises customer service representative helps you order snowmobile parts by phone.

_____ 19. A Cabela's catalog is sent to people who have recently purchased outdoor gear.

_____ 20. A new allergy tablet sample is mailed to all households in a particular city.

_____ 21. Ace Hardware is recognized at a school banquet for hiring marketing education students.

_____ 22. Coupons are placed on or inside product packages.

_____ 23. The sponsor of a paid message is identified.

_____ 24. The Kalamazoo Civic Theatre sends the season schedule to its patrons.

CHAPTER 17 Promotional Concepts and Strategies

Marketing Application 1

DIRECTIONS: *Classify each of the following public relations activities as primarily targeted to employees (E), customers (C), or the general community (GC).*

_____ 1. Perkins Restaurants provides complimentary meals for the Give Kids The World Foundation.

_____ 2. A medical center sponsors a free health and wellness seminar for its staff members.

_____ 3. The U.S. Department of Transportation and the Council run a print advertisement with a logo that reads, "You Could Learn a Lot From A Dummy. Buckle Your Safety Belt."

_____ 4. The Eaton Corporation offers 100 percent tuition reimbursement for marketing support specialists.

_____ 5. A local marketing education program sponsors an end-of-the-year student recognition dinner for students and parents.

_____ 6. A new office building sponsors a free breakfast for area businesspeople followed by a tour of the complex.

_____ 7. A department store offers a free gift wrapping service for the holiday season.

_____ 8. A company recognizes an employee for her work with the Little League in a company newsletter.

_____ 9. A regional sales manager of the AT&T Phone Center allows his store managers to act as judges at a state DECA Career Development Conference.

_____ 10. A local radio station allows its manager to serve as a business advisor to a Junior Achievement program at the high school.

_____ 11. Company associates at the Outback Restaurant get a discount on a dinner for two people.

_____ 12. Stacey and Theo's restaurant provides a free meal to the homeless for Thanksgiving.

_____ 13. The Ford Motor Company provides an employee suggestion awards program.

_____ 14. A local community college plans an open house to celebrate the opening of a new downtown campus location.

_____ 15. A furniture store provides free delivery to customers in a 15-mile radius of the store.

_____ 16. A personal care consultant is available to advise customers on cosmetics selection.

_____ 17. Harding's supermarkets offer to bag your groceries and take them to your car for free.

_____ 18. Pharmacia becomes a civic theater patron and has its name printed in the program.

_____ 19. The Steelcase company promotes people from within the company.

_____ 20. Northwest Airlines supports the Make a Wish Foundation by giving 500 bonus miles to frequent fliers who donate $50 or more.

CHAPTER 17 Promotional Concepts and Strategies

Marketing Application 2

DIRECTIONS: Read the case study below. Then answer the questions that follow.

Fantastic Prizes and Free Gifts Offered through Sweepstakes

Sweepstakes have been popular ways to attract customers for years, but until recently were advertised primarily through print and broadcast media, particularly through targeted mailings. Now, companies are turning to the Internet with their sweepstakes and are finding big audiences. A recent survey ranked several Internet sweepstakes sites among the top 50 sites in numbers of unique visitors.

On iwon.com, Web surfers earn sweepstakes entries for every click. Other sites, such as alladvantage.com and freeride.com, award points redeemable for prizes when users leave an advertising banner visible at the top of the page as they surf. Other companies offer contests as opposed to sweepstakes. In contests, users must demonstrate some skill. Webmillion.com gives points redeemable for sweepstakes entries for correct trivia answers. Web-based giveaways are often cash, but can also be prepaid phone cards, gift certificates for stores and restaurants, and free CDs and books.

The strategy of most Web-based sweepstakes companies is to attract repeat users and then sell the users' demographic information to advertisers. Some simply use the sweepstakes to attract people, then try to sell them magazines, household products, time-share vacations, cruises, books, and flowers. Although purchases are not required to enter most sweepstakes, companies are clearly trying to lure buyers with the chance at free cash. Companies strongly suggest that purchases should be made, and even provide different instructions for entering without a purchase. Two established sweepstakes companies, Publishers Clearing House and American Family Publishers, earn commissions on the products they sell through the sweepstakes.

1. What is the difference between a contest and a sweepstakes?

_____

_____

_____

2. Sweepstakes are an example of a consumer incentive. Why might businesses use sweepstakes as a sales promotional device?

_____

_____

_____

3. Most sweepstakes do not require a participant to purchase anything to enter, but many companies highly suggest that you do. Can you think of some techniques that are used to encourage participants to buy a product?

_____

_____

_____

CHAPTER 17 Promotional Concepts and Strategies

The DECA Connection

Role Play: Sales Promotion Planner

Situation: You are to assume the role of assistant manager for a small independent retailer. The store has a very good community reputation for offering quality merchandise at fair prices. Your store is not large enough to qualify for quantity discounts on its orders, nor does it buy sufficient quantities to acquire its own private label. Because of this, your store needs creative nonprice sales promotions to compete with larger retail chains at full margin prices. Your larger competitors, on the other hand, can and do offer constant sale prices, off-price promotions, and markdowns. You have been asked by the store owner (judge) to come up with a list of several nonprice sales promotions based upon three overall store objectives:

1. Increase customer traffic into the store,

2. Design creative and fun non-price sales promotions, and

3. Increase sales revenues by using effective sales promotions.

Activity: Explain your sales promotion ideas to the owner (judge). Detail the suggested strategies to meet each of these three objectives. Be sure to include ideas that will increase customer traffic through sales promotions that do not emphasize sale prices, off-price reductions, or markdowns, since to compete you must sell at near or full margins.

Evaluation: You will be evaluated on how well you meet the following performance indicators:

- Analyze use of specialty promotions.
- Develop a sales promotion plan.
- Explain the types of promotion.
- Explain the nature of effective communications.
- Persuade others.

DIRECTIONS: *Organize your thoughts around the performance indicators noted above. Use these performance indicators to jot down your ideas during the preparation period. Time your preparation period to last 15 minutes and your role play presentation to last a maximum of ten minutes. After your role play, use the performance indicators to evaluate your efforts.*

Continued on next page

Assessment: Assume each performance indicator is worth 20 points (20 × 5 = 100 points). Use the evaluation levels listed below for judging consistency.

Excellent (16–20) Participant demonstrated the performance indicator in a professional manner; exceeds business standards.

Good (10–15) Participant demonstrated the performance indicator in an acceptable manner; meets minimal business standards; there would be no need for additional formalized training at this time.

Fair (4–9) Participant demonstrated the performance indicator with limited effectiveness; performance generally fell below minimal business standards; additional training would be required to improve knowledge, attitude, and/or skills.

Poor (0–3) Participant demonstrated the performance indicator with little effectiveness or not at all; a great deal of formal training would be needed.

Analyze use of specialty promotions. Score ———

_____

_____

_____

Develop a sales promotion plan. Score ———

_____

_____

_____

Explain the types of promotion. Score ———

_____

_____

_____

Explain the nature of effective communications. Score ———

_____

_____

_____

Persuade others. Score ———

_____

_____

_____

CHAPTER 17 Promotional Concepts and Strategies

Software Activity (Optional)	**Spreadsheet Application**

OBJECTIVE: *To calculate the cost of promotional discounts.*

ACTIVITY: The Cosi Electronics Corporation is introducing a new line of CD players and portable stereo systems. To encourage retail stores to stock the full line of products, Cosi is offering a 12 percent discount off the wholesale price of the CD players and an eight percent discount on the stereo systems. The new CD players and stereos are available in two models. The regular wholesale price for model 640A is $124; for model 750A, $160; for model 2244, $178; and for model 2264, $158. The estimated units that the company plans to ship to stores are shown in the printout below. Use this information to calculate the cost to Cosi of using these promotional discounts.

	A	B	C	D	E	F	G
1	Chapter 17 Promotional Concepts and Strategies						
2							
3							
4			Estimated		Discount		
5	Model	Price	Units	Discount	Cost		
6	640A CD	$124	18,420	12.0%			
7	750A CD	$160	24,640	12.0%			
8	Stereo 2244	$178	32,380	8.0%			
9	Stereo 2264	$158	28,960	8.0%			
10	TOTAL COST						

Spreadsheet Directions

1. Turn on your computer and open your spreadsheet software program.

2. Create a spreadsheet like the one above using your spreadsheet application.

3. Create a formula to calculate the discount cost for each product. Then create a formula to calculate the total of all discount costs.

4. Perform the calculations, then save your work.

5. Print out a copy of your work if your teacher has instructed you to do so. Then answer the questions that follow.

Continued on next page

Interpreting Results

1. What is the total cost of offering the promotional discounts for this new product line?

_____

_____

_____

_____

2. If the company has budgeted a total of $2,000,000 for promotional discounts, how much money is available? If the response from dealers results in a total promotional cost that is 10 percent higher than the current figure, will the cost be under or over budget?

_____

_____

_____

_____

_____

_____

Drawing Conclusions

3. Promotional discounts are offered to try to increase sales of a product. Can you think of at least one situation when a promotional discount might not be to the advantage of the company offering it? Explain your answer.

_____

_____

_____

_____

_____

_____

_____

_____

_____

_____

_____

CHAPTER 18 Visual Merchandising and Display

Vocabulary Review

DIRECTIONS: *Read each sentence, noting the underlined word or phrase. Then, from the four choices that follow, select the term that could best replace the underlined text. Circle your choice.*

1. The <u>total exterior</u> of a business includes the entranceways, display windows, marquee, and the design and setting of the building itself.

   a. display **b.** entrance **c.** layout **d.** storefront

2. The <u>exhibit</u> of spring clothing was visually appealing to customers.

   a. display **b.** formal balance **c.** marquee **d.** store layout

3. Placing large items on each side creates <u>a regular arrangement</u> in a display.

   a. direction **b.** formal balance **c.** informal balance **d.** proportion

4. A <u>canopy</u> extends out over a store's entrance.

   a. banner **b.** marquee **c.** storefront **d.** signs

5. The <u>floor space allocation</u> is used to facilitate sales and serve the customer.

   a. display **b.** storefront **c.** store layout **d.** personnel space

6. Red and green are <u>opposite colors</u> and create great contrasts.

   a. adjacent colors **c.** complementary colors
   b. analogous colors **d.** transparent colors

7. The <u>coordination of all the physical elements</u> projected the right image to the customers.

   a. direction **b.** display **c.** shape **d.** visual merchandising

8. Props and signs should always be in <u>the correct relationship</u> to the merchandise.

   a. aisles **b.** direction **c.** line **d.** proportion

9. Blue and green are <u>located next to each other on the color wheel</u> and blend well.

   a. adjacent colors **c.** matching colors
   b. complementary colors **d.** transparent colors

10. The <u>object used to display a store's name</u> should be original and easily recognizable.

    a. billboard **b.** exterior **c.** sign **d.** spectacular

11. The <u>interactive point-of-purchase display</u> is playing an increasingly important role in sales merchandising.

    a. a fixture **b.** interior display **c.** kiosk **d.** window display

12. The <u>strongest visual element</u> of a display attracts the viewer's attention first, above all else.

    a. direction **c.** informal balance
    b. focal point **d.** line

CHAPTER 18 Visual Merchandising and Display

Fact and Idea Review

DIRECTIONS: *In each series of items, circle the one that does not belong. Then explain your choice.*

1. advertising   interior displays   storefront   store layout   store interior

_____

_____

2. entrances   marquee   store layout   window displays

_____

_____

3. dressing rooms   personnel space   restaurant space   recreational areas for children

_____

_____

4. fixtures   floors   interior displays   store layout   walls

_____

_____

5. abstract setting   color   direction   line   proportion

_____

_____

6. adjacent   complementary   color   lighting

_____

_____

7. balance   formal   informal   proportion

_____

_____

Student	Date
Class	Teacher

CHAPTER 18 Visual Merchandising and Display

Marketing Application 1

DIRECTIONS: *Read the case study below. Then answer the questions that follow.*

Taking a Different Approach

In a major departure from its established merchandising approach, the Walgreen Company has made a shift from strip mall to stand-alone stores. Although Walgreens had historically steered clear of competition with major grocery and discount stores, the company's new strategy puts it in direct competition with discounting behemoths and is so far producing profitable results. Research shows the typical Walgreens customer spends only about $10 per visit and stays in the store only 14 minutes.

By leasing strip-mall space, the company avoided huge cash outlays when opening stores, and could count on each store being profitable very quickly. A freestanding store can cost $3 million to build and usually takes two to three years to show a profit. Even so, the Walgreen Company has been aggressive in its move to freestanding stores. In 1992, only 230 Walgreens stores were stand-alones; today, half of the 3,051 Walgreens stores in 43 states are freestanding.

The new Walgreens stores, at approximately 15,000 square feet in size, are miniscule compared to the typical Wal-Mart, which can top 150,000 square feet. However, the Walgreen Company is banking that they can attract customers with conveniences such as a 24-hour drive-through, and by ensuring customers have a quick, hassle-free visit.

One new store in Buffalo Grove, Ill., is close to both a Jewel/Osco supermarket and a Wal-Mart. This prototype store showcases the company's new store design strategy. The new store has wide aisles and a center aisle for prominent display of seasonal items. The store also has a larger assortment of high-margin food items like snacks, cereals, and frozen foods than the Walgreens strip-mall stores carry. The company's core business remains prescription drugs, and the company has an e-commerce pharmacy to increase customer convenience and prescription drug sales.

Research by the store design firm Retail Design Associates showed that improved theme, colors, lighting, and signage can improve a store's sales from ten to 300 percent. Effective store design can entice shoppers into a store; the right mix of merchandise and competitive prices can keep them as customers. The Walgreen Company has seen the concrete proof of this theory. Customer traffic in strip-mall stores that were converted to stand-alones increased ten percent. More importantly, store revenue in those same stores increased 30 percent.

1. Explain why the Walgreen Company is changing its store locations to compete more directly with large supermarkets and discount stores.

_____

_____

_____

_____

_____

_____

2. The look of every store should conform to customer expectations. What would you suggest to a retailer considering a store design change?

_____
_____
_____
_____
_____
_____
_____

3. Speculate on why the Walgreen Company is willing to take the risk of moving its stores away from strip-malls.

_____
_____
_____
_____
_____
_____
_____

4. In tough economic times, retailers often decide to cut back on staff or inventory, but are reluctant to skimp on store design. Explain this decision and some possible problems it may create.

_____
_____
_____
_____
_____
_____
_____
_____

CHAPTER *18* Visual Merchandising and Display

Marketing Application 2

DIRECTIONS: *Form teams of two and prepare a promotional display using the various artistic considerations involved with display preparation. Depending on the space available and the direction of your instructor, your display can be an interior display or window display for your school store or classroom. Use the space below to design your display before you create it. Your merchandise display will be evaluated by the performance criteria listed on the next page.*

We will need the following props and fixtures:

_____

_____

_____

_____

_____

Continued on next page

Performance Criteria

Your instructor will rate you or your team's completed merchandise display by using the following rating scale.

Rating Scale	1–4	Poor	5–6	Fair
	7–8	Good	9–10	Excellent

Categories: **Your score**

1. **Selling power**
   Does the display give a strong sales message?   _____

2. **Attention-grabbing effect**
   Does the display make striking use of all materials?   _____

3. **Contribution to product image**
   Does the display emphasize and enhance product image?   _____

4. **Timeliness**
   Is the product seasonally appropriate?   _____

5. **Theme usage**
   Does the display use a creative theme appropriate for the product?   _____

6. **Use of color**
   Does the display use color effectively?   _____

7. **Use of artistic elements**
   Were the artistic elements of balance, line, shape, direction, texture,
   proportion, motion, and lighting used creatively?   _____

8. **Arrangement of materials and props**
   Are display materials and props aesthetically pleasing?   _____

9. **Display cards and signs**
   Are display cards and signs easy to read? Do they coordinate and match the
   display?   _____

10. **Overall appearance**
    Was the display clean, neat, and orderly?   _____

Comments:

_____

_____

_____

_____

CHAPTER 18 Visual Merchandising and Display

The DECA Connection

Role Play: Sales Associate

Situation: You are to assume the role of sales associate in the women's apparel department of a large department store. Your department has a reputation for well-designed, professional, and appealing interior displays. A weeklong storewide sales promotion for a new line of clothing has been very successful. In fact, the sale has been so successfully received that there are two more days left on the sale and the store has sold out of the advertised clothing. Since you work evenings, the department manager is not on duty and the store display manager is also unavailable.

Activity: A customer (judge) who has driven several miles to buy the advertised clothing approaches you. You have just informed her that the clothing line is currently out of stock. The customer is very upset. However, the customer notices that the mannequin used for the interior display is wearing the outfit in the exact color she wants and the size the customer wears. The customer insists that you sell her the outfit that is on display. You know you have two days remaining on the sale and how carefully your department manager prepares the interior displays for special sales. You must make a decision on whether to sell the outfit or not. Because the customer is so insistent, you fear that the she will file a formal complaint with management if you don't act appropriately.

Evaluation: You will be evaluated on how well you meet the following performance indicators.

- Explain company selling policies.
- Make decisions.
- Demonstrate problem-solving skills.
- Demonstrate a customer service mindset.
- Demonstrate appropriate creativity.

DIRECTIONS: *Organize your thoughts around the performance indicators noted above. Use these performance indicators to jot down your ideas during the preparation period. Time your preparation period to last 15 minutes and your role play presentation to last a maximum of ten minutes. After your role play, use the performance indicators to evaluate your efforts.*

Continued on next page

Assessment: Assume each performance indicator is worth 20 points (20 × 5 = 100 points). Use the evaluation levels listed below for judging consistency.

Excellent (16–20) Participant demonstrated the performance indicator in a professional manner; exceeds business standards.

Good (10–15) Participant demonstrated the performance indicator in an acceptable manner; meets minimal business standards; there would be no need for additional formalized training at this time.

Fair (4–9) Participant demonstrated the performance indicator with limited effectiveness; performance generally fell below minimal business standards; additional training would be required to improve knowledge, attitude, and/or skills.

Poor (0–3) Participant demonstrated the performance indicator with little effectiveness or not at all; a great deal of formal training would be needed.

Explain company selling policies.   Score ———

_____

_____

Make decisions.   Score ———

_____

_____

Demonstrate problem-solving skills.   Score ———

_____

_____

Demonstrate a customer service mindset.   Score ———

_____

_____

Demonstrate appropriate creativity.   Score ———

_____

_____

CHAPTER 18 Visual Merchandising and Display

Spreadsheet Application

OBJECTIVE: *To analyze test results of visual displays and to choose a new display for national use.*

ACTIVITY: Lantana, a maker of cosmetics and beauty supplies, provides visual displays to the retailers that sell its products. The company has created two new display models and has tested those models in several stores. Total customers passing the display, the number of customers who stopped to look, and the number of customers who bought an item from the product line were all counted. Both display models gained more attention than the display model currently used. Model A will cost $189,800 to place in all stores, while Model B will cost $154,500. Based on the test results, the marketing manager estimates that current sales could be increased by five percent if the Model A display is used, or by three percent if the Model B display is used. The results of the test are shown in the spreadsheet below.

	A	B	C	D	E	F
1	**Chapter 18 Visual Merchandising and Display**					
2						
3						
4		Model A	Model B			
5						
6	Total number of customers passing display	2,890	3,120			
7						
8						
9						
10	Number who stopped at display	980	1,044			
11						
12						
13						
14	Number who bought item	540	520			
15						
16						
17	Of total customers, percentage that bought item					
18						
19						
20		Estimated				
21		Percentage	Total	Sales	Total	
22		Increase	Current Sales	Increase	Projected Sales	
23						
24	Model A	5.0%	$1,200,000			
25						
26	Model B	3.0%	$1,200,000			

Spreadsheet Directions

1. Turn on your computer and open your spreadsheet software program.

2. Create a spreadsheet like the one on page 157 using your spreadsheet application.

3. For Model A and Model B, create a formula to calculate the percentages of total customers who bought an item.

4. Create formulas to calculate the estimated increase in sales for each display model and total projected sales.

5. Perform all calculations, then save your work.

6. Print out a copy of your work if your teacher has instructed you to do so. Then answer the questions that follow.

Interpreting Results

1. What is the percentage of total customers who bought an item?

_____

_____

_____

_____

2. What is the amount of projected increase in sales for each display model?

_____

_____

_____

_____

Drawing Conclusions

3. Make a recommendation to the marketing manager for the display model to be placed in all retail stores. Explain your reasons.

_____

_____

_____

_____

_____

_____

_____

CHAPTER 19 Advertising

Vocabulary Review

DIRECTIONS: *Complete each sentence with one of the terms.*

advertising	local radio advertising	print media
banner ad	media	promotional advertising
broadcast media	national spot radio	specialty media
cost per thousand (CPM)	advertising	transit advertising
direct marketing	network radio advertising	
institutional advertising	online advertising	

1. _____ is a broadcast from a studio to all affiliated radio stations throughout the country.

2. _____ is advertising that is designed to increase sales.

3. _____ attempts to create a favorable impression and goodwill for a business or an organization.

4. _____ includes direct mail sent to a home or business and electronic direct mail delivered to an e-mail address.

5. Newspapers, magazines, direct mail, and billboards are examples of _____ .

6. Radio and television are both examples of _____ .

7. _____ uses public transportation facilities to bring advertising messages to people.

8. _____ is used by national firms to advertise on a local station-by-station basis.

9. Items with an advertiser's name printed on them are called _____ .

10. The _____ is the cost of exposing 1,000 readers to an ad.

11. A(n) _____ is a common form of online advertising.

12. Radio advertising done by a local business for its target market is called _____ .

13. _____ are the agencies, means, or instruments used to convey messages.

14. _____ involves placing advertising messages on the Internet.

15. Any paid form of nonpersonal promotion of ideas, goods, or services by an identified sponsor is called _____ .

CHAPTER 19 Advertising

Fact and Idea Review

DIRECTIONS: *For each of the following statements determine whether the information provided reflects an **advantage** or **disadvantage** for the type of advertising media identified.*

_____ 1. Newspapers have a high readership and a high level of reader involvement.

_____ 2. Magazines are often read more slowly and thoroughly than newspapers.

_____ 3. Many people think of direct-mail advertising as junk mail.

_____ 4. Outdoor advertising is usually viewed very quickly.

_____ 5. Telephone directories are found in 98 percent of American households.

_____ 6. Transit advertising is restricted to certain travel routes.

_____ 7. Radio advertising is a mobile medium.

_____ 8. Television can use all of the necessary elements to produce a creative advertising message.

_____ 9. Online advertising response rates are often as low as one percent.

_____ 10. Radio advertising has a short life span.

_____ 11. Transit advertising has a defined market.

_____ 12. Yellow Pages directories are usually printed yearly.

_____ 13. Outdoor advertising permits easy repetition of a message.

_____ 14. Direct marketing can be flexible and keep competitors from seeing the advertisements.

_____ 15. Magazines have less mass appeal when compared to newspapers within a geographical area.

_____ 16. The life of an advertisement in a newspaper is limited.

_____ 17. Online advertisements can be interactive and reach a global audience.

_____ 18. Magazine advertisers can target regular readers because the characteristics of the readers are known.

_____ 19. Direct-mail advertisers can be selective about who will receive their mailing.

_____ 20. The cost of printed direct mail can be high because of the cost of producing the mailing, maintaining mailing lists, and postage.

CHAPTER 19 Advertising

Marketing Application 1

DIRECTIONS: *Read the case study below. Then answer the questions that follow.*

Changing an Advertising Approach

After years of relying on television to advertise its products, Procter & Gamble (P&G) is changing its strategy to focus more on direct mail, the Internet, and staged events. In 1998, Procter & Gamble spent $1.72 billion on advertising. The next year, it reduced its advertising costs slightly to $1.7 billion. More dramatic is the way P&G spent those advertising dollars. It decreased the total amount spent on television advertising to $1.18 billion, a 7 percent drop. The company pulled back significantly from local TV, decreasing expenses by 30 percent from $163.6 million to $114.5 million. At the same time, it increased magazine advertising expenditures by 17 percent and tripled its newspaper advertising. The company hopes to more accurately reach its target market this way.

P&G is also changing the way it handles its advertising agencies and advertising campaigns. Company personnel will now be involved in advertising campaigns from the beginning, rather than after a budget has been established and a campaign designed, as in the past. The company now consults with its advertising, public relations, Internet, and direct marketing staff before launching any campaign.

In addition, P&G will no longer reimburse advertising agencies based on a straight 15 percent of advertising dollars spent. Under the new policy, agencies will be rewarded based on the success of their assigned products in the marketplace. Sales growth, rather than advertising expenditures, will be an incentive to spend more wisely rather than spend more.

The policy changes are part of an overall company policy to control operating costs. The changed policies have already resulted in different advertising campaigns. A campaign for Bounty paper towels offers lifestyle advice as a way to get women talking about the paper towels. The launch of Physique, a hair-care line, depended heavily on direct mail rather than television. The company spent 60 to 80 percent on direct mail teasers, product samples, and specialty advertising. Only then did television and print advertising begin. Finally, the company sent a mass distribution of Physique to more than 60,000 grocery, drug, and warehouse discount stores. The type of launch may not be successful with products such as laundry detergent, but Procter & Gamble felt it was successful for Physique.

1. Speculate on why P&G has reduced TV spending in favor of increased spending for magazine and local newspapers.

_____

_____

_____

_____

_____

_____

Continued on next page

2. Why did P&G change the way it reimburses advertising agencies? Will this newer approach lower its operating costs? Why or why not?

_____

_____

_____

_____

_____

_____

_____

_____

3. Did the product launch of the Physique hair-care line demonstrate a push or pull marketing strategy for the company? Provide a rationale for your answer.

_____

_____

_____

_____

_____

_____

_____

_____

4. According to company officials, the advertising approach used to launch Physique will not be successful with other P&G product such as laundry detergents. Explain the rationale for this statement.

_____

_____

_____

_____

_____

_____

_____

_____

| Student | | Date | |
| Class | | Teacher | |

CHAPTER 19 Advertising

Marketing Application 2

DIRECTIONS: *Newspapers are measured by standard column inches—each page being 6 columns by 22 inches or 132 column inches total. Use the chart on the next page for display advertising rates from a local newspaper to answer the following questions. The advertising rates are for run-of-paper advertisements and are all based upon a 6-column format.*

1. What is the non-contract rate for a column inch to run in a daily edition (M–Th)? In a Sunday edition?

_____

2. How much more does it cost to advertise per column inch in the Saturday paper than in the daily edition?

_____

3. How much does a column inch cost on a yearly frequency contract for a Saturday ad? For a Friday ad?

_____

4. An advertiser uses a minimum of 30 column inches every week for 52 weeks. What will be the column inch rate for a daily advertisement? What will the advertiser pay to run a 30-column inch ad?

_____

5. How much does it cost Advertiser A, who has a short term frequency contract, to buy 30 column inches in a Monday paper?

_____

6. How much more does it cost Advertiser A to buy 30 column inches on Sunday than a Tuesday?

_____

7. Advertiser B buys 2,500 column inches to use in Monday editions of the newspaper over a 12-month period. What does Advertiser B pay to run the advertisements for the contract year?

_____

8. If Advertiser B bought 5,000 column inches in the Monday editions at the bulk space contract rate rather than 2,500, how much would the advertiser save per column inch?

_____

DISPLAY ROP ADVERTISING RATES
Based on a 6-column format

		Daily (M–Th)	Friday	Saturday	Sunday
Non-contract Rates		$27.83	$29.44	$30.82	$35.29
Yearly Frequency Contract Minimum number of column inches to be used every week for 52 weeks		**Cost Per Column Inch**			
Inches	1	17.00	17.99	18.83	21.56
	3	16.85	17.83	18.66	21.37
	7	16.53	17.49	18.31	20.96
	15	16.21	17.15	17.95	20.55
	30	15.90	16.82	17.61	20.16
	60	15.64	16.55	17.32	19.83
	90	15.46	16.36	17.12	19.60
	120	15.35	16.24	17.00	19.46
	240	15.24	16.12	16.88	19.32
	300	14.76	15.62	16.35	18.72
	360	14.31	15.14	15.85	18.15
Short Term Frequency Contract Separates day insertions and minimum number of column inches for 13 times during a 90-day period		**Cost Per Column Inch**			
Inches	1	18.52	19.59	20.51	23.48
	3	18.37	19.44	20.34	23.29
	7	18.05	19.10	19.99	22.89
	15	17.87	18.91	19.79	22.66
	30	17.42	18.43	19.29	22.09
	60	17.16	18.16	19.00	21.76
Bulk Space Contract To be used at will within a 12-month contract year.					
Inches	125	20.13	21.30	22.29	25.52
	175	17.89	18.93	19.81	22.68
	375	17.59	18.61	19.48	22.30
	750	17.30	18.30	19.16	21.94
	1,500	16.98	17.96	18.81	21.53
	2,500	16.78	17.75	18.58	21.28
	5,000	16.49	17.45	18.26	20.91
	10,000	16.19	17.13	17.93	20.53
	15,000	16.01	16.94	17.73	20.30
	25,000	15.78	16.70	17.48	20.01
	50,000	15.47	16.37	17.13	19.62
	75,000	15.35	16.24	17.00	19.46

CHAPTER **19** Advertising

The DECA Connection

Role Play: Retail Marketing Specialist

Situation: You are to assume the role of marketing specialist for the advertising department of a large retail store chain that seeks to promote its new e-commerce Web site. You have been charged with the promotion of the Web site based upon three overall company objectives:

1. Increase store revenues through gaining new customers,
2. Increase store revenues through increasing sales to existing customers; and,
3. Reduce operating costs involved with servicing existing customers.

Activity: Provide ideas to promote the store's new Web site to your promotional manager (judge) using strategies to meet the three objectives. In your presentation be sure to include existing advertising methods to promote the Web site and other plans to increase sales to new and existing customers. You should also address how the new Web site could be used to reduce the cost of sales and operating costs.

Evaluation: You will be evaluated on how well you meet the following performance indicators:

- Develop Web site design/components.
- Explain the nature of overhead/operating costs.
- Identify ways that technology impacts business.
- Explain the types of advertising media.
- Demonstrate appropriate creativity.

DIRECTIONS: *Organize your thoughts around the performance indicators noted above. Use these performance indicators to jot down your ideas during the preparation period. Time your preparation period to last 15 minutes and your role play presentation to last a maximum of ten minutes. After your role play, use the performance indicators to evaluate your efforts.*

_____

_____

_____

_____

_____

_____

_____

_____

Continued on next page

Assessment: Assume each performance indicator is worth 20 points (20 × 5 = 100 points). Use the evaluation levels listed below for judging consistency.

Excellent (16–20) Participant demonstrated the performance indicator in a professional manner; exceeds business standards.

Good (10–15) Participant demonstrated the performance indicator in an acceptable manner; meets minimal business standards; there would be no need for additional formalized training at this time.

Fair (4–9) Participant demonstrated the performance indicator with limited effectiveness; performance generally fell below minimal business standards; additional training would be required to improve knowledge, attitude, and/or skills.

Poor (0–3) Participant demonstrated the performance indicator with little effectiveness or not at all; a great deal of formal training would be needed.

Develop Web site design/components. Score _____

_____

_____

_____

Explain the nature of overhead/operating costs. Score _____

_____

_____

_____

Identify ways that technology impacts business. Score _____

_____

_____

_____

Explain the types of advertising media. Score _____

_____

_____

_____

Demonstrate appropriate creativity. Score _____

_____

_____

_____

CHAPTER 19 Advertising

Spreadsheet Application

OBJECTIVE: *To evaluate the effectiveness of different types of advertising media.*

ACTIVITY: The Apollo Company recently completed a survey of customers who had purchased a bottle of its Spring Joy perfume. The company wanted to know the number of customers who learned about the product from its magazine, newspaper, billboard, or television ads, or from its in-store promotions. The results of the survey are shown in the spreadsheet below. The number beside each type of ad is the number of customers who bought the product after seeing it advertised.

	A	B	C	D	E	F	G
1	**Chapter 19 Advertising**						
2							
3	**Source of Customer**	Number of	Percentage				
4	**Product Knowledge**	Buyers	of Total				
5							
6	Magazines	180					
7	Newspapers	94					
8	Television	108					
9	Billboards	14					
10	In-store promotions	41					
11	Other	34					
12	**TOTAL BUYERS**						

Continued on next page

Spreadsheet Directions

1. Turn on your computer and open your spreadsheet software program.

2. Create a spreadsheet like the one on page 167 using your spreadsheet application.

3. Enter a formula to calculate the total number of buyers responding to the survey.

4. Enter a formula to calculate the percentage of the total for each type of ad.

5. Perform the calculations, then prepare a pie chart showing the percentage for each type of advertising media and for the in-store promotions.

6. Save your work. Print out a copy of your work if your teacher has instructed you to do so. Then answer the questions that follow.

Interpreting Results

1. Of the advertising media given, which had the ads that were seen by the largest percentage of buyers? the smallest?

_____

_____

2. If you had 1,200,000 customers, how many of them might you expect to see your ad if it were placed on a billboard?

_____

_____

_____

Drawing Conclusions

3. Which two advertising media would you recommend to a local retailer that wants to advertise a special weekend sale? Explain your reasons.

_____

_____

_____

_____

_____

_____

_____

_____

CHAPTER 20 Print Advertisements

Vocabulary Review

DIRECTIONS: *Match each term in the left column with the correct sentence in the right column. Write the letter of the phrase in the blank by the term.*

_____ 1. ad layout

_____ 2. advertising agencies

_____ 3. advertising proof

_____ 4. alliteration

_____ 5. clip art

_____ 6. copy

_____ 7. headline

_____ 8. illustration

_____ 9. print advertisement

_____ 10. pun

_____ 11. signature

_____ 12. slogan

_____ 13. typeface

_____ 14. advertising campaign

a. Companies that work with business clients to develop advertising campaigns.

b. The words that get the readers' attention, arouse their interest, and lead them to read the rest of the ad.

c. Computer-generated images that are placed in a print advertisement.

d. A headline writing technique that involves the humorous use of a word that suggests two or more meanings.

e. The distinctive identification symbol or logo for a business.

f. A catchphrase or small group of words that are combined in a special way to present an advertising message.

g. A rough draft that shows the general arrangement and appearance of a finished ad.

h. This usually includes a headline, copy, illustrations, and a signature.

i. The selling message contained in a written advertisement.

j. This shows exactly how an ad will appear when printed.

k. The photograph or drawing used in a print advertisement.

l. The style of printing type used in a print advertisement.

m. A headline writing technique that involves repeating initial consonant sounds.

n. The creation and coordination of a series of advertisements around a particular theme to promote a product.

CHAPTER **20** Print Advertisements

Fact and Idea Review

DIRECTIONS: *Categorize each ad element below as a* **headline, copy, illustration,** *or* **signature.**

_____ 1. Intrepid 🔘 The New Dodge
A DIVISION OF THE CHRYSLER CORPORATION

_____ 2. "A nagging cough with congestion. Or a cough with a painful sore throat. Take new Drixoral Liquid Caps. You can't buy a more powerful liquid cap for long-lasting cough relief."

_____ 3. "Introducing the New Ford Explorer."

_____ 4. ⓔ **ENTERPRISE RENT-A-CAR** 🚗

_____ 5. A painting of Nestle Sweet Success Healthy Shake on a brick wall.

_____ 6. There is a difference™ **IBM**®

_____ 7. "COROLLA. Where promises are kept. And new ones made every day."

_____ 8. "The fear of choosing the wrong fund, of losing money. How to conquer it? First, choose an amount of money that doesn't make you nervous. Start small. Invest monthly. At Janus Funds, you can open an account for as little as $50 a month."

_____ 9. "Milk. What a surprise!"

_____ 10. A photo of an International truck.

_____ 11. "Only a car this quiet could make such noise." (Nissan)

_____ 12. ▲**DELTA AIR LINES** YOU'LL LOVE THE WAY WE FLY™

_____ 13. "FIRST AGAIN." (Prodigy)

_____ 14. A picture of a clear blue sky. (Lufthansa)

_____ 15. "Sound this big from a radio?" (Bose)

_____ 16. **Mobil**®

_____ 17. "The 2005 Grand Marquis. Setting the standard for all other cars in your class would be enough to satisfy most people. Not our engineers. They restyled the exterior for a sleeker, more dynamic appearance."

Student	Date
Class	Teacher

CHAPTER 20 Print Advertisements

Marketing Application 1

DIRECTIONS: *Read the case study below. Then answer the questions that follow.*

Yellow Pages Remain Popular with Advertisers

The Internet may be the fastest way to find some information, but when someone needs to find a restaurant, doctor, mechanic, or a pizza, they are still more likely to reach for the good, old-fashioned phone book. That's one of the reasons why print Yellow Pages are still profitable.

Internet Yellow Pages are growing dramatically, but spending on print Yellow Pages ads continues to rise because businesses know that they will get a very high return on their advertising dollars. Yellow Pages ads average $29 of return for every $1 spent, according to research by CRM Associates. Not surprisingly, one-third of all American businesses advertise in at least one Yellow Pages directory.

Even so, print Yellow Pages usage has declined over the past 10 years. In 1989, people referred to the Yellow Pages 17.7 billion times, according to the Yellow Pages Publishers Association. By 1999, the Yellow Pages was receiving only 15.6 billion annual references. Despite that drop, advertising expenditures in print Yellow Pages for both local and national businesses continue to grow, rising 5.5 percent in 1999—from $11.99 billion to $12.65 billion—according to a report from New York's McCann-Erickson.

Several Yellow Pages publishers have created their own Internet directories: BellSouth produces RealPages.com and SBC communications produces SmartPages.com. They are even bundling print and online advertising options for their customers. Online directory assistance has become increasingly popular. The Kelsey Group estimates that online directory advertising lookups in the United States reached 2.4 billion in 2002.

1. Why are Yellow Pages publishers not afraid of online versions of this type of print media?

_____

2. Why do print versions of the Yellow Pages still dominate the online versions of the Yellow Pages?

_____

_____

_____

3. Speculate why overall consumer usage of print Yellow Pages has declined.

_____

_____

_____

CHAPTER *20* Print Advertisements

Marketing Application 2

DIRECTIONS: *Create a one-item newspaper advertising layout for a real or invented store of your choice using a piece of paper or a posterboard. Your advertising layout must contain five elements: a headline, an illustration, copy, the price, and a signature. Use one of the standard layouts illustrated below. Your layout can use illustrations, or artwork produced by yourself or obtained from newspapers or magazines.*

Standard layouts:

Your completed advertising layout will be judged and the performance areas noted below: using the following rating scale:

Rating Scale	1–2 needs significant improvement	5–7 good
	3–4 needs minor improvement	8–9 excellent
		10 exceptional

Performance areas:	Your score
General format	
1. Ad is well organized and easy to follow	———
2. Ad is clean and uncluttered	———
3. White space is appropriate	———
Headline	
4. Headline attracts attention	———
5. Aimed at a target audience	———
Illustration	
6. Illustration demonstrates a benefit or shows product in use	———
7. Illustration is large enough	———

Performance areas:	Your score
Copy	
8. Written in terms of benefits	———
9. Copy complete and specific	———
10. Grammar and spelling appropriate	———
Price	
11. Clear and visible	———
Signature	
12. Signature complete (name, address, telephone, hours, and slogan)	———

CHAPTER **20** Print Advertisements

The DECA Connection

Role Play: Advertising Proofreader

Situation: You are to assume the role of an intern at a local newspaper. The manager (judge) of the advertising department has asked you to proofread and edit advertising copy written for a firm of CPAs (certified public accountants). The firm hopes to attract new clients, either businesses or individuals. They have requested that the newspaper advertising department design the rest of the ad. They would like to see a sketch of the proposed ad layout that makes use of the copy they provided.

Activity: Your job is to proofread the ad copy and make corrections necessary for spelling, grammar, punctuation, and accuracy. Run-on sentences should be corrected and missing information should be added. Rewrite the ad copy and sketch an ad layout for the firm. Be sure to include all parts of a print ad in your sketch. You will present the rewritten ad copy and your proposed ad layout on two separate sheets of paper to your manager (judge).

Ad Copy

GROAN! Its that time of year again! No, it's not time to set you're clocks ahead but it is time too get ahead start on your tax return. Roderik & Stacy, CPAs, is a full-service accounting firm that provides financail services to businesses and to individuals and we can make your life a lot easier by releiving you of the burden of keeping up with the latest changes in tax laws. Call us today for free as estimate.

Evaluation: You will be evaluated on how well you meet the following performance indicators:

- Explain parts of a print advertisement.
- Write promotional messages that appeal to targeted markets.
- Use proper grammar and vocabulary.
- Evaluate effectiveness of advertising.
- Make oral presentations.

DIRECTIONS: *Organize your thoughts around the performance indicators noted above. Use these performance indicators to jot down your ideas during the preparation period. Time your preparation period to last 15 minutes and your role play presentation to last a maximum of ten minutes. After your role play, use the performance indicators to evaluate your efforts.*

_____

_____

_____

_____

Continued on next page

Assessment: Assume each performance indicator is worth 20 points (20 × 5 = 100 points). Use the evaluation levels listed below for judging consistency.

Excellent   (16–20)   Participant demonstrated the performance indicator in a professional manner; exceeds business standards.

Good   (10–15)   Participant demonstrated the performance indicator in an acceptable and effective manner; meets at least minimal business standards; there would be no need for additional formalized training at this time.

Fair   (4–9)   Participant demonstrated the performance indicator with limited effectiveness; performance generally fell below minimal business standards; additional training would be required to improve knowledge, attitude, and/or skills.

Poor   (0–3)   Participant demonstrated the performance indicator with little effectiveness or not at all; a great deal of formal training would be needed.

Explain parts of a print advertisement.   Score ———

_____

_____

_____

Write promotional messages that appeal to targeted markets.   Score ———

_____

_____

_____

Use proper grammar and vocabulary.   Score ———

_____

_____

_____

Evaluate effectiveness of advertising.   Score ———

_____

_____

_____

Make oral presentations.   Score ———

_____

_____

_____

CHAPTER 20 Print Advertisements

| Software Activity (Optional) | **Word Processing Application** |

OBJECTIVE: To prepare written elements for a printed ad.

ACTIVITY: You have been asked to write a print ad to promote a new line of umbrellas. Use the following information to write a headline (15 words or fewer) and copy for the ad:

- Giant size
- All nylon
- Crayon-box solid colors; Rainbow plaids
- Bamboo handle
- Price: $14.00

Word Processing Directions

1. Turn on your computer and open your word processing software program.

2. Write copy for the ad. Proofread and edit your work to make sure it is correct.

3. Save your work. Print out a copy of your work if your teacher has instructed you to do so. Then answer the questions that follow.

Evaluating Results

1. How does the copy give reasons why the umbrella is a good buy?

_____

_____

_____

_____

_____

_____

2. What kind of writing techniques did you use in your ad in order to make it more effective?

_____

_____

_____

_____

3. Would your headline and ad copy work in all media?

_____

_____

_____

_____

_____

4. What images would you add to make your ad ready for publication in a magazine, and why?

_____

_____

_____

_____

_____

5. What is the target audience for your ad, and how does your ad speak to that audience?

_____

_____

_____

_____

_____

_____

CHAPTER 21 Channels of Distribution

Vocabulary Review

DIRECTIONS: *Match each definition with the correct term.*

agents	e-tailing	intermediaries
brick-and-mortar retailers	exclusive distribution	rack jobbers
channel of distribution	indirect distribution	retailers
direct distribution	integrated distribution	selective distribution
drop shippers	intensive distribution	wholesalers
e-marketplace		

_____ 1. They sell goods to the final consumer.

_____ 2. This involves no intermediaries.

_____ 3. Intermediaries who do not own the goods they sell.

_____ 4. Selling products over the Internet to the consumer.

_____ 5. An online shopping location.

_____ 6. This involves one or more intermediaries.

_____ 7. Those who buy large quantities of goods from manufacturers and store the goods to resell them to other businesses.

_____ 8. Channel members that help move products from the producer or manufacturer to the final user.

_____ 9. This involves protected territories for product distribution in a given geographic area.

_____ 10. The path a product takes from the producer or manufacturer to the consumer.

_____ 11. Those who sell goods to consumers through their own stores.

_____ 12. This involves use of a limited number of outlets in an area to sell a product.

_____ 13. This involves use of all suitable outlets to sell a product.

_____ 14. Wholesalers that manage inventory and merchandising for retailers.

_____ 15. Wholesalers that own the goods they sell but do not physically handle the actual product.

_____ 16. When a manufacturer acts as wholesaler and retailer for its products.

CHAPTER 21 Channels of Distribution

Fact and Idea Review

DIRECTIONS: *Circle the letters of all choices that accurately complete the sentence or answer the question.*

1. Intermediaries provide value to producers because they

   a. provide expertise in areas producers do not have, such as displaying and merchandising products.

   b. reduce the number of contacts required to reach the final consumer.

   c. may have contacts and ongoing relationships with potential customers that producers do not have.

   d. may reduce a company's selling expenses.

2. Intermediaries that take ownership of goods are classified as

   a. agents.   c. manufacturers' agents.

   b. brokers.   d. merchant intermediaries.

3. Non-store retailing operations include

   a. automatic retailing (vending machines).   c. TV home shopping.

   b. direct mail and catalogs.   d. online retailing.

4. Industrial goods can be marketed

   a. by agents.   c. using direct distribution.

   b. by distributors.   d. using indirect distribution.

5. A retail stationery store that sells its products to customers for their personal use and to businesses for use in their operations would be considered

   a. a retailer in the consumer market.

   b. an industrial distributor in the industrial market.

   c. a producer in any market.

   d. a user of multiple channels of distribution.

6. For a small manufacturer that wants to sell its products in a new marketplace, the most economical decision would be to

   a. hire a direct sales force who could be trained to sell the manufacturer's products.

   b. hire independent sales agents to sell its products.

   c. maintain complete control over its sales function.

   d. relinquish some control over how sales are made to keep costs down.

7. A franchised operation is an example of what type of distribution policy?

   a. intensive   c. exclusive

   b. selective   d. integrated

CHAPTER 21 Channels of Distribution

Marketing Application 1

DIRECTIONS: *The following news briefs on Tupperware are related to distribution planning. Read them and answer the questions that follow.*

Tupperware and the Home Shopping Network

Tupperware Corporation, a $1.1 billion multinational company, is one of the world's leading direct sellers and the major supplier of food storage containers, with products reaching consumers in more than 100 countries. Tupperware's core distribution policy makes use of an independent sales force and a home-party format for selling.

Tupperware's sales consultants get paid a 35 percent commission on sales, plus other bonuses and benefits. They are required to purchase a sample kit when they first get started, which costs $20 or $65, depending on the products in the kit.

In May 1999, Tupperware entered into an agreement with the Home Shopping Network to air television specials to sell Tupperware products. The Home Shopping Network program features specials from home shopping parties happening across America during each broadcast. The Home Shopping Network is the pioneer in electronic retailing. It has 24-hour programming reaching more than 70 million households.

1. According to the above news brief, what is Tupperware's core distribution policy?

_____

_____

_____

2. How would you classify Tupperware's independent sales force?

_____

_____

_____

_____

_____

3. The news brief addresses an agreement Tupperware has with the Home Shopping Network. How does that agreement alter Tupperware's traditional channel of distribution, if at all?

_____

_____

_____

_____

Continued on next page

Tupperware's Web Site

Tupperware has a Web site, which allows consumers to purchase Tupperware products online.

4. How does Tupperware's venture into online selling change its basic channel of distribution philosophy, if at all?

_____

_____

_____

_____

_____

5. If you were a Tupperware sales consultant, how would you react to Tupperware's Web site? Why?

_____

_____

_____

_____

_____

_____

Tupperware's Sales Consultants and the Internet

The Tupperware Corporation has a special program for its 75,000 U.S sales agents to bring them low cost Internet access. My.tupperware.com is a Web site specifically designed for use by Tupperware's sales consultants. Special software permits them to personalize their Web sites with product information and promote Tupperware parties. Online sales go through Tupperware's main Web site, but consultants will earn sales credit and commission on all sales that originate from their personal Web site.

6. How does Tupperware's service, my.tupperware.com, help its sales consultants?

_____

_____

_____

_____

_____

_____

CHAPTER 21 Channels of Distribution

Marketing Application 2

DIRECTIONS: *For each of the following scenarios, identify the current channel of distribution being used. Then recommend a channel of distribution or multiple channels for the product. Indicate the intensity of distribution desired for the product. Provide rationale for both recommendations.*

Scenario #1

A manufacturer of home health care products has just developed a new home blood pressure monitoring machine. At present the company sells the majority of its other consumer health care products through mass merchandisers, like Kmart and Wal-Mart, as well as through drugstore chains, like CVS, Rite Aid, and Genovese. Over the years, solid relationships have been established with these retailers.

1. What is the current channel of distribution being used by this company for its consumer health products?

   _____

2. What channel(s) of distribution do you recommend for the new home blood pressure machine? Why?

   _____

   _____

   _____

   _____

   _____

   _____

3. What intensity of distribution do you recommend: intensive, selective, or exclusive? Why?

   _____

   _____

   _____

   _____

   _____

Continued on next page

Scenario #2

A small importer of bags of all sizes and purposes is seeking national exposure. Some of the bags are designed for laptop computers, while other bags are designed to keep food warm and are marketed to food catering and food delivery businesses, such as pizza restaurants that deliver. Duffel bags are designed for use as promotional gifts for clients or as employee prizes for outstanding performance. All bags are unique in that they are designed specifically for the client, and, in many cases, include the client's logo. Currently, the owner does all the business-to-business selling himself. The owner would like to increase sales while controlling his selling expenses.

4. What channel of distribution is being used currently by this importer of specialty bags?

_____

_____

_____

_____

5. What channel(s) of distribution do you recommend for these products? Why?

_____

_____

_____

_____

_____

_____

_____

6. Discuss the additional selling expenses that will be incurred with your plan and how your plan keeps those expenses in line with sales.

_____

_____

_____

_____

_____

CHAPTER 21 Channels of Distribution

The DECA Connection

Role Play: Distributor

Situation: You are to assume the role of employee of Sky Millwork. Your company is a local distributor of XYZ Windows. As a distributor, you sell these windows through your own showroom to general building contractors, as well as to distributors in the construction trade. A new Home Depot is slated to open in your territory in the next few months. As the person who has direct contact with most of your company's customers, you have heard first hand how worried your customers are about their new competitor. They fear Home Depot because it is a large chain with a lot of clout and bargaining power. Several of your customers have asked if your company will be selling XYZ Windows to the new Home Depot. You feel obligated to share these concerns with your supervisor (judge).

Activity: Write a memo to your supervisor (judge) explaining the current customers' concerns regarding the new Home Depot. Request a meeting to discuss this issue. Suggest a plan that will allow Sky Millwork to benefit from Home Depot's reputation by selling them XYZ products, but at the same time will not ruin your company's relationship with current, loyal customers.

Evaluation: You will be evaluated on how well you meet the following performance indicators:

- Explain the nature of channels of distribution.
- Evaluate channel members.
- Explain the nature of channel strategies.
- Explain the nature of channel member relationships.
- Write informational messages.

DIRECTIONS: *Organize your thoughts around the performance indicators noted above. Use these performance indicators to jot down your ideas during the preparation period. Time your preparation period to last 15 minutes and your role play presentation to last a maximum of ten minutes. After your role play, use the performance indicators to evaluate your efforts.*

Continued on next page

Assessment: Assume each performance indicator is worth 20 points (20 × 5 = 100 points). Use the evaluation levels listed below for judging consistency.

Excellent (16–20) Participant demonstrated the performance indicator in a professional manner; exceeds business standards.

Good (10–15) Participant demonstrated the performance indicator in an acceptable and effective manner; meets at least minimal business standards; there would be no need for additional formalized training at this time.

Fair (4–9) Participant demonstrated the performance indicator with limited effectiveness; performance generally fell below minimal business standards; additional training would be required to improve knowledge, attitude, and/or skills.

Poor (0–3) Participant demonstrated the performance indicator with little effectiveness or not at all; a great deal of formal training would be needed.

Explain the nature of channels of distribution.   Score ———

———————————————————————————————

———————————————————————————————

———————————————————————————————

Evaluate channel members.   Score ———

———————————————————————————————

———————————————————————————————

———————————————————————————————

Explain the nature of channel strategies.   Score ———

———————————————————————————————

———————————————————————————————

———————————————————————————————

Explain the nature of channel member relationships.   Score ———

———————————————————————————————

———————————————————————————————

———————————————————————————————

Write informational messages.   Score ———

———————————————————————————————

———————————————————————————————

———————————————————————————————

CHAPTER 21 Channels of Distribution

Spreadsheet Application

OBJECTIVE: *To analyze channels of distribution.*

ACTIVITY: The Paresi Company makes specialty food items such as cookies and candies. The company uses several marketing channels to distribute its products. Paresi products are sold through company stores, direct mail catalogs, specialty stores, and online. The printout below shows the channels used and the sales resulting from each channel. You are evaluating sales for the past three years to find out whether the proportion of sales for each channel has changed. The company wants to make sure that its advertising and promotion dollars are directed toward the channels that deliver the strongest sales.

	A	B	C	D	E	F	G
1	Chapter 21 Channels of Distribution						
2							
3							
4			Previous Year		Last Year		This Year
5		Previous Year	Percentage	Last Year	Percentage	This Year	Percentage
6		Sales	of Total	Sales	of Total	Sales	of Total
7							
8	Company stores	$1,848,900		$1,760,800		$2,084,600	
9	Mail order	$1,680,400		$2,988,600		$3,140,900	
10	Specialty stores	$1,200,780		$1,480,900		$1,690,200	
11	Electronic marketplace	$400,250		$785,100		$1,248,300	
12							
13	TOTAL SALES						

Spreadsheet Directions

1. Turn on your computer and open your spreadsheet software program.

2. Create a spreadsheet like the above using your spreadsheet application.

3. First, enter a formula to calculate total sales for each year.

4. Next, calculate the sales for company stores as a percentage of total sales for each year. Copy these formulas to all remaining rows.

5. Save your work. Print out a copy of your work if your teacher has instructed you to do so. Then answer the questions that follow.

Continued on next page

Interpreting Results

1. Which is the most important channel of distribution for the company? Is its portion of sales growing or decreasing?

_____

_____

_____

_____

_____

2. Which channel of distribution has increased in importance most over the past three years?

_____

_____

_____

_____

_____

Drawing Conclusions

3. Assume that you are the marketing manager for the Paresi Company. Make a recommendation for allocating advertising dollars to each channel of distribution. Explain the reasons for your recommendation.

_____

_____

_____

_____

_____

_____

_____

_____

_____

_____

_____

_____

_____

CHAPTER 22 Physical Distribution

Vocabulary Review

DIRECTIONS: *Match each definition with the correct term.*

bonded warehouse	express delivery services	private warehouse
carload	exempt carrier	public warehouse
common carrier	freight forwarder	storage
contract carrier	physical distribution	ton-mile
distribution center	private carrier	transportation

_____ 1. A warehouse designed to speed the delivery of goods and minimize storage costs.

_____ 2. This type of carrier transports goods for just one business.

_____ 3. Holding goods until they are sold.

_____ 4. The marketing function of moving goods from a seller to a buyer.

_____ 5. A private company that combines shipments from several different businesses and delivers them to their destinations.

_____ 6. A facility designed to meet the specific needs of its owner.

_____ 7. Imported or domestic products cannot be removed from this type of warehouse until the required federal tax is paid.

_____ 8. The logistics involved with transporting, storing, order processing, stock handling, and inventory control of materials and products.

_____ 9. This type of carrier is a for-hire carrier that provides equipment and drivers for specific routes according to agreements between the carrier and the shipper.

_____ 10. This offers storage and handling to any business or individual that will pay for its use.

_____ 11. This term represents the minimum number of pounds of freight needed to fill a railroad boxcar.

_____ 12. The movement of one ton (2000 lbs) of freight one mile.

_____ 13. This type of carrier provides transportation services to any business in its operating area for a fee.

_____ 14. These carriers are free from direct regulation of rates and operating procedures.

_____ 15. These carriers specialize in delivering small, lightweight packages and high priority mail weighing less than 150 pounds.

CHAPTER 22 Physical Distribution

Fact and Idea Review

DIRECTIONS: **A.** *In each series of items, circle the one that does not belong. Then explain your choice on the line below.*

1. common carrier   contract carrier   private carrier   public carrier

   _____

2. Fishyback service   intermodal transportation   physical distribution   piggyback service

   _____

3. air carrier   express delivery   freight forwarder   U.S. Postal Service

   _____

4. pipelines   storage   transportation   waterways

   _____

5. air carrier   distribution center   pipeline   waterway

   _____

DIRECTIONS: **B.** *Decide which form of transportation—**air carrier, motor carrier, pipeline, railroad,** or **waterway**—each of the following phrases describes, and write the appropriate term in the blank. Some terms will be used more than once.*

_____ 1. This form of transportation can handle large quantities at relatively low cost and is rarely affected by weather.

_____ 2. The cheapest way to transport freight but also the slowest.

_____ 3. This form of transportation carries approximately two percent of the ton-miles of freight moved in the United States.

_____ 4. This form of transportation is used for virtually all intracity shipping.

_____ 5. The most expensive form of distribution but also the fastest.

_____ 6. This form of transportation handles nearly 87 percent of the shipments weighing less than 1,000 pounds.

_____ 7. This form of transportation moves nearly six percent of the total intercity ton-miles of freight.

_____ 8. The oldest form of transportation of large quantities.

CHAPTER **22** Physical Distribution

Marketing Application 1

DIRECTIONS: *Write the preferred form of transportation when shipping each product in the circumstances described (**air carrier, motor carrier, pipeline, railroad, waterway**).*

_____   1. Oil shipped from an oil field in Oklahoma to a refinery in Houston, Texas.

_____   2. Iron ore transported from Duluth, Minnesota, to the steel mills of Gary, Indiana.

_____   3. Cut flowers transported from Hawaii to the mainland.

_____   4. Gasoline transported from a refinery to a local service station.

_____   5. Corn transported from a farm to a local grain elevator.

_____   6. Beef transported from a meatpacker to a supermarket.

_____   7. An overnight letter transported from Phoenix to New York City.

_____   8. Furniture transported from a distribution center to a store.

_____   9. Natural gas transported from Alaska to Vancouver, British Columbia.

_____   10. Merchandise shipped from a warehouse to a discount store.

_____   11. Coal transported from a mine in Pennsylvania to a power plant in Detroit, Michigan.

_____   12. Lumber transported from Seattle, Washington, to Tokyo, Japan.

_____   13. Farm equipment manufactured in Canada transported to a warehouse in Wisconsin.

_____   14. Vaccine transported from Atlanta, Georgia, to Los Angeles.

_____   15. Sugar transported from the port of New Orleans to Europe.

_____   16. Lobsters transported from Maine to a restaurant in San Francisco.

_____   17. Gasoline shipped from a Texas oil refinery to Chicago, Illinois.

_____   18. Steel transported from Gary, Indiana, to Dallas, Texas.

_____   19. Grain transported from Milwaukee, Wisconsin, to Cleveland, Ohio.

_____   20. Limestone shipped from a quarry off Lake Huron to Detroit, Michigan.

CHAPTER 22 Physical Distribution

Marketing Application 2

DIRECTIONS: *Read the case study below. Then answer the questions that follow.*

A New Way to Buy Baseball Cards

Once a staple of dime-store counters, baseball cards are moving to the Internet. The largest maker of baseball cards, The Topps Company, Inc., has announced plans to sell a new line of premium, extra glossy baseball cards through its Web site.

Topps will continue to sell its trading cards in stores and stadiums, which remain its principle distribution system. The new "etopps" cards will be deluxe cards available exclusively through the company's Web site during "Initial Player Offerings." The deluxe cards will be sold individually for $3 to $12. The company will either send them directly to the customer or hold them in the customer's portfolio so the cards can later be sold through eBay.com, the Internet auction site. Collectors could buy a Mark McGwire card for something like $3, for example, then sell it a few months later on eBay without ever actually seeing the card themselves. eBay is expected to resell one to five percent of every new etopps card Topps sells on topps.com.

Topps began selling baseball cards in 1951 and now controls 37 percent of the trading card market. While Topps does not believe the move to selling deluxe, limited-edition cards on the Internet will alienate distributors or young collectors, other trading card companies have so far not followed Topps' lead. Upper Deck, Fleer, and Pacific Trading Cards have announced no similar distribution plans. Critics say Topps' new strategy does not support the secondary or collectible market. More importantly, distributing deluxe cards over the Internet does nothing to address the business's real problem—primarily that today's kids are not as interested in collecting baseball cards as their parents were. Whether Topps will be able to attract buyers to single cards when they are accustomed to buying packs is yet to be seen.

1. What are some potential risks for Topps by adding another distribution channel for its cards?

_____

_____

_____

_____

2. Unlike its competitors, Topps is pursuing an online distribution strategy. Speculate on the company's rationale for this move.

_____

_____

_____

_____

CHAPTER 22 Physical Distribution

The DECA Connection

Role Play: Distribution Planner

Situation: You are to assume the role of assistant manager of a retail outlet located on the site of the Big B Ranch in Montana. The Big B Ranch is unique because it raises buffalo and sells the meat to specialty stores and restaurants. The ranch specializes in buffalo steaks, ribs, and hamburger (bulk and patty). The retail store also sells the product directly to consumers who visit the ranch, but retail sales are limited to a fairly small geographic area. Buffalo meat is very nutritious, tasty, and low in fat and cholesterol compared with beef. The business market for the product is very specialized and focused on quality restaurants and independent grocery stores. The ranch has its own private carrier to deliver its products to area restaurants and stores. Because of limited distribution, it is difficult for potential consumers to purchase the products. Past experience has indicated that many people prefer buffalo to beef after they have had an opportunity to try it. The ranch owner (judge) believes that with proper advertising and better distribution, more consumers would try the products.

Activity: The ranch owner (judge) has asked you to develop a marketing and distribution plan for selling the product to consumers through the Internet. You are to present your ideas to the owner (judge). As you prepare your ideas, be sure to consider how the product would be marketed, distributed, and what type of transportation carrier you would use for local, in-state (outside of the local area), and out-of-state deliveries.

Evaluation: You will be evaluated on how well you meet the following performance indicators:

- Describe the use of technology in the distribution function.
- Explain the relationship between customer service and distribution.
- Explain shipping processes.
- Select advertising media.
- Demonstrate orderly and systematic behavior.

DIRECTIONS: *Organize your thoughts around the performance indicators noted above. Use these performance indicators to jot down your ideas during the preparation period. Time your preparation period to last 15 minutes and your role play presentation to last a maximum of ten minutes. After your role play, use the performance indicators to evaluate your efforts.*

_____

_____

_____

_____

_____

Continued on next page

Assessment: Assume each performance indicator is worth 20 points (20 × 5 = 100 points). Use the evaluation levels listed below for judging consistency.

Excellent (16–20) Participant demonstrated the performance indicator in a professional manner; exceeds business standards.

Good (10–15) Participant demonstrated the performance indicator in an acceptable manner; meets minimal business standards; there would be no need for additional formalized training at this time.

Fair (4–9) Participant demonstrated the performance indicator with limited effectiveness; performance generally fell below minimal business standards; additional training would be required to improve knowledge, attitude, and/or skills.

Poor (0–3) Participant demonstrated the performance indicator with little effectiveness or not at all; a great deal of formal training would be needed.

Describe use of technology in the distribution function.   Score ———

_____

_____

_____

Explain the relationship between customer service and distribution.   Score ———

_____

_____

_____

Explain shipping processes.   Score ———

_____

_____

_____

Select advertising media.   Score ———

_____

_____

_____

Demonstrate orderly and systematic behavior.   Score ———

_____

_____

_____

_____

CHAPTER 22 Physical Distribution

Software Activity (Optional)

Spreadsheet Application

OBJECTIVE: *To evaluate the cost of distributing goods.*

ACTIVITY: The Nugen Company has central distribution centers in five regions of the country. The company uses its own trucks to transport goods from the distribution centers to stores. The company is expanding its distribution facilities in three of the regions to meet increased demand. The spreadsheet below shows the additional shipping needs for each of the three regions. Each company truck can haul 55,000 pounds of goods per load. The number of trips that can be made by a truck during a week varies by region and is shown in the spreadsheet. Use the information given to determine the number of trucks the company needs to buy to handle the additional shipments.

	A	B	C	D	E	F	G
1	Chapter 22 Physical Distribution						
2							
3		Shipping Needs	Number of	Number of	Number of		
4		Per Week	Pounds Per	Trips	Trucks		
5		(in Pounds)	Truck	Per Week	Needed		
6							
7	Region A	2,000,000	55,000	2			
8	Region B	1,500,000	55,000	3			
9	Region C	2,750,000	55,000	2			
10							
11				Total Trucks			

Spreadsheet Directions

1. Turn on your computer and open your spreadsheet software program.

2. Create a spreadsheet like the one above using your spreadsheet application.

3. Calculate the number of trucks needed for each region based on the shipment weights and the trips per week. Then calculate the total number of trucks needed. Enter the appropriate formula for each calculation.

Continued on next page

4. Complete the calculations, then save your work.

5. Print out a copy of your work if your teacher has instructed you to do so. Then answer the questions that follow.

Interpreting Results

1. How many trucks are needed for all regions to handle the extra shipping? Which region needs the most trucks?

_____

_____

2. If each truck costs $120,000 to operate per year, what is the total annual operating cost of the added trucks?

_____

_____

Drawing Conclusions

3. Suppose that 30 percent of the additional shipping needs could be handled by train at a total cost of $2,200,000. Would you recommend shipping only by truck or also by rail shipments? Why or why not?

_____

_____

_____

_____

_____

_____

_____

_____

_____

_____

_____

_____

_____

_____

_____

_____

CHAPTER 23 Purchasing

Vocabulary Review

DIRECTIONS: *Match each definition with the correct term.*

centralized buying	open-to-buy	six-month merchandise plan
consignment buying	organizational buyers	want slips
decentralized buying	resident buying offices	wholesale and retail buyers
memorandum buying	reverse auction	

_____ 1. Purchase goods for resale.

_____ 2. Budget that estimates planned purchases for a six-month period.

_____ 3. Buying for all branches in a chain store operation at a central location.

_____ 4. Arrangement in which goods are paid for only after they are purchased by the consumer.

_____ 5. Local store managers or their designated buyers are authorized to make purchases for their individual stores in a chain store operation.

_____ 6. Amount of money left for buying goods.

_____ 7. Arrangement in which the supplier agrees to take back any unsold goods by a certain date.

_____ 8. Customer requests for items not carried in the store.

_____ 9. Retailers' representatives in the central market.

_____ 10. They buy goods for use in business and buy in much greater quantities than average consumers do.

_____ 11. Companies post what they want to buy on the Internet and suppliers bid for the contract.

CHAPTER 23 Purchasing

Fact and Idea Review

DIRECTIONS: *Circle the letters of all the choices that accurately complete each of the following sentences.*

1. A purchasing agent for a manufacturing business is involved with
   a. production planning.
   b. the preparation and/or implementation of a master production schedule.
   c. materials requirement planning.
   d. buying goods for resale purchases.

2. Business people who buy goods for resale include
   a. industrial buyers.
   b. purchasing agents.
   c. retail buyers.
   d. wholesale buyers.

3. In manufacturing and service businesses, the people responsible for purchasing are called
   a. purchasing managers.
   b. industrial buyers.
   c. procurement managers.
   d. wholesale buyers.

4. Criteria that buyers use to select supply sources include
   a. production capabilities.
   b. previous experience with a vendor.
   c. product offerings and terms (price, discounts, dating, etc.).
   d. services offered.

5. When projecting planned sales on a six-month merchandise plan, the firm's sales goal for the current year is derived from a study of
   a. last year's sales.
   b. current market conditions.
   c. current economic conditions.
   d. analysis of the competition.

6. On a merchandise plan, planned retail reductions take into account reductions in the selling price, as well as shortages of merchandise caused by
   a. defective merchandise returned to the vendor.
   b. clerical mistakes.
   c. employee pilferage.
   d. customer shoplifting.

7. B2B e-commerce covers online selling and purchasing of goods and services via
   a. companies' own Web sites.
   b. electronic exchanges.
   c. online auctions.
   d. online reverse auctions.

CHAPTER 23 Purchasing

Marketing Application 1

DIRECTIONS: *Use the following exercise to review the calculations for a merchandise plan. Following each element, write the formula used to obtain that figure.*

Assume you are a gift store manager and you are completing the merchandise plan entries for the month of December. Last year's December sales totaled $112,000. You are projecting a three percent increase in sales for this year. During the month of December, you usually maintain a 3:1 stock-to-sales ratio. Last year's reductions were $7,000. This year you hope to reduce that amount by five percent. Assume an EOM stock figure for December of $250,000.

1. Planned sales _____

   Previous sales _____

   Desired increase _____

   Calculation of planned sales _____

2. Beginning-of-the-month stock _____

   Stock-to-sales ratio _____

   Planned sales _____

   Calculation of BOM _____

3. Planned reductions _____

   Last year's reductions _____

   Desired decrease _____

   Calculation of planned reductions _____

4. Planned purchases _____

   Planned sales _____

   EOM Stock _____

   Planned reductions _____

   BOM stock _____

   Calculation of planned purchases _____

5. Planned purchases at cost with 55 _____
   percent markup on retail.

   Planned purchases at retail _____

   Cost equivalent percentage
   (100 − MU% retail) _____

   Planned purchases at cost _____

CHAPTER 23 Purchasing

Marketing Application 2

DIRECTIONS: *Compare and contrast the deals offered by suppliers X, Y, and Z and decide with which you would do business. Provide a rationale for your selection by reviewing the criteria buyers use in selecting supply sources. The product is men's cotton/ polyester blend shirts to which you will add your own private label.*

Vendor X (present vendor)
Vendor X has been your source of supply for the past ten years and is located in the United States. Resource file data indicates that Vendor X has recently been bought out by a large corporation, and since then deliveries have been one to two weeks late, which is why you are looking for a new vendor. You have been paying $5.85 per shirt with FOB factory freight prepaid and dating terms of 3/10, net 45.

Vendor Y
Vendor Y is a potential new source of supply and is located abroad (China). A visit to the manufacturing facility revealed that Vendor Y has the production capabilities to deliver the quantities needed at significantly lower prices than Vendor X and Vendor Z. Deliveries will take longer, so purchasing must be done earlier. Vendor Y offers FOB destination charges reversed and ROG dating of 2/10, net 30. The price of one shirt less the quantity discount (for which you would qualify) is $2.75. Tariffs will be $.25 per shirt, and shipping costs have been projected to be $.50 per shirt, based on shipping by boat. Hidden costs include frequent trips abroad to monitor the manufacturing process for quality-control purposes.

Vendor Z
Vendor Z is a potential new source of supply. It is in the U.S. and has the capacity to make frequent deliveries. It has its own delivery trucks and an excellent reputation for servicing its customers. Its production facilities are smaller than Vendor X and Vendor Y, but worker productivity appears to be higher. Vendor Z offers FOB destination (no charge for shipping) and dating terms of 2/10, net 30. The price per shirt with the quantity discount is $6.50.

Note: All three vendors offer UPC labeling and will take care of your private labeling and packaging requirements but will not agree to consignment or memorandum buying arrangements.

_____

_____

_____

_____

_____

_____

_____

_____

CHAPTER 23 Purchasing

The DECA Connection

Role Play: Online Purchasing Consultant

Situation: You are to assume the role of employee of a locally owned restaurant. The owner (judge) is not knowledgeable about computers and their use. Since you have worked in all areas of the restaurant, including ordering supplies and checking in the supplies when they arrived, the owner wants your input about the benefits and risks of purchasing online.

B2B purchases online are expected to double in each of the next three years. Your research indicates hospitals and physicians, as well as hotels, are buying goods and services online through e-commerce exchanges. The restaurant industry is next in line to realize the benefits of B2B purchasing over the Internet. If estimates are correct, the cost of traditional purchasing using paper forms runs around $100 per purchase order, while the same process online typically costs around $5. Since supplies are bought more quickly and efficiently, warehousing and storage of supplies (especially perishable items) can be reduced significantly. Checking on orders is faster because computerized data can be accessed quickly and easily.

Activity: Discuss the pros and cons of buying online versus buying restaurant supplies in the traditional manner with the owner (judge) in his/her office.

Evaluation: You will be evaluated on how well you meet the following performance indicators:

• Explain the nature and scope of purchasing.

• Explain types of business risk.

• Explain the nature of risk management.

• Review performance of vendors.

• Identify factors affecting a business's profit.

DIRECTIONS: *Organize your thoughts around the performance indicators noted above. Use these performance indicators to jot down your ideas during the preparation period. Time your preparation period to last 15 minutes and your role play presentation to last a maximum of 10 minutes. After your role play, use the performance indicators to evaluate your efforts.*

_____

_____

_____

_____

_____

Continued on next page

Assessment: Assume each performance indicator is worth 20 points (20 × 5 = 100 points). Use the evaluation levels listed below for judging consistency.

Excellent (16–20) Participant demonstrated the performance indicator in a professional manner; exceeds business standards.

Good (10–15) Participant demonstrated the performance indicator in an acceptable and effective manner; meets at least minimal business standards; there would be no need for additional formalized training at this time.

Fair (4–9) Participant demonstrated the performance indicator with limited effectiveness; performance generally fell below minimal business standards; additional training would be required to improve knowledge, attitude, and/or skills.

Poor (0–3) Participant demonstrated the performance indicator with little effectiveness or not at all; a great deal of formal training would be needed.

Explain the nature and scope of purchasing. Score ———

_____

_____

Explain types of business risk. Score ———

_____

_____

_____

Explain the nature of risk management. Score ———

_____

_____

_____

Review performance of vendors. Score ———

_____

_____

_____

Identify factors affecting a business's profit. Score ———

_____

_____

_____

CHAPTER 23 Purchasing

Database Application

OBJECTIVE: *To add a new field of information to a database file of suppliers.*

ACTIVITY: The Brewster Corporation is updating its database of information about the suppliers from which it purchases items used to operate the business. Several of the company's suppliers have added online services and have e-mail addresses. Messages asking for quotes or availability of stock can now be sent via e-mail. The printout below shows a list of suppliers used by the Brewster Corporation.

Company	Address	City/State/Zip	Telephone	Fax	Terms	Shipping
Practical Business Solutions	914 South Lane Center	Dallas, TX 75212	(555) 982-4478	(555) 982-4479	2/15, n/30, EOM	FOB Destination
Bryant Equipment Corp.	1229 St. Paul Street	Springfield, MA 01105	(555) 688-4501	(555) 688-7802	2/10 n/30	FOB FFP
McAvoy Plastics & Coatings, Inc.	648 Industrial Drive	Lansing, MI 48932	(555) 278-4401	(555) 278-4405	Net 30	FOB Destination
Riverton Corp.	928 Briggs Road	Columbus, OH 43223	(555) 899-4801	(555) 899-4802	Net 30	FOB Destination
Topper Machinery Company, Inc.	150 E. Willson Road	Knoxville, TN 37922	(555) 688-7888	(555) 688-9802	2/10, n/45	FOB Destination
Landings Design & Construction Co.	12 Coppersmith Road	Billings, MT 59106	(555) 277-8801	(555) 277-8860	2/10, n/30, EOM	FOB Shipping Point
Lawrence Manufacturing Co.	1214 Hunter Street	Lawrence, KS 66046	(555) 989-0142	(555) 989-2445	1/10, n/30	FOB Destination

Continued on next page

Database Directions

1. Turn on your computer and open your database software program.

2. Create a database like the one on page 201.

3. Create a new field called "e-mail address" and place it after the fax telephone number. Add a fictional e-mail address for each company.

4. Save your data. Print out a copy of your work if your teacher has instructed you to do so. Then answer the questions that follow.

Interpreting Results

1. How does adding a field in a database change the information that can be retrieved from the database?

_____

_____

_____

_____

_____

2. In what different ways could this database be sorted?

_____

_____

_____

_____

Drawing Conclusions

3. Can you have either too much or too little information in a database? Explain why each situation might cause difficulty for someone searching a database for information.

_____

_____

_____

_____

_____

_____

_____

_____

CHAPTER 24 Stock Handling and Inventory Control

Vocabulary Review

DIRECTIONS: *Match each statement with the correct term.*

basic stock list	model stock list	receiving record
dollar control	never-out list	source marking
inventory management	perpetual inventory system	stockkeeping unit
inventory turnover	physical inventory system	unit control
just-in-time (JIT)	real-time inventory	

_____ 1. Tracks inventory on a constant basis.

_____ 2. A stock plan used to monitor staple items.

_____ 3. When the seller or manufacturer puts the price on the merchandise before it is delivered to a retailer.

_____ 4. Measuring quantities of merchandise that a business handles during a stated period of time.

_____ 5. Number of times the average inventory is sold and replaced in a given time period.

_____ 6. In this system, stock is visually inspected and counted.

_____ 7. The planning and monitoring of the total inventory investment.

_____ 8. Each item or a group of related items.

_____ 9. A stock plan used to monitor fashionable items.

_____ 10. An inventory system in which suppliers deliver parts and materials just before they are needed for use.

_____ 11. A form used to describe the goods received by a business.

_____ 12. An Internet technology that connects applications, data, and users.

_____ 13. The process of buying and storing merchandise for sale while controlling costs.

_____ 14. A stock plan used for best-selling items that make up a high percentage of sales volume.

CHAPTER 24 Stock Handling and Inventory Control

Fact and Idea Review

DIRECTIONS: *In each series of items, circle the one that does not belong. Then explain your choice on the line below.*

1. blind   direct   inventory   quality   spot
_____
_____

2. apron   dock   invoice   purchase order   receiving record
_____
_____
_____

3. stock transfer   preretailing method   source marking   UPC
_____
_____

4. dollar control   stock turnover   unit control   working capital
_____
_____

5. dollar control   sales   purchases   stock shortages   unit control
_____
_____

6. dollar control   brands   colors   sizes   unit control
_____
_____

7. annual inventory count   perpetual inventory   physical inventory   visual control
_____
_____

8. stock shrinkage   electronic data exchange   UPC   SCM
_____
_____
_____

9. basic stock   model stock   never-out   SKU
_____
_____

CHAPTER 24 Stock Handling and Inventory Control

Marketing Application 1

1. Assume you are responsible for taking an inventory in the stationery department of a school store. Complete the inventory form below, by filling in the heading and calculating the necessary extensions (total retail value for each item and for the entire stationery inventory).

_____ School Store

INVENTORY FORM

Date _____ 20 --   Counted by _____

Page Number _____   Checked by _____

Description of Merchandise	Units on Hand	Unit Price		Total Retail Value
refrigerator magnets	45	$	.99	
5" x 8" note cards	25		.79	
filler notebook paper	38	1	.19	
erasers	60		.29	
pencils	115		.15	
medium-point pens	45		.39	
fine-point pens	51		.39	
computer paper (250 ct.)	10	10	.59	
typewriter ribbons	20	1	.98	
posterboard (white)	15		.59	
posterboard (colored)	10		.79	
protractors	5	2	.19	
rulers (6")	6		.39	
rulers (12")	12		.79	
pocket portfolios	12		.79	
Total Retail Value				

Continued on next page

2. You are a stockroom employee at Michelmann's Department Store. Every item in the store has a storage control card like the one below to which action is posted weekly and when merchandise is moved to the sales floor.

Fill in the card for the Proctor-Silex four-slice toaster (stock No. 12374), located in Housewares. The store tries to have a maximum of 25 and a minimum of 5 such toasters in stock at all times. As merchandise is issued (moved to the sales floor and sold), the quantity of toasters on hand is adjusted. Transactions for two months are as follows:

Date Received			Date Issued		
3/4/—	Ordered	0*	3/5/—	Ordered	3†
3/11/—	Ordered	0	3/13/—	Ordered	5
3/18/—	Ordered	6	3/20/—	Ordered	8
3/25/—	Ordered	10	3/25/—	Ordered	3
4/1/—	Ordered	0	4/3/—	Ordered	12
4/8/—	Ordered	0	4/10/—	Ordered	5
4/15/—	Ordered	15	4/19/—	Ordered	12
4/22/—	Ordered	3	4/22/—	Ordered	1

*Initial quantity on hand is 25.
†Quantity sold is always the same as that ordered by sales personnel.

Article			Size		Max.		Location			Stock No.	
			Unit		Min.						

RECEIVED			ISSUED			BALANCE	RECEIVED			ISSUED			BALANCE
DATE	ORDER	QUAN	DATE	ORDER	QUAN		DATE	ORDER	QUAN	DATE	ORDER	QUAN	

CHAPTER 24 Stock Handling and Inventory Control

Marketing Application 2

DIRECTIONS: *Read the case study below. Then answer the questions that follow.*

Apple Reaches Out to Retailers

In an effort to improve flagging sales, Apple Computer Inc. has stepped out of self-imposed isolation and returned to retail stores. During most of the 1990s, Apple sold its computers only through its own Web site, CompUSA, and a few other specialty retailers.

That distribution was a conscious choice by the computer maker and was in reaction to inventory problems and the expense of maintaining relationships with retail stores. Retail outlets that did carry Apple products had trouble keeping them in stock and complained that the company's policies were too rigid. Apple at one point mandated that dealers had to sell at least $500,000 worth of product to carry Apple.

The policy was unprofitable for many retailers and for Apple. Now, with the success of the new iMac line, Apple has decided that it will broaden its presence in retail stores. The company is getting its products in more stores and working with distributors to get Apple computers into specialty shops. Apple experts help design the display space in stores and provide sales demonstrations for customers. Apple representatives also provide training on Apple software for retail salespeople.

Retail stores are willing to work with Apple again, because in addition to the popular iMac, Apple introduced PowerBook laptops and G4 desktops that are attracting new customers. The company has solved its inventory problems, so it is able to keep retailers stocked. Plus, the colorful Apple computers look good in displays. National retailer Sears Roebuck & Co. sells Apple computers now. However, another retailer, Best Buy, refused to carry all five colors of the iMac, so Apple pulled its products from Best Buy stores.

Getting into more retail establishments seems to be working for Apple. About half of all Apples that aren't sold to schools are sold through retail stores. Apple's own online store handles about 20 percent of its sales. With increased retail outreach successful in the United States, Apple is planning similar efforts in Europe and Japan.

Apple has been advertising under the slogan "Think different," and the company has shown that it can think differently, even about its own marketing and distribution. The company hopes that the combination of increased distribution, successful product lines, and catchy advertising will increase sales.

1. What are some of the costs involved with maintaining effective dealer networks for a computer company like Apple?

   _____

   _____

   _____

   _____

Continued on next page

2. What did Apple do to alienate many retailers from carrying its products before the new strategy was implemented?

_____

_____

_____

_____

_____

_____

_____

3. Why does Apple believe that it must expand on its retailer network?

_____

_____

_____

_____

_____

_____

4. Why do you think Apple maintains its own online store instead of totally relying on its dealer network?

_____

_____

_____

_____

_____

_____

_____

_____

CHAPTER 24 Stock Handling and Inventory Control

The DECA Connection

Role Play: Supermarket Assistant Manager

Situation: You are to assume the role of assistant manager of a large supermarket that has over 27,000 individual stockkeeping units. The store uses point-of-sale terminals for all selling transactions. Your store is located in a state that does not require all stockkeeping units to be individually price marked. However, the state does require that shelf labels and signs accurately reflect the price of each item to be sold. Your state also penalizes a store for overcharging. Because of a busy weekend and some newly hired stockpersons, shelf prices and signs were not changed to accurately reflect the price on several sale items. Accordingly, an irate customer (judge) has approached you complaining about being overcharged. The customer is shouting loudly in front of several customers that your store has a reputation for overcharging customers on sale items. This is not a correct allegation, since your store genuinely tries to be fair and honest with its pricing practices. However, the customer is a regular customer and really believes that it is a common practice in your store to overcharge customers. The customer's sales receipt indicates that there has been overcharge on four sales items for a total of approximately $3.59.

Activity: The manager has asked you to handle the disgruntled customer (judge) in a manner that will not embarrass the customer and do further damage to the store's reputation. Remember that the customer is a regular shopper and that under state law your store incurs a financial penalty for overcharging customers of twice the amount of the overcharge up to a $10 maximum. You must resolve the situation to the satisfaction of the customer and gain a commitment from the customer to continue shopping at your store.

Evaluation: You will be evaluated on how well you meet the following performance indicators:

- Handle customer/client complaints.
- Demonstrate problem-solving skills.
- Interpret business policies to customers/clients.
- Explain the nature of positive customer/client relations.
- Describe the role of business ethics in pricing.

DIRECTIONS: *Organize your thoughts around the performance indicators noted above. Use these performance indicators to jot down your ideas during the preparation period. Time your preparation period to last 15 minutes and your role play presentation to last a maximum of ten minutes. After your role play, use the performance indicators to evaluate your efforts.*

_____

_____

_____

_____

Continued on next page

Assessment: Assume each performance indicator is worth 20 points (20 × 5 = 100 points). Use the evaluation levels listed below for judging consistency.

Excellent (16–20) Participant demonstrated the performance indicator in a professional manner; exceeds business standards.

Good (10–15) Participant demonstrated the performance indicator in an acceptable manner; meets minimal business standards; there would be no need for additional formalized training at this time.

Fair (4–9) Participant demonstrated the performance indicator with limited effectiveness; performance generally fell below minimal business standards; additional training would be required to improve knowledge, attitude, and/or skills.

Poor (0–3) Participant demonstrated the performance indicator with little effectiveness or not at all; a great deal of formal training would be needed.

Handle customer/client complaints.   Score ———

_____

_____

_____

Demonstrate problem-solving skills.   Score ———

_____

_____

_____

Interpret business policies to customers/clients.   Score ———

_____

_____

_____

Explain the nature of positive customer/client relations.   Score ———

_____

_____

_____

Describe the role of business ethics in pricing.   Score ———

_____

_____

_____

CHAPTER 24 Stock Handling and Inventory Control

Software Activity (Optional)

Spreadsheet Application

OBJECTIVE: *Track inventory.*

ACTIVITY: Inventory management is the process of buying and storing merchandise for sale while controlling costs for ordering, shipping, handling, and storage. As inventory manager, you place orders for new merchandise at the end of each week. With the aid of a spreadsheet, you track the daily sales of each item in the department to determine how much to order.

Inventory and sales information for five products in your department are shown in the spreadsheet below. Based on past sales records, you have estimated the "Planned Weekly Stock Level." This is the level that you need at the beginning of each week. Your computer has also generated information on the beginning inventory level and sales of each item for the past six days.

Use a spreadsheet to calculate the ending inventory for each product. Then calculate the number of each product that you must order to bring your inventory back up to the "Planned Weekly Stock Level."

	A	B	C	D	E	F	G	H	I	J	K
1	Chapter 24 Stock Handling and Inventory Control										
2		Planned									
3		Weekly									
4	Stock	Stock	Beginning	Day 1	Day 2	Day 3	Day 4	Day 5	Day 6	Ending	Amount to
5	Number	Level	Inventory	Sales	Sales	Sales	Sales	Sales	Sales	Inventory	Order
6	17345	55	65	5	6	3	9	5	4		
7	35567	105	104	12	10	4	20	3	3		
8	97365	25	25	2	14	6	0	2	1		
9	55677	60	62	4	5	3	0	0	4		
10	9785	40	38	1	0	0	3	5	7		

Spreadsheet Directions

1. Turn on your computer and open your spreadsheet software program.

2. Create a spreadsheet like the one above using your spreadsheet application.

3. Enter a formula to calculate the current Ending Inventory for Stock Number 17345.

4. Copy the formula to appropriate cells in all remaining rows.

5. Enter the formula to calculate Amount to Order for Stock Number 17345. Copy the formula to appropriate cells in all remaining rows.

6. After completing your calculations, save your work.

7 Print out a copy of your work if your teacher has instructed you to do so. Then answer the questions that follow. *Continued on next page*

Interpreting Results

1. List the Ending Inventory levels for each of the five products.

_____

_____

_____

2. At the end of the week, how many of each item must be ordered, based on Planned Weekly Stock Levels?

_____

_____

_____

Drawing Conclusions

3. How are the Planned Weekly Stock Levels determined?

_____

_____

_____

_____

4. Does using these calculations to place orders for merchandise ensure that the business will not run out of product next week?

_____

_____

_____

_____

5. Does an ending inventory of 0 at the end of week indicate that the manager made an excellent buying decision?

_____

_____

_____

CHAPTER 25 Price Planning

Vocabulary Review

DIRECTIONS: *Match each definition with the correct term.*

bait and switch advertising	loss leader	price discrimination
break-even point	market position	price fixing
elastic demand	market share	return on investment
inelastic demand	price	unit pricing

_____ 1. Marketer's relative standing/rank in relation to competitors.

_____ 2. Competitors agree on certain price ranges within which they set their own prices.

_____ 3. Calculation used to determine the relative profitability of a product.

_____ 4. An item priced at or below cost to draw customers into a store.

_____ 5. Value of money (or its equivalent) placed on a good or service.

_____ 6. Demand that is affected by a change in price.

_____ 7. Charging different prices to similar customers in similar situations.

_____ 8. This allows customers to compare prices in relation to a standard unit or measure, such as an ounce or a pound.

_____ 9. Refers to demand that is barely, if at all, affected by a change in price.

_____ 10. Point at which sales revenue equals the costs and expenses of making and distributing a product.

_____ 11. A firm's percentage of the total sales volume generated by all competitors in a given market.

_____ 12. Advertisements of a low price on an item that the advertiser has no intention of selling.

CHAPTER 25 Price Planning

Fact and Idea Review

DIRECTIONS: *Circle the letter of the phrase that best completes each of the following sentences.*

1. The prices a business charges its customers for its products are important because they establish and maintain a firm's
   a. image, competitive edge, and profits.
   b. ability to control competition.
   c. costs and expenses.
   d. ability to manipulate elastic and inelastic consumer demand.

2. Assume your firm's sales increased from $3 million last year to $10 million this year. However, the market leader still enjoys a 40 percent share of the $200 million widget market. The other four competitors had sales this year of $53 million, $38 million, $12 million, and $7 million, respectively. For this year, your firm's market position would be
   a. 1.5 percent. b. five percent. c. last. d. fifth.

3. If you sell a product for $18.98 and it costs you $16.50 to make and market it, your return on investment for that product would be
   a. 13 percent. b. 15 percent. c. 87 percent. d. 115 percent.

4. To maintain a firm's profits in the face of rising costs and expenses or declining sales, businesses might do all of the following except
   a. reduce the size of the product to maintain or lower the price.
   b. decrease the price by reducing the number of product features.
   c. improve product quality and increase the number of features to justify a higher price.
   d. maintain prices while increasing product size and or features.

5. A manufacturer plans to produce 300,000 dolls that will be sold to wholesalers and retailers for $15 each. Unit costs and expenses associated with making and distributing one doll are $12. The point at which this manufacturer will break even is
   a. 375,000 dolls. c. 240,000 dolls.
   b. 200,000 dolls. d. 100,000 dolls.

6. When a person is at a vacation resort where the only food service available is affiliated with the resort, prices will most likely be higher than normal because
   a. the food service would be classified as a luxury.
   b. the law of diminishing marginal utility says so.
   c. all consumers are brand loyal.
   d. the demand is inelastic because of the lack of substitutes.

7. The federal law that prohibits sellers from offering one price to one customer and another price to another customer in the same class of trade is the
   a. Sherman Antitrust Act. c. Robinson-Patman Act.
   b. Clayton Antitrust Act. d. Resale Price Maintenance Act.

CHAPTER 25 Price Planning

Marketing Application 1

DIRECTIONS: *Read the article below. Then answer the questions that follow.*

Newspaper Cost-Cutting Measure

Due to lower than average advertising revenues and increasing paper costs, newspapers are cutting the length of their newspapers instead of increasing their prices. The *Dallas Morning News* reduced the amount of space designated for stock tables, sports results, television listings, and comics. Other newspapers across the nation are facing the same problem and many have elected to cut some of their comic strips, which caused a fury among dedicated followers. To avoid offending these comic-strip readers, some newspapers have shrunk the size of comic strips so that they fit into a smaller space, while others have conducted surveys to determine which comic strips to cut. The results of the survey, however, have been skewed toward older readers who prefer longtime favorites and who are still the mainstay for newspaper readership.

In some cases, comic strips that have been cut have been reinstated due to popular demand. The *Salt Lake Tribune,* which cut its weekday comics section from three pages to two pages, and in so doing retired comic strips *Judge Parker* and *Mary Worth*. Readers responded with e-mails, phone calls, and faxes asking for those comic strips to be restored. A few weeks later the two comic strips were restored and a newer one was cut instead.

Some syndicated comic strips can cost several hundred dollars a week per strip. Newsprint prices increased 10 percent from 2003 to 2004, and those increases are expected to continue.

1. What two major factors have impacted newspapers' profits?

_____

_____

_____

_____

_____

_____

_____

_____

_____

_____

_____

_____

Continued on next page

2. How have newspapers responded to their current financial situation?

_____

_____

_____

_____

_____

_____

_____

3. Why do you think newspapers did not elect to increase their prices, given their financial situation?

_____

_____

_____

_____

_____

_____

_____

_____

4. If you were on the newspaper staff, what recommendations would you make to increase revenue and/or cut expenses?

_____

_____

_____

_____

_____

_____

_____

_____

_____

CHAPTER 25 Price Planning

Marketing Application 2

DIRECTIONS: *Read the article below. Then answer the questions that follow.*

160 Auto Parts Dealers Sue Wal-Mart & Others for Monopolistic Pricing

New York – A coalition of auto parts retailers and warehouse distributors filed an antitrust suit here against Wal-Mart Stores and Sam's Club, Bentonville, Arkansas; Auto-Zone, Memphis, Tennessee; Advance Auto, Roanoke, Virginia; and 13 auto parts manufacturers. The coalition said the manufacturers that sell auto parts to the retailers named in the suit engage in monopolistic pricing practices. The plaintiffs claim those manufacturers named in the suit sell parts to Wal-Mart, Sam's, AutoZone and other defendants named at substantially lower per-unit prices than [to] other distributors and that those prices are lower than the manufacturers' direct costs. Those actions, according to the suit, violate both the Robinson-Patman Act and the [Clayton] Antitrust Act. The plaintiffs claim they are unable to compete because of the price discrimination, and will be driven out of business by the practice. The suit also alleges the defendant auto parts manufacturers have failed to comply with the Sarbanes-Oxley (effective in September 2003) corporate governance statute by not reporting they are selling below cost to their largest customers in their SEC filings.
From Supermarketnews.com, October 29, 2004.

1. What three laws are the plaintiffs using as the basis for their suit against the auto parts manufacturers and large retailers that sell auto parts? Note the purpose of each law.

_____

_____

_____

_____

_____

_____

_____

_____

_____

_____

_____

Continued on next page

2. If you were a lawyer for one of the 13 manufacturers named in this case, what points might you argue regarding the lower prices offered to your larger customers?

_____

_____

_____

_____

_____

_____

_____

3. If you were a lawyer for Wal-Mart, Sam's Club, AutoZone, or Advance Auto, how could you dispute the allegations that the companies are driving smaller auto parts retailers and warehouse distributors out of business?

_____

_____

_____

_____

_____

_____

_____

_____

4. Who do you think will win this case – plaintiffs or the defendants? Why?

_____

_____

_____

_____

_____

_____

_____

CHAPTER 25 Price Planning

The DECA Connection

Role Play: Assistant Manager

Situation: You are to assume the role of assistant manager of an independent coffee café. You are faced with a dilemma regarding a special promotion you planned for the store's anniversary. You were going to slash prices on cups of coffee and bags of coffee beans due to a price cut you were told you would be receiving from your wholesale supplier. Today you received a fax from your coffee supplier that rescinded the 10 percent cut because of bad weather in Brazil, where one-third of the world's coffee is produced. In a trade paper, you learned that Starbucks, a competitor, is increasing its coffee prices by about seven cents a cup in order to defray operating expenses related to rent and wage increases. The article did not mention the reduced supply of coffee beans from Brazil due to the bad weather, so you are not sure if the Starbucks will be increasing its prices even more in anticipation of higher coffee prices in the near future.

Activity: The owner of the store (judge) is meeting with you to discuss the upcoming anniversary promotion. With all the information you now have, you must decide what to do about coffee prices and how you are going to handle the special promotion. You know the owner's goals for pricing include maintaining market share, getting a fair return on investment, and meeting the competition.

Evaluation: You will be evaluated on how well you meet the following performance indicators:

- Adjust prices to maximize profitability.
- Explain factors affecting pricing decisions.
- Explain the principles of supply and demand.
- Describe the concept of price.
- Describe the role of business ethics in pricing.

DIRECTIONS: *Organize your thoughts around the performance indicators noted above. Use these performance indicators to jot down your ideas during the preparation period. Time your preparation period to last 15 minutes and your role play presentation to last a maximum of ten minutes. After your role play, use the performance indicators to evaluate your efforts.*

_____

_____

_____

_____

_____

_____

Continued on next page

Assessment: Assume each performance indicator is worth 20 points (20 × 5 = 100 points). Use the evaluation levels listed below for judging consistency.

Excellent (16–20) Participant demonstrated the performance indicator in a professional manner, exceeds business standards.

Good (10–15) Participant demonstrated the performance indicator in an acceptable manner; meets minimal business standards; there would be no need for additional formalized training at this time.

Fair (4–9) Participant demonstrated the performance indicator with limited effectiveness; performance generally fell below minimal business standards; additional training would be required to improve knowledge, attitude, and/or skills.

Poor (0–3) Participant demonstrated the performance indicator with little effectiveness or not at all; a great deal of formal training would be needed.

Adjust prices to maximize profitability. Score _____

_____

_____

Explain factors affecting pricing decisions. Score _____

_____

_____

Explain the principles of supply and demand. Score _____

_____

_____

_____

Describe the concept of price. Score _____

_____

_____

_____

Describe the role of business ethics in pricing. Score _____

_____

_____

_____

_____

CHAPTER 25 Price Planning

Spreadsheet Application

OBJECTIVE: *To calculate break-even units for different manufacturing levels.*

ACTIVITY: The Martinez Company makes equipment for racket sports. The company has developed a new tennis racket. The marketing manager has asked you to analyze the cost of manufacturing and selling this new racket. You are to determine the units that must be sold to break even at three different manufacturing volumes. The unit manufacturing costs decrease as the number of units manufactured increases. See the printout below for the cost for each manufacturing level. The sales expenses for this new racket are estimated at three percent of the selling price of $79.50. Marketing expenses will average four percent of the selling price.

	A	B	C	D	E	F	G
1	Chapter 25 Price Planning						
2							
3		Unit			Total		Break-
4		Manufacturing	Sales	Marketing	Unit	Total	Even
5		Cost	Expenses	Expenses	Cost	Cost	Point
6	20,000	28.50					
7	30,000	27.35					
8	40,000	27.00					

Spreadsheet Directions

1. Turn on your computer and open your spreadsheet software program.

2. Create a spreadsheet like the one above using your spreadsheet application.

3. Enter a formula to calculate the sales expenses.

4. Enter a formula to calculate the marketing expenses.

5. Enter a formula to calculate the total unit cost for each manufacturing level (add columns B, C, and D). Then enter a formula to find the total cost for each level.

6. Enter a formula to calculate the break-even points.

7. Save your work. Print out a copy of your work if your teacher has instructed you to do so. Then answer the questions that follow.

Continued on next page

Interpreting Results

1. What is the total unit cost at each level of manufacturing?

_____

_____

_____

_____

_____

2. What is the break-even point at each level of manufacturing?

_____

_____

_____

_____

_____

Drawing Conclusions

3. Assume that this model of racket is manufactured only once a month. The marketing manager has estimated average sales of 22,000 rackets a month. To avoid having excess inventory, the company wants to have no more than 10,000 rackets in stock when it next manufactures this model in one month. Make a recommendation for the number of units to manufacture now. Explain your reasons for choosing this number.

_____

_____

_____

_____

_____

_____

_____

_____

_____

_____

_____

CHAPTER 26 Pricing Strategies

Vocabulary Review

DIRECTIONS: *Match each definition with the correct term.*

bundle pricing	flexible-price policy	promotional pricing
cost-plus pricing	markup pricing	seasonal discounts
discount pricing	penetration pricing	skimming pricing
EDLP	prestige pricing	trade discounts

_____ 1. All costs and expenses are calculated and then the desired profit is added to arrive at a price.

_____ 2. The price of a new prodct is set very high to capitalize on the high demand during its introductory period.

_____ 3. Prices are reduced for a short period of time.

_____ 4. The seller offers reductions from the usual price.

_____ 5. These are offered to buyers who are willing to buy in advance of the customary buying season.

_____ 6. The initial price for a new product is set very low in order to encourage as many people as possible to buy it.

_____ 7. A company sets prices consistently low with no intention of offering discounts in the future.

_____ 8. Prices are higher than average to suggest status and an upscale image to the consumer.

_____ 9. Some manufacturers quote prices to wholesalers and retailers in this way.

_____ 10. Arriving at a price by adding a dollar amount to the cost of an item.

_____ 11. This permits customers to bargain for merchandise.

_____ 12. Including several products in a package that is sold at a single price.

CHAPTER 26 Pricing Strategies

Fact and Idea Review

DIRECTIONS: *Circle the letter of the word or phrase that best completes each of the following sentences.*

1. Cost-plus pricing is used primarily by
   a. consumers.   b. manufacturers.   c. retailers.   d. wholesalers.

2. The consumer's perceived value of an item is the basis for
   a. competition-oriented pricing.
   b. cost-oriented pricing.
   c. demand-oriented pricing.
   d. markup-oriented pricing.

3. Skimming pricing permits marketers to
   a. cover the research and development costs incurred in designing the product.
   b. enjoy a bargain image.
   c. lure customers away from higher-priced brands.
   d. raise their product's price in the future without affecting customer loyalty.

4. A retail department store that has price tags on all of its merchandise is practicing a
   a. flexible-price policy.
   b. penetration pricing policy.
   c. skimming pricing policy.
   d. one-price policy.

5. The main goal of marketers is to keep products in the
   a. decline stage.   b. growth stage.   c. introduction stage.   d. maturity stage.

6. A marketer who wants to project a quality image would price a sweater at
   a. $153.50.   b. $149.99.   c. $150.   d. $147.59.

7. To suggest a bargain and help increase sales volume, some businesses make it a practice to
   a. price items in multiples, like 3 for $1.
   b. use prestige pricing.
   c. set prices that end in even numbers, like $30.
   d. price just above round amount, like $31.

8. A special type of promotional discount that goes directly to buyers when they sell back an old model of the product they are purchasing is called a
   a. rebate.
   b. loss leader.
   c. trade-in allowance.
   d. special deal.

9. A store that prices all of its sweaters at $50, $75, and $100 is following
   a. bundle pricing.
   b. an EDLP policy.
   c. a price-lining policy.
   d. a discount pricing policy.

CHAPTER 26 Pricing Strategies

Marketing Application 1

DIRECTIONS: *Read the article below. Then answer the questions that follow.*

Costco—A Warehouse Retailer With Low Prices

With a combination of low markups, bare bones design, and a wide merchandise mix, the warehouse retailer Costco is able to offer customers low prices every day.

Costco stores are the epitome of no frills. They are warehouses with merchandise stacked to the rafters. While Costco carries only a few brands and sizes, it offers an impressive range of products, from groceries to household products, from clothing, books, and records to automotive equipment and even luxury items. Fresh food accounts for ten percent of Costco's annual sales. Costco customers can get their photos processed in the hour it takes to pick up fresh salmon, Waterford crystal, and motor oil. Customers can also get an eye exam and have glasses made, and at some locations they can fill up with gas that is as much as 25 cents a gallon cheaper than retail gas stations.

Costco relies on a predictable pricing strategy. It keeps markups at between 10 and 14 percent above cost, well below the minimum 25 percent for most retailers. And Costco avoids selling items at cost to attract customers, instead relying on a low markup to ensure that prices on all items stay low every day. In addition, Costco charges all its customers a membership fee: $45 for a business owner and the general public, and $100 for an executive membership with added features.

Costco does not have as many stores as Sam's Club, a major competitor. There are about 300 Costcos compared with around 530 Sam's Clubs (a subsidiary of Wal-Mart). Another competitor is BJ's Wholesale Club, with around 150 locations. Regardless of number of locations, Costco manages to generate greater annual sales per store, $112 million, which is significantly higher than the $63 million per store for Sam's Club and $46 million for BJ's Wholesale Club.

1. How does Costco demonstrate cost-oriented, demand-oriented, and competition-oriented pricing?

_____

_____

_____

_____

_____

_____

_____

_____

_____

Continued on next page

2. Is Costco's pricing policy more representative of a one-price policy or a flexible-price policy? Explain your answer.

_____

_____

_____

_____

_____

_____

3. How is Costco able to keep its prices so low and still be profitable?

_____

_____

_____

_____

_____

_____

_____

_____

4. Why do you think Costco's annual sales per store exceed those of its competitors?

_____

_____

_____

_____

_____

_____

_____

_____

CHAPTER 26 Pricing Strategies

Marketing Application 2

DIRECTIONS: *Use the six steps in setting a price to demonstrate how a luggage manufacturer would price a newly designed piece of luggage. The case has wheels and a retractable handle for pulling. It is 14½ inches wide by 9 inches deep by 22 inches high and weighs 9 pounds empty. This new model is approved as carry-on luggage for airline flights. It can be made of a heavy-duty polyester fabric or a water resistant tapestry fabric with leather trim.*

1. *Determine pricing objectives.* Do you want to generate a certain sales volume, take away market share from competitors, or establish a prestigious or value-oriented image?

   _____

   _____

   _____

   _____

   _____

2. *Study costs.* It costs $43.50 to make and market this piece of luggage. The company would like to get a return on investment on this new design of 10–20 percent. Determine the floor, midrange, and ceiling prices (plus 10, 15, and 20 percent, respectively) that would be charged to retailers. Then, assuming that the retailers would charge customers at least double their cost, determine what the retail prices would be for this item.

   _____

   _____

   _____

   _____

   _____

3. *Estimate demand.* Who will be your final target market, and what will that group be willing to pay? This design is similar to the type of luggage flight attendants use. Research indicates that it is fast becoming the luggage of choice for female business travelers and other people who don't like waiting for their luggage in airline terminals.

   _____

   _____

   _____

   _____

   _____

Continued on next page

4. *Study competition.* With whom will you compete? Research indicates that the Verdi brand retails for a $130, which means the price to the retailer is estimated to be between $50 and $65. The Destination brand retails for $99.99, which means the price to the retailer was probably between $40 and $50. Other competitors have prices somewhere between those two.

_____

_____

_____

_____

_____

5. *Decide on a pricing strategy.* Will it be skimming, going-rate, or penetration? Why?

_____

_____

_____

_____

_____

_____

6. *Set price.*

  a. What will be the suggested retail price for the luggage? Explain.

_____

_____

_____

_____

_____

  b. What is the price you will charge retailers for this luggage? Explain.

_____

_____

_____

_____

_____

_____

CHAPTER 26 Pricing Strategies

The DECA Connection

Role Play: Assistant Buyer

Situation: You are to assume the role of assistant buyer for fragrances in an upscale department store. You are always on the lookout for new product ideas. After seeing advertisements for French perfume and other toiletries for dogs in *Elle* and *Vogue*, two fashion magazines, you decide to conduct a little research. You learn that a celebrity is about to launch her own doggie perfume and that the doggie toiletries market has not as yet been tapped. Research indicates that the French perfume for dogs is retailing for $38 in other upscale department stores. Your store's customary markup based on cost for high-end toiletries is between 60 percent and 100 percent, depending on the brand. The celebrity's doggie perfume will cost the store $22.50.

Activity: Write a memo to your buyer (judge) detailing your discovery of doggie perfume and toiletries and providing a suggested retail price for the celebrity's doggie perfume. You need to take cost, demand, and competition into account when providing your rationale. You should also provide a pricing strategy for the new, innovative product, as well as strategies to sell more than one product in the line. Explain any psychological pricing ideas you have, as well as any ideas about promotional pricing to launch this new line.

Evaluation: You will be evaluated on how well you meet the following performance indicators:

- Select an approach for setting a base price.
- Identify strategies for pricing new products.
- Select product mix pricing strategies.
- Use psychological pricing to adjust base prices.
- Select promotional pricing strategies used to adjust base prices.

DIRECTIONS: *Organize your thoughts around the performance indicators noted above. Use these performance indicators to jot down your ideas during the preparation period. Time your preparation period to last 15 minutes and your role play presentation to last a maximum of ten minutes. After your role play, use the performance indicators to evaluate your efforts.*

_____

_____

_____

_____

_____

_____

_____

Continued on next page

Assessment: Assume each performance indicator is worth 20 points (20 × 5 = 100 points). Use the evaluation levels listed below for judging consistency.

Excellent (16–20) Participant demonstrated the performance indicator in a professional manner, exceeds business standards.

Good (10–15) Participant demonstrated the performance indicator in an acceptable manner; meets minimal business standards; there would be no need for additional formalized training at this time.

Fair (4–9) Participant demonstrated the performance indicator with limited effectiveness; performance generally fell below minimal business standards; additional training would be required to improve knowledge, attitude, and/or skills.

Poor (0–3) Participant demonstrated the performance indicator with little effectiveness or not at all; a great deal of formal training would be needed.

Select an approach for setting a base price. Score _____

_____

_____

_____

Identify strategies for pricing new products. Score _____

_____

_____

_____

Select product mix pricing strategies. Score _____

_____

_____

_____

Use psychological pricing to adjust base prices. Score _____

_____

_____

_____

Select promotional pricing strategies used to adjust base prices. Score _____

_____

_____

_____

_____

CHAPTER 26 Pricing Strategies

Software Activity (Optional)	Spreadsheet Application

OBJECTIVE: *To determine the best price for a new product.*

ACTIVITY: The Sun Protection Company has conducted research asking customers the maximum price they would be willing to pay for a new sunblock cream with an SPF of 40. The number of customers saying they would buy the product at each price is shown in the spreadsheet below. Prices below $3.50 were omitted from the table because they are unprofitable. The company plans to sell its new sunblock cream in one city first to test market acceptance. Assume that the research group represents five percent of the total market of potential buyers in the test city.

	A	B	C	D	E	F	G	H
1	Chapter 26 Pricing Strategies							
2								
3								
4		Number		Estimated				
5		of	Total	Retail				
6	Price	Customers	Market	Sales				
7								
8	$3.99	500						
9	$4.49	1,100						
10	$4.99	800						
11	$5.49	600						
12	$5.99	200						
13								
14	TOTAL	3,200						

Continued on next page

Spreadsheet Directions

1. Turn on your computer and open your spreadsheet software program.

2. Create a spreadsheet like the one on page 231 using your spreadsheet application.

3. Enter a formula to calculate the total market at each price (assuming the research group to be five percent of the total market).

4. Enter a formula to calculate the total for the "Total Market" column.

5. Enter a formula to calculate the estimated retail sales at each price level.

6. Perform all calculations.

7. Save your work. Print out a copy of your work if your teacher has instructed you to do so. Then answer the questions that follow.

Interpreting Results

1. Which price would get the largest market share?

_____

_____

_____

2. What is the number of total potential buyers when all prices are included?

_____

_____

_____

Drawing Conclusions

3. Assume that Sun Protection's major competitor sells its sunblock cream for $4.39. Make a recommendation for pricing Sun Protection's new sunblock. Explain your reasons for choosing that price.

_____

_____

_____

_____

_____

_____

_____

_____

CHAPTER 27 Pricing Math

Vocabulary Review

DIRECTIONS: *Fill in the puzzle blanks by using terms from the chapter. Then read down the column of boxed entries to discover the mystery phrase.*

Clues

1. The difference between sales revenue and the cost of goods sold is called _____ profit.

2. To determine the percentage markup based on cost, you would divide _____ by the cost of the item.

3. You can use a visual device, known as the _____ box, to help you when calculating the retail price of an item for which you know only cost and percentage markup on retail.

4. To determine net profit before taxes, _____ must be deducted from gross profit.

5. Cash, seasonal, and promotional are types of _____.

6. To encourage employees to buy the products a business resells or manufactures, employees are often granted a(n) _____ discount.

7. _____ discounts are based on manufacturers' list prices.

8. The difference between an item's final sale price and its cost is called the _____ markup.

9. A quantity discount that is dependent on reaching a minimum amount of purchases over an extended period of time is called a _____ quantity discount.

10. The correlation between markup percentage based on cost and markup percentage based on retail can be seen in a markup _____ table.

Mystery Phrase

1. __ __ __ __ ⦾ __ __

2. __ __ ⦾ __ __ __ __ __

3. __ __ __ __ __ ⦾ __ __

4. __ __ __ ⦾ __ __ __ __

5. __ __ ⦾ __ __ __ __ __

6. __ __ ⦾ __ __ __ __

7. __ ⦾ __ __ __ __

8. __ __ ⦾ __ __ __

9. ⦾ __ __ __ __

10. __ __ __ __ __ ⦾ __ __

Mystery Phrase: _____

CHAPTER 27 Pricing Math

Fact and Idea Review

DIRECTIONS: *Circle the letter of the word or phrase that best completes each of the following sentences.*

1. For a business to be successful, its markup (like its gross profit) must be

    a. high enough to cover expenses and provide the profit sought.

    b. low.

    c. lower than its costs.

    d. the same as its costs.

2. The formula for calculating retail price is

    a. cost − markup = retail price.

    c. retail price + cost − markup = final retail price.

    b. cost + markup = retail price.

    d. retail price = markup − cost.

3. Most retailers choose to express their markup percentage on retail prices because

    a. future markdowns and discounts are calculated on a retail basis.

    b. manufacturers express their markup percentages in retail terms.

    c. profits are generally calculated on the cost of goods sold.

    d. markup on retail sounds like a higher percentage when compared with markup based on cost.

4. Maintained markup is

    a. always the same as the initial markup.

    b. always different from the initial markup.

    c. calculated when the initial retail price is different from the final sale price.

    d. generally calculated when sales tax is added to the purchase price.

5. A $50,000 invoice has payment terms of 2/10, net 30. If the buyer takes advantage of the discount, the net amount payable will be

    a. $40,000.   b. $45,000.   c. $49,000.   d. $49,900.

6. A manufacturer offers a five percent cumulative quantity discount for total purchases that equal or exceed $10,000 in one calendar year (January 1 through December 31). The one business that would be permitted the discount is

    a. Dana Dimples, which purchased goods worth $3,000 in January, $2,500 in February, and $4,300 in April.

    b. Lia Look-Alikes, which purchased goods worth $3,000 in January, $4,000 in March, and $6,000 in December.

    c. Lauren's Laughs, which purchased goods worth $9,000 in August.

    d. Charlie's Champs, which purchased goods worth $9,979 in June and $2,000 on January 15 of the following year.

CHAPTER 27 Pricing Math

Marketing Application 1

DIRECTIONS: *Complete the following pricing math problems. Record your answers in the spaces provided.*

1. Determine the retail price for a calculator that a business wants to mark up $3.49 above its cost of $6.50.

2. Determine the markup percentage based on both retail and cost for a hand-held hair dryer that sells in the store for $17.95 and costs the business $10.77.

3. Use the markup equivalents table to determine the markup percentage based on cost and the retail price for a child's bicycle that cost the business $43.99 and has a markup on retail of 33⅓ percent.

4. Use the retail box to determine the retail price and markup in dollars for a coffee machine that costs a business $15.78. The retail markup percentage used by the firm is 61.5 percent.

5. Sally's Dinettes has an invoice dated March 10 that totals $65,429 for an order of tables and chairs it purchased from George's Manufacturing. George's terms are 3/15, net 60. How much will Sally's Dinettes pay for that order if the check is mailed on March 16?

6. The Shop Vac Wet/Dry Vacuum is purchased by a wholesaler with trade discounts of 45 percent and 10 percent off the list price of $70. Determine the wholesaler's cost.

7. Baseballs are on special for the week. During the promotion, customers can buy three baseballs for $26.99. What is the retail price for a customer who wants to buy two baseballs?

CHAPTER 27 Pricing Math

Marketing Application 2

DIRECTIONS: *Study the problem below. Then answer the questions that follow.*

1. The school store has purchased 72 T-shirts and 72 pairs of boxer shorts with the school's mascot and name on them. The cost was $5.75 each. Choose two possible retail prices, calculate the unit dollar markup and markup percentage based on the retail price for each. Then compare each price's profitability by calculating the gross profit for each, assuming all items sell. Based on everything you know about cost-, demand-, and competition-oriented pricing strategies, settle on a realistic price for the new items and provide rationale for your answer. The school store would like a total gross profit of $600, assuming all 144 items sell at that price.

A		B	
Suggested Retail Price		Suggested Retail Price	
Cost	$5.75	Cost	$5.75
Markup in dollars		Markup in dollars	
Markup % (retail)		Markup % (retail)	
Gross Profit		Gross Profit	

Retail price selected and rationale:

_____

_____

What if you had to mark down 40 items at the end of the season by 25 percent? Would you still make the required $600 gross profit? Show your calculations.

_____

_____

_____

_____

_____

_____

_____

CHAPTER 27 Pricing Math

The DECA Connection

Role Play: DECA Fundraiser

Situation: You are to assume the role of fundraising chairperson for your DECA chapter. A local electronics wholesaler is willing to sell your DECA chapter new, brand-name electronics for a fundraiser. The selected products are discontinued models, all of which are under full warranty. This wholesaler also has a Web site where its products are displayed with suggested retail prices. He is offering to sell DECA these discontinued items at 40 percent off the suggested retail prices. It is up to DECA members to decide how much to mark up the goods in order to make a profit from the fundraiser. A few of the items and their suggested retail prices are as follows: Digital Video Camcorder $799.95; Portable CD Player $49.95; Cordless Digital Phone $59.95; Portable DVD Player $1,299.95; Digital Ready DVD Player $249.95; Wizard Organizer $39.95; and Microwave Half Pint Size $99.95. The wholesaler is willing to let you return any unopened boxed items for full credit. However, you must purchase all products that will be used for display purposes because they will no longer be classified as "new" after the DECA electronics sale. You need a pricing plan for the sale of those displayed products at the end of the sale.

Activity: Prepare a report to share with the DECA treasurer (judge) that details the cost, markup, and suggested sale price you would recommend for this fundraiser. The treasurer will want to know how you plan to present this proposal to the entire DECA membership.

Evaluation: You will be evaluated on how well you meet the following performance indicators:

• Explain the nature and scope of the pricing function.
• Explain the use of technology in the pricing function.
• Determine the cost of a product.
• Determine discounts and allowances used to adjust base prices.
• Set prices.

DIRECTIONS: *Organize your thoughts around the performance indicators noted above. Use these performance indicators to jot down your ideas during the preparation period. Time your preparation period to last 15 minutes and your role play presentation to last a maximum of ten minutes. After your role play, use the performance indicators to evaluate your efforts.*

_____

_____

_____

_____

_____

_____

Continued on next page

Assessment: Assume each performance indicator is worth 20 points (20 × 5 = 100 points). Use the evaluation levels listed below for judging consistency.

Excellent (16–20) Participant demonstrated the performance indicator in a professional manner, exceeds business standards.

Good (10–15) Participant demonstrated the performance indicator in an acceptable manner; meets minimal business standards; there would be no need for additional formalized training at this time.

Fair (4–9) Participant demonstrated the performance indicator with limited effectiveness; performance generally fell below minimal business standards; additional training would be required to improve knowledge, attitude, and/or skills.

Poor (0–3) Participant demonstrated the performance indicator with little effectiveness or not at all; a great deal of formal training would be needed.

Explain the nature and scope of the pricing function. Score _____

_____

_____

_____

Explain the use of technology in the pricing function. Score _____

_____

_____

_____

Determine the cost of a product. Score _____

_____

_____

_____

Determine discounts and allowances used to adjust base prices. Score _____

_____

_____

_____

Set prices. Score _____

_____

_____

_____

_____

CHAPTER **27** Pricing Math

Spreadsheet Application

OBJECTIVE: *To calculate cost, selling price, and markup for products.*

ACTIVITY: To establish prices, a marketer must take into account costs or expenses and the desired profit. The difference between the retail price and the cost is the markup. If you know the cost and the retail price, you can calculate the markup. In most business situations, markup is expressed as a percentage rather than as a dollar amount because percentages are more meaningful when making comparisons. The percentage markup is determined by dividing the dollar markup by the selling price.

   Your company sells the twelve products shown in the printout below. For some of the products, the cost and desired markup are known and you must calculate the selling price. For other products, the planned selling price is known and you must calculate cost based on the desired markup. If the cost and selling price are both known, you will need to calculate the markup. Calculate the markup percentage on retail for all the products.

	A	B	C	D	E
1	**Chapter 27 Pricing Math**				
2					
3					
4				**Selling**	**Markup**
5	**Item**	**Cost**	**Markup**	**Price**	**Percentage**
6					
7	1	$10.45	$10.49		
8	2	$72.16		$145.47	
9	3		$0.71	$1.46	
10	4	$4.35		$8.70	
11	5	$83.12	$82.88		
12	6	$13.17		$25.75	
13	7	$0.49		$1.00	
14	8	$2.69	$2.56		
15	9		$12.49	$25.00	
16	10	$2.34		$4.69	
17	11	$71.25	$71.74		
18	12		$0.34	$0.59	

Continued on next page

Spreadsheet Directions

1. Start your spreadsheet software program.

2. Create a spreadsheet like the one on page 239 using your spreadsheet application.

3. Calculate the following:
   - Find the selling price by adding cost and markup.
   - Find the cost by subtracting markup from selling price.
   - Find the markup by subtracting cost from selling price.
   - Find the markup percentage on retail by dividing markup by the selling price.

4. After completing your calculations, save your work.

5. Print out a copy of your work if your teacher has instructed you to do so. Then answer the following questions.

Interpreting Results

1. Which product shows the highest dollar markup? Which product shows the lowest dollar markup?

2. Which product shows the highest markup percentage? Which product shows the lowest markup percentage?

Drawing Conclusions

3. Does the highest markup percentage produce the greatest profit for the marketer?

4. How do market prices affect the selling price a marketer establishes for his/her products? Explain.

CHAPTER 28 Marketing Research

Vocabulary Review

DIRECTIONS: *Complete each sentence with the correct term. Some of the terms may be used more than once.*

attitude research	marketing information system	product research
database	marketing research	qualitative research
market intelligence	media research	quantitative research

1. _____ involves the process and methods used to gather information.

2. Research that answers questions of "how many" and how much" is known as _____.

3. In order to conduct marketing research, businesses need a(n) _____ that regularly generates, stores, analyzes, and distributes marketing information.

4. A(n) _____ is a collection (or file) of related information about a specific topic.

5. The type of research that tries to answer questions about "why" or "how" is called _____.

6. _____ is used to identify opportunities, solve problems, implement plans and monitor performance.

7. _____ is concerned with the size, location, and/or makeup of the market for a particular product or service.

8. Research that is designed to obtain information on how people feel about certain products, services, or ideas is called _____.

9. Customer, employee, and industrial satisfaction surveys are used to gather information about existing products and services and are examples of techniques used in _____.

10. Researching the effectiveness of a printed advertising message for recall, communication, and persuasive ability is an example of _____.

11. The use of random samples and opinion polls that can be generalized to the entire population are important elements in _____.

CHAPTER 28 Marketing Research

Fact and Idea Review

DIRECTIONS: *Classify each of the following marketing research activities as examples of* **attitude research, market research, media research,** *or* **product research,** *and label it accordingly.*

_____ 1. A gubernatorial candidate conducts an opinion survey on law enforcement issues prior to an election campaign.

_____ 2. Your family receives in the mail a product sample and cents off coupon for reformulated Cheer laundry detergent.

_____ 3. A local radio station asks you to complete a mail-in diary on your listening habits.

_____ 4. A new, purple mustard is available in Cincinnati for a limited time.

_____ 5. Sales of Ivory liquid soap are tracked for a 12-month period.

_____ 6. Polaris predicts that its new all-terrain vehicles will be bought by 35,000 customers.

_____ 7. A Web site records the number clicks on a banner ad.

_____ 8. The Gallup Organization conducts a random sample survey about the impact of technology on Americans.

_____ 9. McDonald's test markets pizzas in selected stores in the Midwest.

_____ 10. Ford Motor Company offers a $1,500 rebate on Escorts during the month of February to increase its sales penetration of the sub-compact market.

_____ 11. Blockbuster Video has a "two-for-one" price special on Tuesdays to increase its rentals.

_____ 12. Fortune magazine has a subscriber survey with each new subscription to determine the most effective advertising message for a particular advertiser.

_____ 13. Whirlpool Corporation surveys high-income appliance owners to determine their demographic and psychographic characteristics.

_____ 14. To predict next year's economic outlook, the U.S. government releases statistics on new building starts.

_____ 15. Marriott asks overnight guests to complete a customer satisfaction survey.

CHAPTER **28** Marketing Research

Marketing Application 1

DIRECTIONS: *Review the database chart on the next page titled The Jet Set (America's Most Wealthy), prepared by a company specializing in compiling mailing lists.*

1. Speculate on how companies can compile such large amounts of information.

   _____

   _____

   _____

   _____

2. The company that compiles this database uses an Affluence Model to score and categorize every household in the United States according to its net worth (defined as assets minus liabilities), real estate values, financial holdings, business equity, attitudes/consumption, and occupational characteristics. What are the advantages of this model?

   _____

   _____

   _____

3. What types of companies would be interested in marketing their products to America's most wealthy?

   _____

   _____

4. What five states have the largest number of aircraft owners? How many aircraft owners are in the database?

   _____

   _____

5. What state has the largest number of attorneys in the database? The smallest?

   _____

   _____

6. What category under America's Most Wealthy has the highest number of people in the database? What category has the smallest number of people in the database?

   _____

   _____

Continued on next page

THE JET SET
(AMERICA'S MOST WEALTHY)

	Highest Salaried Executives at Home Address	Social Register	Prominent Medical Specialists	Attorneys	Wealthy At Home	Prominent Americans	Yacht Owners 30'+	Wealthy Women	Corporation Presidents At Manufacturing Firms	Aircraft Owners
AL	593	211	6,679	5,842	18,658	1,941	535	1,767	4,937	2,763
AK	44	10	770	1,764	21,791	283	513	1,543	90	6,525
AZ	435	200	7,778	6,960	26,608	2,659	245	2,825	2,847	5,136
AR	304	6	3,672	4,451	9,388	791	99	873	2,393	2,351
CA	3,957	1,988	67,089	78,001	219,136	32,118	11,486	23,367	18,787	29,323
CO	713	238	7,341	11,242	27,686	2,996	150	3,298	4,289	4,173
CT	2,843	1,686	9,573	8,808	36,392	9,645	554	4,017	6,187	1,983
DE	156	136	1,419	1,271	6,833	681	394	529	5,294	2,119
DC	133	684	4,370	12,839	6,718	3,701	209	1,517	80	310
FL	1,874	1,420	26,722	28,747	153,176	10,467	7087	11,945	14,817	12,658
GA	1,137	194	11,112	13,737	36,183	4,987	720	3,792	8,129	4,960
HI	163	37	2,619	2,835	7,609	739	198	796	1,987	578
ID	150	20	1,432	1,680	6,914	435	64	615	1,194	1,893
IL	4,173	729	25,632	36,629	67,496	14,722	2046	8,001	21,167	7,043
IN	1,406	18	9,161	11,009	25,868	3,255	388	2,778	9,890	3,806
IA	624	8	5,202	6,526	14,035	1,550	240	1,644	5,064	2,586
KS	703	6	4,823	5,673	14,751	1,839	63	1,672	3,247	3,322
KY	552	60	6,426	8,063	12,529	1,476	431	1,464	4,240	1,681
LA	518	144	8,224	12,954	24,876	1,692	1,368	1,919	2,746	2,672
ME	277	295	2,537	2,336	13,409	1,146	915	1,172	1,856	1,216
MD	1,183	1,187	14,677	9,742	60,115	10,639	3,689	8,276	4,610	2,706
MA	2,758	2,323	20,006	15,437	54,532	11,823	3,304	6,243	6,690	3,141
MI	1,921	98	21,183	17,479	80,103	7,364	4,630	6,490	15,104	6,675
MN	1,261	41	9,691	12,263	31,392	3,076	738	3,269	8,306	4,617
MI	265	46	3,472	5,234	10,922	799	370	996	2,569	1,832
MO	1,234	476	11,504	12,556	25,535	4,226	343	3,071	8,301	4,272
MT	75	22	1,305	1,788	5,868	361	21	579	1,479	1,823
NE	415	10	3,086	3,283	8,179	911	35	938	1,665	1,749
NV	118	19	1,797	2,280	10,271	575	179	834	2,239	2,426
NH	413	258	2,189	2,154	11,438	1,350	385	1,192	2,090	1,471
NJ	4,054	894	19,870	15,637	64,166	26,358	2,018	6,695	6,937	3,572
NM	123	74	2,929	3,173	8,763	1,119	16	1,159	1,531	2,243
NY	5,990	4,460	56,690	46,472	126,743	38,723	5,434	16,981	8,962	6,352
NC	1,229	180	12,321	9,830	42,632	3,876	880	4,761	5,360	4,878
ND	94	1	1,263	911	4,605	271	12	436	576	1,150
OH	3,585	581	23,811	27,482	69,729	8,736	2,457	6,880	19,959	7,295
OK	559	17	5,839	10,073	17,526	1,512	100	1,884	4,359	3,906
OR	360	76	6,230	6,307	24,495	1,478	928	2,215	6,513	5,127
PA	3,773	3,168	31,929	20,543	70,831	13,469	1,592	8,463	19,145	5,969
RI	397	236	2,634	1,820	8,160	1,273	0	769	2,344	361
SC	473	235	5,902	4,802	22,453	1,855	416	2,986	3,020	1,875
SD	87	1	1,098	973	4,143	278	14	450	915	1,042
TN	822	108	9,787	10,661	22,483	2,579	574	2,528	4,998	3,348
TX	3,447	453	30,091	35,291	104,069	13,701	1,759	10,448	18,787	16,434
UT	265	13	3,284	3,331	9,781	769	64	792	2,408	1,481
VT	171	192	1,376	1,289	5,233	784	133	598	1,277	501
VA	1,352	692	12,491	21,219	48,121	11,375	1,684	4,542	3,405	3,363
WA	632	114	10,139	11,475	57,827	2,773	3,422	4,228	3,756	6,542
WV	240	10	3,779	2,987	5,695	611	80	717	2,199	981
WI	1,526	57	9,753	9,671	31,308	3,302	805	3,076	9,997	4,053
WY	64	32	671	939	3,261	336	6	350	558	802
TOTALS	59,641	24,164	557,701	588,482	1,804,132	273,531	65,490	188,763	309,444	209,467
	$50/M	$45/M	$50/M	$50/M	$60/M	$45/M	$50/M	$60/M	$55/M	$50/M

CHAPTER 28 Marketing Research

Marketing Application 2

DIRECTIONS: *Read the case study below. Then answer the questions that follow.*

Prepaid phone cards present more info at much less cost

In industries as disparate as consumer goods, automotive, hospitality, pharmaceutical, and health care, prepaid phone cards have been used successfully to conduct marketing research. The Health Communication Research Institute (HCRI) provides prepaid phone cards to patients in Sacramento when they leave a doctor's office or the hospital. When the patient first uses the phone card, he or she is connected to an automated service that asks five or six questions and records the responses. After answering the questions, the patient is rewarded with 30 minutes of free long-distance service.

Several companies have done similar research, compiling surveys of three to ten questions which are recorded by a professional announcer onto an automated system. Questions can cover customer satisfaction, attitude, use of service, or even a customer's perception of a product. The automated phone service conducts the interview, then sorts the results, delivering them either graphically as bar graphs or textually. Some companies deliver the results in a printed report, others provide a secure Web site where businesses can view the results of their automated survey in real time.

A marketing research campaign using prepaid phone cards is significantly cheaper to operate than other marketing research methods. According to the marketing research firm Market Facts Inc., direct mail campaigns cost approximately $10 per person, telemarketing interviews can cost $20 per person, and focus groups can cost $200 to $250 per person. By contrast, an automated voice survey with as many as ten questions and that offers prepaid phone service as a reward can be completed for as little as $5 per person, and sometimes less.

According to recent research conducted by MCI WorldCom, an interactive phone survey with an immediate reward nets a 25 percent response rate, compared with a 10 percent response rate for telemarketing and a two percent response rate for direct mail, when both offer compensation in return for a response.

1. What are some ways marketing researchers could reward people for completing marketing surveys?

_____

_____

_____

_____

_____

_____

Continued on next page

2. How have interactive telephone surveys changed the way survey results are collected and reported?

_____

_____

_____

_____

_____

_____

_____

3. Why do you think the survey response rates for interactive phone surveys are better than traditional telemarketing and direct mail response rates?

_____

_____

_____

_____

_____

_____

_____

4. What are some advantages of automated voice surveys compared with other methods of collecting marketing research?

_____

_____

_____

_____

_____

_____

_____

CHAPTER 28 Marketing Research

The DECA Connection

Role Play: Marketing Research Consultant

Situation: You are to assume the role of employee of a bed and breakfast lodging establishment. The B & B has recently completed remodeling and restoring a large 1850s farmhouse in a beautiful and historically significant part of New England. Because of the large expenditures for remodeling and landscaping, the B & B has limited resources for conducting marketing research. You strongly believe in the importance of marketing research to learn about the demographics of your customers, their interests, and their overall satisfaction with their stay at your bed and breakfast. However, the owner (judge) is more concerned about the overall appearance of the building and grounds. The owner believes that word of mouth alone will sell the business and that a marketing information database and marketing research itself is too costly and unnecessary.

Activity: Convince the owner (judge) about the overall importance of marketing research and the need for a marketing research database of past guests to help the business grow and prosper. You must also identify for the owner the type of marketing research that you would use to collect information about customer satisfaction about their stay. Remember that you are on a very limited budget and your marketing research efforts must be effective, but cost a minimum amount of money.

Evaluation: You will be evaluated on how well you meet the following performance indicators:

- Discuss the need for marketing information.
- Develop a marketing information system.
- Explain the nature of marketing research in a marketing information system.
- Identify information monitored for marketing decision making.
- Persuade others.

DIRECTIONS: *Organize your thoughts around the performance indicators noted above. Use these performance indicators to jot down your ideas during the preparation period. Time your preparation period to last 15 minutes and your role play presentation to last a maximum of ten minutes. After your role play, use the performance indicators to evaluate your efforts.*

_____

_____

_____

_____

_____

Continued on next page

Assessment: Assume each performance indicator is worth 20 points (20 × 5 = 100 points). Use the evaluation levels listed below for judging consistency.

Excellent (16–20) Participant demonstrated the performance indicator in a professional manner, exceeds business standards.

Good (10–15) Participant demonstrated the performance indicator in an acceptable manner; meets minimal business standards; there would be no need for additional formalized training at this time.

Fair (4–9) Participant demonstrated the performance indicator with limited effectiveness; performance generally fell below minimal business standards; additional training would be required to improve knowledge, attitude, and/or skills.

Poor (0–3) Participant demonstrated the performance indicator with little effectiveness or not at all; a great deal of formal training would be needed.

Discuss the need for marketing information.   Score _____

_____

_____

_____

Develop a marketing information system.   Score _____

_____

_____

_____

Explain the nature of marketing research.   Score _____

_____

_____

_____

Identify information monitored for marketing decision making.   Score _____

_____

_____

_____

Persuade others.   Score _____

_____

_____

_____

_____

CHAPTER 28 Marketing Research

Software Activity (Optional)

Database Application

OBJECTIVE: *Evaluate customer responses to a questionnaire.*

ACTIVITY: Marketers use questionnaires and interviews to gather information about why customers buy certain products or patronize certain businesses. The Olympic Health Club recently conducted a marketing research survey to find out about customers' opinions of the health club. The customers' responses were all recorded in a database. Customers responded to the following questions.

1. How would you rate the exercise facilities in this health club?
   - A. Excellent
   - B. Above Average
   - C. Average
   - D. Below Average
   - E. Poor

2. Please indicate your age category:
   - A. 21 and under
   - B. 22–35
   - C. 36–45
   - D. 46–55
   - E. over 55

On the printout below, you will find the customers' responses.

Customer	Age Category	Question #1 Response
1	A	A
2	B	A
3	A	B
4	A	A
5	E	A
6	D	D
7	E	E
8	A	B
9	B	A
10	A	A
11	E	E
12	D	B
13	A	A
14	B	A
15	C	A

Continued on next page

Database Directions

1. Start your database software program.

2. Create a database like the one on page 249 using your database application.

3. Sort the responses for question 1 by type of response. The database will sort these responses alphabetically.

4. Save your sorted database.

5. Print out a copy of your work if your teacher has instructed you to do so.

6. Answer the following questions.

Interpreting Results

1. Did the customers who responded "excellent" to question 1 fall into any type of age pattern? How many customers responded "excellent"?

_____

_____

_____

_____

_____

2. Did the customers who responded "below average" or "poor" fall into any type of age or gender pattern? How many customers responded with these answers?

_____

_____

_____

Drawing Conclusions

3. Assuming that these 15 customers represent the typical customers at Olympic Health Club, what is a characteristic of the majority of the customers of the health club?

_____

_____

4. Based on these responses, what recommendations would you make to the owner of Olympic Health Club?

_____

_____

_____

_____

_____

CHAPTER 29 Conducting Marketing Research

Vocabulary Review

DIRECTIONS: *Match each definition with the correct term.*

data analysis	point-of-sale research	secondary data
experimental method	primary data	survey method
forced-choice questions	problem definition	validity
observation method	reliability	
open-ended questions	sample	

_____ 1. "Do you have any suggestions to improve our service?" is an example of this type of questions.

_____ 2. Information that has already been collected and used for some other purpose.

_____ 3. Research technique that gathers information from people directly through the use of interviews or questionnaires.

_____ 4. When survey questions measure what was intended to be measured.

_____ 5. Research technique in which information is gained about customer behavior and preferences by viewing and recording people's actions.

_____ 6. Information obtained for the first time and used for a specific problem or issue under study.

_____ 7. Compiling, analyzing, and interpreting the results of primary and secondary data collection.

_____ 8. Part of the target population that is assumed to represent the entire population.

_____ 9. Questions that are either two-choice, multiple choice, rating, or ranking.

_____ 10. Form of research that combines natural observation with personal interviews to get people to explain their buying behavior.

_____ 11. This identifies the research issue and the information that might be needed to solve it.

_____ 12. Research technique often used to test new package designs, levels of media usage, and new promotions.

_____ 13. This condition exists when a research technique produces nearly identical results in repeated trials.

CHAPTER 29 Conducting Marketing Research

Fact and Idea Review

DIRECTIONS: *Demonstrate your knowledge of primary and secondary data research techniques by classifying each of the following situations as either primary (P) or secondary (S) research.*

_____ 1. Black & Decker sends out a survey to past purchasers of its portable drill.

_____ 2. An aspiring entrepreneur studies the U.S. census data to obtain information on single heads of households in Phoenix, Arizona.

_____ 3. Jewel/Osco Supermarkets conducts a focus group regarding customer attitudes toward its meat department.

_____ 4. Gantos Fashions examines operating ratios available from Dun & Bradstreet for apparel stores of its size.

_____ 5. A local Ace hardware store owner purchases demographic data regarding population, housing, education, and income from CACI Marketing Systems, a business information company.

_____ 6. Taco Bell records the number of used ticket stubs turned in from a hockey game promotional tie-in.

_____ 7. A local mall conducts personal interviews with customers.

_____ 8. McDonald's gives out a free breakfast sandwich for each customer questionnaire that is turned in by March 31.

_____ 9. Quebec's maple syrup makers conduct a taste test of various flavored syrups to market in different countries.

_____ 10. To determine the popularity of its talk shows, a radio station has listeners complete listening diaries.

_____ 11. When forecasting this year's summer sales, a heating and air conditioning firm reviews last year's sales for the months of June to August.

_____ 12. When developing new toys, Mattel Inc. creates a room for observing children playing with toy prototypes.

_____ 13. An independent floral shop uses the Internet to search for commercial directories and potential suppliers.

_____ 14. Post uses a syndicated service to track its retail cereal sales by brand.

_____ 15. Coca-Cola uses an interactive telephone survey to obtain information about a new product.

_____ 16. Kmart hires a mystery shopping service to obtain information about its customer service.

CHAPTER 29 Conducting Marketing Research

Marketing Application 1

DIRECTIONS: *A national consumer product manufacturer uses secondary data from a computer analysis of the Census of the Population to analyze population growth patterns. The information will be used to assist the company in its sales forecasting efforts by state, population, race, and ethnicity. The results of the analysis are summarized in the table on page 254. Study it and answer the questions that follow.*

1. What five states are projected to have the greatest percentage growth rates for the period from 1995–2025?

   _____

   _____

2. What five states are projected to have the slowest percentage growth rates for the period from 1995–2025?

   _____

   _____

3. According to the chart, which state had the smallest percentage of Caucasians in 2000? What is the total percentage of minorities in this state?

   _____

   _____

   _____

4. By the year 2025 California is projected to be home to 41 percent of the nation's 21 million citizens of Asian descent. Using this information, how many Asians will reside in California in 2025?

   _____

5. Why is secondary data available from the U.S. Census Bureau important for consumer product manufacturers?

   _____

   _____

   _____

Continued on next page

2000 POPULATION
RACE/ETHNICITY

State	1995 pop. (in millions)	2000 pop. (mill.)	Change 1995–2000	2025 pop. est. (mill.)	Change 1995–2025	Caucasian	Black	Native American	Asian	Hispanic[1]
AL	4.25	4.45	5%	5.22	23%	73.3%	25.5%	0.4%	0.8%	.8%
AK	.60	.65	8%	.89	47%	74.3%	4.4%	14.2%	7.0%	4.7%
AZ	4.22	4.80	14%	6.41	52%	88.6%	3.7%	5.5%	2.2%	22.3%
AR	2.48	2.63	6%	3.06	23%	83.1%	15.6%	0.6%	0.7%	1.3%
CA	31.59	32.52	3%	49.29	56%	78.5%	7.5%	0.9%	13.2%	32.7%
CO	3.75	4.17	11%	5.19	38%	91.7%	4.7%	1.0%	2.6%	14.3%
CT	3.28	3.28	0%	3.74	14%	87.5%	9.9%	0.2%	2.4%	8.8%
DE	.72	.77	7%	.86	20%	78.6%	19.2%	0.3%	2.0%	3.3%
DC	.55	.52	6%	.66	18%	35.4%	61.7%	0.0%	2.9%	7.7%
FL	14.17	15.23	8%	20.71	46%	82.6%	15.3%	0.3%	1.8%	15.7%
GA	7.20	7.88	9%	9.87	37%	69.0%	28.9%	0.2%	1.8%	2.4%
HI	1.19	1.26	6%	1.81	53%	33.7%	2.5%	0.5%	63.4%	8.5%
ID	1.16	1.35	16%	1.74	50%	96.6%	0.6%	1.6%	1.3%	7.1%
IL	11.83	12.05	2%	13.44	14%	80.8%	15.5%	0.2%	3.5%	10.5%
IN	5.80	6.05	4%	6.55	13%	90.4%	8.3%	0.3%	1.0%	2.3%
IA	2.84	2.90	2%	3.04	7%	96.1%	2.1%	0.3%	1.5%	1.9%
KS	2.57	2.67	4%	3.11	21%	90.6%	6.5%	1.0%	1.9%	5.2%
KY	3.86	4.00	3%	4.31	12%	91.9%	7.2%	0.2%	0.7%	0.8%
LA	4.34	4.43	2%	5.13	18%	65.4%	32.7%	0.5%	1.4%	2.7%
ME	1.24	1.26	1%	1.42	15%	98.4%	0.4%	0.5%	0.7%	0.6%
MD	5.04	5.28	5%	6.27	24%	67.2%	28.2%	0.3%	4.2%	4.1%
MA	6.07	6.20	2%	6.90	14%	89.1%	6.7%	0.2%	4.0%	7.0%
MI	9.55	9.68	1%	10.08	6%	82.9%	14.8%	0.6%	1.7%	2.7%
MN	4.61	4.83	5%	5.51	20%	92.5%	3.3%	1.3%	2.9%	2.0%
MS	2.70	2.82	4%	3.14	16%	63.1%	36.0%	0.3%	0.7%	0.7%
MO	5.32	5.54	4%	6.25	17%	87.1%	11.3%	0.4%	1.1%	1.6%
MT	.87	.95	9%	1.12	29%	92.5%	0.3%	6.4%	0.7%	2.1%
NE	1.64	1.71	4%	1.93	18%	93.5%	4.2%	0.9%	1.3%	3.6%
NV	1.53	1.87	22%	2.31	51%	86.4%	7.4%	1.7%	4.5%	14.8%
NH	1.15	1.22	7%	1.44	25%	98.0%	0.7%	0.2%	1.1%	1.4%
NJ	7.95	8.18	3%	9.56	20%	78.8%	15.2%	0.2%	5.8%	12.8%
NM	1.69	1.86	10%	2.61	55%	86.8%	2.6%	9.1%	1.6%	39.5%
NY	18.14	18.15	0%	19.83	9%	75.8%	18.2%	0.4%	5.7%	15.5%
NC	7.20	7.78	8%	9.35	30%	75.2%	22.3%	1.2%	1.2%	1.6%
ND	.64	.66	3%	.73	14%	93.5%	0.8%	4.8%	0.9%	0.9%
OH	11.15	11.32	2%	11.74	5%	86.9%	11.7%	0.2%	1.2%	1.6%
OK	3.28	3.37	3%	4.06	24%	81.8%	8.4%	8.3%	1.5%	3.7%
OR	3.14	3.40	8%	4.35	38%	93.2%	1.9%	1.5%	3.4%	5.7%
PA	12.07	12.20	1%	12.69	5%	88.0%	10.0%	0.1%	1.8%	2.7%
RI	.99	1.00	1%	1.14	15%	91.4%	5.4%	0.4%	2.8%	7.6%
SC	3.67	3.86	5%	4.65	26%	69.0%	30.0%	0.2%	0.9%	1.1%
SD	.73	.78	7%	.87	19%	91.0%	0.6%	7.7%	0.6%	1.0%
TN	5.26	5.66	8%	6.67	27%	82.4%	16.4%	0.2%	1.0%	1.0%
TX	18.72	20.12	7%	27.19	45%	84.1%	12.6%	0.5%	2.8%	29.2%
UT	1.95	2.21	13%	2.89	48%	94.5%	1.0%	1.7%	2.8%	6.3%
VT	.59	.62	5%	.68	16%	98.4%	0.3%	0.3%	1.0%	1.0%
VA	6.62	7.00	6%	8.47	28%	75.7%	20.2%	0.3%	3.8%	3.8%
WA	5.43	5.86	8%	7.81	44%	88.8%	3.3%	1.8%	6.1%	6.1%
WV	1.83	1.84	1%	1.85	1%	96.1%	3.2%	0.1%	0.6%	0.6%
WI	5.12	5.33	4%	5.87	15%	91.1%	6.1%	0.9%	1.9%	2.6%
WY	.48	.53	9%	.69	45%	95.6%	1.1%	2.5%	0.8%	6.7%

[1] Hispanics can be of any race.

Source: Computer analysis of U.S. Census Bureau data. More detailed information is available on the Census Bureau's World Wide Web site: http://www.census.gov

CHAPTER 29 Conducting Marketing Research

Marketing Application 2

DIRECTIONS: *A restaurant at a resort location conducted a customer satisfaction survey over the summer season in an effort to provide the best possible dining experience for its patrons. The results of the survey are summarized in the table below. Study it and answer the questions that follow.*

1. Was your reservation in order?	95% Yes	5% No		
2. Cleanliness	65% Excellent	20% Good	15% Fair	
3. Food Quality	75% Excellent	20% Good	5% Fair	0% poor
4. Beverage Quality	70% Excellent	20% Good	10% Fair	0% poor
5. Friendliness of Staff	50% Excellent	30% Good	10% Fair	10% poor
6. Were you served in a timely manner?	40% Excellent	20% Good	30% Fair	10% poor
7. Overall Value	50% Excellent	30% Good	15% Fair	5% poor
8. Would you return?	75% Yes	25% No		

9. Any recommendations or comments?

_____

_____

_____

10. How can you be reached?

Name _____

Address _____

City _____ State, Zip _____

Telephone _____

E-mail _____

Continued on next page

1. What questions on the survey would you classify as forced-choice questions and which questions would you classify as open-ended?

_____

_____

2. Given the responses to Questions 1–4, what conclusion would you draw?

_____

_____

_____

_____

3. Given the responses to Questions 5–8, what conclusions would you draw?

_____

_____

_____

_____

4. Why do you think the restaurant would want the names and addresses of its patrons?

_____

_____

_____

_____

5. Given the results of this survey, what recommendations would you make to the management about how the restaurant could be improved?

_____

_____

_____

_____

_____

_____

_____

_____

CHAPTER 29 Conducting Marketing Research

The DECA Connection

Role Play: Marketing Researcher

Situation: You are to assume the role of marketing researcher for a nationally recognized hotel/resort chain. The chain wants to build a database and study individuals who would likely vacation at a luxury resort and hotel complex. Your company is also interested in the following information: the time of year that individuals would most likely take a vacation of four or more days; favored geographical locations of planned vacations; amenities and activities favored; transportation methods used to get to a vacation resort; number of vacations taken per year; number of weekend trips taken per year; hotel chains that potential customers would consider; how individuals pay for their vacations; and whether respondents would like additional information about vacation packages. Your company also wants ideas on how to encourage responses to the study.

Activity: Your supervisor (judge) has asked you to design a survey questionnaire that will provide the needed information. You must also recommend a plan to encourage high responses to the survey. Your survey must include a section for the name and address of the respondent and can have no more than ten questions. You will meet with your supervisor to discuss your ideas for the survey.

Evaluation: You will be evaluated on how well you meet the following performance indicators:

- Identify information monitored for marketing decision making.
- Collect marketing information from others.
- Write marketing reports.
- Explain the nature of marketing research in a marketing information system.
- Make oral presentations.

DIRECTIONS: *Organize your thoughts around the performance indicators noted above. Use these performance indicators to jot down your ideas during the preparation period. Time your preparation period to last 15 minutes and your role play presentation to last a maximum of ten minutes. After your role play, use the performance indicators to evaluate your efforts.*

_____

_____

_____

_____

_____

_____

Continued on next page

Assessment: Assume each performance indicator is worth 20 points (20 × 5 = 100 points). Use the evaluation levels listed below for judging consistency.

Excellent (16–20) Participant demonstrated the performance indicator in a professional manner, exceeds business standards.

Good (10–15) Participant demonstrated the performance indicator in an acceptable manner; meets minimal business standards; there would be no need for additional formalized training at this time.

Fair (4–9) Participant demonstrated the performance indicator with limited effectiveness; performance generally fell below minimal business standards; additional training would be required to improve knowledge, attitude, and/or skills.

Poor (0–3) Participant demonstrated the performance indicator with little effectiveness or not at all; a great deal of formal training would be needed.

Identify information monitored for marketing decision making. Score _____

_____

_____

_____

Collect marketing information from others. Score _____

_____

_____

_____

Write marketing reports. Score _____

_____

_____

_____

Explain the nature of marketing research. Score _____

_____

_____

_____

Make oral presentations. Score _____

_____

_____

_____

CHAPTER 29 Conducting Marketing Research

Software Activity (Optional)

Database Application

OBJECTIVE: Track marketing research using marketing information systems.

ACTIVITY: FMB-Maynard Allen Bank recently surveyed customers to learn whether they were satisfied with the quality of service they received in their local branch. This market research was stored in a database. Here is a sampling of the questions:

Question 1: In general, how satisfied are you with the service provided at the FMB branch office you visit most often?

A. Very Satisfied
B. Somewhat Satisfied
C. Neither Satisfied Nor Dissatisfied
D. Somewhat Dissatisfied
E. Very Dissatisfied

Question 2: Check one:
_____ Male   _____ Female

Question 3: Please indicate your age category.

A. 21 and under
B. 22–35
C. 36–45
D. 46–55
E. over 55

On the printout below you will find the responses to these questions that were entered into the database.

Customer	Question 1	Question 2	Question 3
1	A	M	B
2	A	F	A
3	B	M	B
4	A	M	B
5	A	F	C
6	D	F	C
7	E	F	E
8	B	M	B
9	A	M	A
10	A	M	B
11	E	F	E
12	B	F	C
13	A	M	D
14	A	M	B
15	A	M	C

Continued on next page

Database Directions

1. Turn on your computer and open your spreadsheet software program.

2. Create a database like the one on page 259 using your database application.

3. Sort the responses based on Question 1. Then answer Question 1 below. Save your sorted database. Print out a copy of your work if your teacher has instructed you to do so.

4. Sort the responses based on Question 2. Then answer Question 2 below. Save your sorted database to a new file. Print out a copy of your work if your teacher has instructed you to do so.

5. Sort the responses based on Question 3. Then answer Question 3 below. Save your sorted database to a new file. Print out a copy of your work if your teacher has instructed you to do so.

6. Answer the remaining questions.

Interpreting Results

1. What were the number of responses to each possible response in Question 1?

_____

_____

2. Who were more dissatisfied with the quality of service—males or females?

_____

_____

3. Were any age groups more or less satisfied with the quality of service than others?

_____

_____

Drawing Conclusions

4. As a market researcher hired to help the bank review its customer service, would you suggest that the bank make changes based on these responses?

_____

_____

_____

5. Based on these responses, what recommendations would you make?

_____

_____

_____

_____

CHAPTER 30 Product Planning

Vocabulary Review

DIRECTIONS: *Fill in the puzzle blanks by using terms and concepts found in the chapter. Then read down the column of circled entries to discover the Mystery Phrase.*

Clues

1. Anything a person receives in an exchange.
2. Involves making decisions related to packaging, labeling, warranties, guarantees, branding, and product mix.
3. All the different items that a company makes or sells.
4. The number of product items offered within each product line.
5. An alteration to an existing product.
6. Introduction, growth, maturity, and decline.
7. The number of different product lines a business manufactures or sells.
8. The effort that a business makes to identify, place, and sell its products.
9. An example is all the different canned soups made by Campbell's.
10. The first step in new product development.
11. Evaluating a new product measures this.
12. Computer generated diagram that shows retailers how and where products within a category should be displayed.

13. A specific model, brand, or size of a product within a product line.
14. Dropping a product.
15. A process for marketing and selling products that treats each product classification as an individual business unit.

1. ◯ __ __ __ __ __
2. __ ◯ __ __ __ __ __ __ __
3. __ __ ◯ __ __ __ __ __ __
4. __ __ __ ◯ __ __ __ __ __
5. __ __ __ __ ◯ __ __ __ __
   __ __ __ __ __ __ __ __ __
6. __ __ __ __ __ ◯ __ __ __ __
7. __ __ __ __ __ __ ◯ __ __ __
8. ◯ __ __ __ __ __ __ __
   __ __ __ __ __ __
9. __ __ __ __ __ __ __ __ ◯ __ __
10. __ __ __ __ __ __ ◯ __ __ __
11. __ __ __ __
    __ __ __ __ __ __ __ __ ◯ __
12. __ __ __ ◯ __ __ __ __
13. __ __ __ __ __ __ ◯ __ __ __
14. __ __ __ __ __ __ ◯ __ __
15. __ __ __ ◯ __ __ __ __
    __ __ __ __ __ __ __ __

Mystery Phrase: _____

CHAPTER **30** Product Planning

Fact and Idea Review

DIRECTIONS: *Read each of the following statements about product life cycles and then select the stage in the life cycle that is characterized by the statement (**introduction, growth, maturity,** and **decline**). Write your answer on the line preceding each statement.*

_____ 1. During this phase of the product life cycle, sales level off.

_____ 2. Discounting the product is typical in this stage of the product life cycle.

_____ 3. In this stage, company efforts are focused on promotion.

_____ 4. This stage of the product life cycle is usually the least profitable.

_____ 5. During this stage, advertising is focused on consumer satisfaction rather than new product benefits.

_____ 6. In this stage of the product life cycle, most of the target market owns the product.

_____ 7. Profits drop until they are smaller than costs in this stage of the product life cycle.

_____ 8. Decisions need to be made in this stage to improve the product to gain additional sales.

_____ 9. Selling or licensing the product often occurs in this stage.

_____ 10. Competition is likely to offer new products in order to compete in this stage of the life cycle.

_____ 11. Companies spend more of their advertising dollars fighting off the competition in this stage of the product life cycle.

_____ 12. Management needs to make decisions about how long to continue supporting a product in this stage of the product life cycle.

_____ 13. Modernizing or altering a product sometimes occurs at this stage.

_____ 14. The major goal at this stage is to draw attention to the product.

_____ 15. Companies work on building sales by increasing product awareness in this stage of the product life cycle.

_____ 16. At this stage, the product is enjoying success as demonstrated by rising sales and profits.

CHAPTER **30** Product Planning

Marketing Application 1

DIRECTIONS: *Try your hand at developing new product strategies. In the first column below, list five well-known products. In the second column, describe a possible product expansion. In the third column suggest a possible product modification. Your ideas for product expansion and modification should be original and not currently being used.*

Product	Product Expansion	Product Modification
Example: Palm Tungsten personal digital assistant (PDA)	Add another type of PDA with more power and memory	Create a PDA with a built-in cell phone

CHAPTER 30 Product Planning

Marketing Application 2

DIRECTIONS: *Read the case study below. Then answer the questions that follow.*

Repositioning an Established Product Line

During World War II, Procter & Gamble developed a moisturizer to treat burns. That moisturizer later took on a new life. In 1962, it was tinted a light pink, named Oil of Olay, and marketed to women.

In the 1990s, P&G expanded the Oil of Olay line to include other skin-care products and cosmetics. But the company realized that it needed to update the product line to attract younger buyers. After product research found that young women avoid any product that seems like it would be oily, company executives decided to remove the word *oil* from the name. Oil of Olay became simply the Olay line of beauty products. Along with the new name came new packaging and a new logo.

After research showed that women don't like having wet washcloths by their sinks, P&G expanded the Olay line to include disposable paper washcloths called Olay Daily Facials. Using information gathered through market research, the company developed a new advertising campaign to promote desired features of the product, using television commercials, outdoor ads, and in-store and direct mail samples.

P&G hoped the newly repositioned line would boost the sales of the old, established Olay line by keeping the existing customer base and attracting new customers.

1. What techniques did P&G use to reposition its Olay product line?

   _____

   _____

   _____

   _____

2. Speculate on the type of research P&G did to evaluate customer acceptance of the product.

   _____

   _____

   _____

   _____

3. Why might P&G have involved different divisions in the development of Daily Facials?

   _____

   _____

   _____

CHAPTER 30 Product Planning

The DECA Connection

Role Play: Product Planner

Situation: You are to assume the role of employee in the marketing department of Sheldon Sound Systems, an established electronics manufacturer. One of your company's product lines is audio players and speakers. The company makes models in several sizes. Bookshelf speakers were introduced in 1996. Sales of those speakers have grown steadily. However, in recent years, younger consumers have begun to view the company as stodgy and old-fashioned. The company has seen its sales drop among Generation Y consumers, the 70 million people born between 1977 and 1997. The company is concerned because this market is nearly as large as the baby boom generation (born between 1946 and 1964) and three times the size of Generation X (born between 1965 and 1976). The industry trend seems to be moving toward smaller and more technologically advanced products.

Activity: Your supervisor (judge) has asked you to recommend strategies to reposition the Sheldon product line to better meet the needs of a generation of potential customers who want advanced technology and more portability built into their products. Your task is to identify the steps and strategies that you would use to change the image of the Sheldon product line. Your suggested strategies must aim to create an image that appeals to the desired target market. Your strategies could involve positioning by price, quality, features, benefits, or unique characteristics. You will present your ideas to your supervisor.

Evaluation: You will be evaluated on how well you meet the following performance indicators:

- Explain the concept of marketing strategies.
- Explain the concepts of market and market identification.
- Develop strategies to position a product/business.
- Explain the nature of marketing plans.
- Develop a marketing plan.

DIRECTIONS: *Organize your thoughts around the performance indicators noted above. Use these performance indicators to jot down your ideas during the preparation period. Time your preparation period to last 15 minutes and your role play presentation to last a maximum of 10 minutes. After your role play, use the performance indicators to evaluate your efforts.*

_____

_____

_____

_____

_____

Continued on next page

Assessment: Assume each performance indicator is worth 20 points (20 × 5 = 100 points). Use the evaluation levels listed below for judging consistency.

Excellent (16–20) Participant demonstrated the performance indicator in a professional manner, exceeds business standards.

Good (10–15) Participant demonstrated the performance indicator in an acceptable manner; meets minimal business standards; there would be no need for additional formalized training at this time.

Fair (4–9) Participant demonstrated the performance indicator with limited effectiveness; performance generally fell below minimal business standards; additional training would be required to improve knowledge, attitude, and/or skills.

Poor (0–3) Participant demonstrated the performance indicator with little effectiveness or not at all; a great deal of formal training would be needed.

Explain the concept of marketing strategies. Score _____

_____

_____

Explain the concepts of market and market identification. Score _____

_____

_____

_____

Develop strategies to position a product/business. Score _____

_____

_____

_____

Explain the nature of marketing plans. Score _____

_____

_____

_____

Develop a marketing plan. Score _____

_____

_____

_____

_____

CHAPTER **30** Product Planning

Presentation Application

ACTIVITY: With a successful product already attracting loyal customers on the market, companies often seek to expand their profits by expanding their product lines. In order to do this well, a company must identify its goals for the new product, and consider how the product will fit into the product mix in the stores where it intends to sell it.

Practice Situation

The McCallum Foods Corporation is developing a new candy to add to its successful line of peanut and chocolate candies. Nutty Chewy Bits will be peanuts coated with caramel and milk chocolate. As part of the product development process, McCallum Foods has hired you to help it determine how Nutty Chewy Bits will build on the company's image and appeal to new markets, as well as how it should position the product.

First, identify how this new candy will build on the company's image, increase sales, and appeal to new markets. Then determine where Nutty Chewy Bits will fit within the product mix of the stores where McCallum hopes to sell the candy, and how the company should best position the product. Then prepare a slide presentation, presenting your ideas about adding Nutty Chewy Bits to the McCallum Foods product line. Be as specific as possible.

Beginning with a title slide, create a series of slides to present your ideas to the head of McCallum Foods. You should include at least one slide to describe how Nutty Chewy Bits will build on the company's image, one slide on the product mix, and at least one slide on proposed product placement.

[slide 1]
Title Slide

[slide 2]
Build on Company's Image
Increase Sales
Appeal to New Markets

[slide 3]
Product Mix

[slide 4]
Product Positioning

Continued on next page

Presentation Directions

1. Start your presentation software.

2. Follow your software's instructions to create a title slide. Save your file as **CH30PROB**.

3. Develop a minimum of four more slides based on the information you have compiled about the proposed launch of Nutty Chewy Bits. Include clip art or other appropriate art and graphics to illustrate your ideas.

4. Save your work.

5. Print out a copy of your slides if your teacher has instructed you to do so.

6. Answer the following questions.

Interpreting Results

1. Which is the most important step of the product line expansion process?

_____

_____

_____

2. Exchange a copy of your slide presentation with a classmate. Check whether your classmate's ideas are concisely and clearly written. Suggest any additional ideas that could improve the company's launch of the new candy. Be specific.

_____

_____

_____

_____

_____

_____

Drawing Conclusions

3. If the company follows all your product planning advice, will Nutty Chewy Bits be guaranteed a successful launch? Explain.

_____

_____

_____

_____

_____

_____

_____

CHAPTER **31** Branding, Packaging, and Labeling

Vocabulary Review

DIRECTIONS: *Complete the crossword puzzle by using key terms from the chapter.*

Across

3. The legal authorization by a trademarked brand owner to allow another company to use its brand, brand mark, or trade character for a fee.

4. The physical container or wrapping for a product.

7. A personified brand mark.

8. A branding strategy that uses an existing brand name for a new or improved product in the line.

9. The word, group of words, letters, or numbers that can be spoken. (2 words)

10. A brand name, brand mark, trade character, or a combination of these that is given legal protection.

11. Name, term, design, or symbol that identifies a business or organization.

12. An information tag or imprinted message that is attached to a product or its package.

13. Another term for a producer brand.

14. Products that have no brand name.

Down

1. Identifies the company or division of a company. (2 words)

2. A branding strategy used by companies offering a combination of manufacturer, private, and generic brands. (2 words)

5. A brand owned and initiated by wholesalers and retailers. (2 words)

6. The part of a brand that is a symbol, design, or distinctive coloring or lettering. (2 words)

7. This works well when two or more companies' brands complement each other.

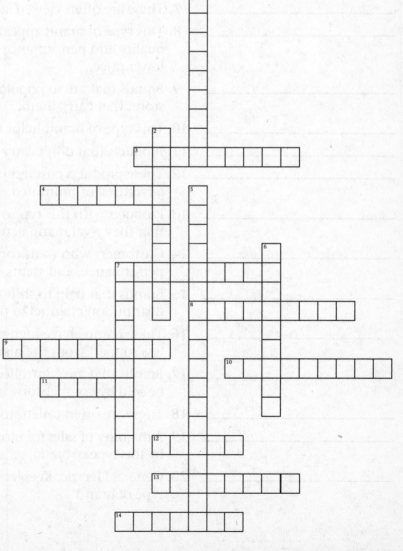

CHAPTER 31 Branding, Packaging, and Labeling

Fact and Idea Review

DIRECTIONS: *Read the statements listed below and classify each statement as typical of* **national, private distributor,** *or* **generic** *brands.*

_____ 1. Brand owned and initiated by producers.

_____ 2. These products are promoted by stressing quality.

_____ 3. Brand owned and initiated by wholesalers and retailers.

_____ 4. This type of brand is priced 30 to 50 percent lower than nationally advertised brands.

_____ 5. This type of product is generally sold in supermarkets and discount stores.

_____ 6. Brands that are popular with retailers because of high gross margins.

_____ 7. These are often viewed as "no frills" products.

_____ 8. This type of brand appeals to customers who want the quality and performance of manufacturers' brands but at a lower price.

_____ 9. Brands that are so popular that they attract customers to stores that carry them.

_____ 10. This type of brand helps to promote store loyalty.

_____ 11. Products that don't carry a company identity.

_____ 12. These products cost less because they are not usually advertised or promoted.

_____ 13. Products with this type of brand often become so popular that they rival manufacturers' brands.

_____ 14. Customers who want consistent quality, dependable product performance, and status often desire this type of brand.

_____ 15. Brands that help to shift the balance of power in the distribution channel to the retailer.

_____ 16. These brands have higher advertising costs because there is less support from the manufacturer.

_____ 17. Brands that are controlled by retailers because they cannot be sold by competitors.

_____ 18. These are often called store or dealer brands.

_____ 19. A majority of sales for most product categories are represented by this type of brand.

_____ 20. General Electric, Keebler, and Hershey are examples of this type of brand.

CHAPTER **31** Branding, Packaging, and Labeling

Marketing Application 1

DIRECTIONS: *Read the case study below. Then answer the questions that follow.*

Dodge sees NASCAR Building Brand and Sales

After years off the race track, Dodge returned to the NASCAR circuit in 2001. Dodge, a division of DaimlerChrysler, raced in one of the series of the National Association for Stock Car Auto Racing (NASCAR). In addition, the 3,000 Dodge dealers of North America sponsored a two-car racing team.

With the most loyal fans of any sport in America, NASCAR is growing quickly. Attendance grew steadily and significantly throughout the 1990s, and NASCAR races can be depended on to attract more television viewers than baseball or basketball games. NASCAR fan loyalty is double the fan loyalty for pro football, baseball, and basketball. Fans love NASCAR's down-to-earth drivers, in addition to the excitement of racing.

NASCAR racing features American-made sedans outfitted for the racetrack. They look very different from the single-seat, open-wheeled race cars of Indy and Formula One racing. Several manufacturers race their sedans in NASCAR: General Motors races the Pontiac Grand Prix and Chevrolet Monte Carlo; the Ford Motor Company competes with its Taurus; Dodge added the Intrepid R/T sedan to the track.

In addition to attention on the track, Dodge hoped to make money from branded merchandise sold at NASCAR retail outlets, online stores, during NASCAR events, and at Dodge dealerships. NASCAR merchandise includes clothing, flags, key chains, license plates, decals, and other race-related items. Some top NASCAR teams generate as much as $10 million in annual profits from merchandise sales. While Dodge and Dodge dealers are no doubt pleased with the percentage of sales they receive, the main goal of the new racing program is enhancing Dodge's brand image.

1. Why are the Dodge dealers willing to sponsor a Dodge car in NASCAR races?

   _____

   _____

2. Even though top NASCAR teams generate profits from merchandise sales, what is the main reason for a car manufacturer to get involved with a racing series?

   _____

   _____

3. What is it about NASCAR fans that makes Dodge think sponsoring a NASCAR team can pay off?

   _____

   _____

   _____

CHAPTER 31 Branding, Packaging, and Labeling

Marketing Application 2

DIRECTIONS: *Create your own brand for a product. Give your product a brand name, brand mark, trade name, trade character, and trademark. In the space below, draw a package and label for your product. Make sure the brand name, brand mark, trade name, trade character, and trademark are clearly identified. Below the drawing, note any appropriate information, such as a product guarantee, directions for use, safety instructions, ingredients, date of manufacture, and manufacturer's name and address.*

CHAPTER 31 Branding, Packaging, and Labeling

The DECA Connection

Role Play: Sports Marketing Consultant

Situation: You are to assume the role of an employee of a sports marketing consulting firm that performs a variety of integrated branding services for local and national sports teams. Your company provides branding services such as brand valuation, brand research, strategies, naming, and corporate identification for sports teams. Your firm has also helped financial institutions and manufacturers negotiate contracts with sports teams to place their corporate brand on new sports arenas in different communities. Through corporate branding of sports arenas, team owners receive additional revenue and corporate sponsors receive tremendous promotional value by being associated with a popular sports team.

Activity: A shopping mall developer has approached your firm to explore the feasibility of having a newly developed mall named after a local sports team. Your company has been asked to prepare a proposal. Your supervisor (judge) has asked you to develop the possible branding elements that would be necessary for a shopping mall naming proposal. You will present your ideas to your supervisor.

Evaluation: You will be evaluated on how well you meet the following performance indicators:

- Explain the nature of branding.
- Develop strategies to position a product/business.
- Describe factors used by marketers to position products/businesses.
- Demonstrate orderly and systematic behavior.
- Make oral presentations.

DIRECTIONS: *Organize your thoughts around the performance indicators noted above. Use these performance indicators to jot down your ideas during the preparation period. Time your preparation period to last 15 minutes and your role play presentation to last a maximum of ten minutes. After your role play, use the performance indicators to evaluate your efforts.*

_____

_____

_____

_____

_____

_____

_____

Continued on next page

Assessment: Assume each performance indicator is worth 20 points (20 × 5 = 100 points). Use the evaluation levels listed below for judging consistency.

Excellent (16–20) Participant demonstrated the performance indicator in a professional manner, exceeds business standards.

Good (10–15) Participant demonstrated the performance indicator in an acceptable manner; meets minimal business standards; there would be no need for additional formalized training at this time.

Fair (4–9) Participant demonstrated the performance indicator with limited effectiveness; performance generally fell below minimal business standards; additional training would be required to improve knowledge, attitude, and/or skills.

Poor (0–3) Participant demonstrated the performance indicator with little effectiveness or not at all; a great deal of formal training would be needed.

Explain the nature of branding. Score _____

_____

_____

_____

Develop strategies to position a product/business. Score _____

_____

_____

_____

Describe factors used by marketers to position products/businesses. Score _____

_____

_____

_____

Demonstrate orderly and systematic behavior. Score _____

_____

_____

_____

Make oral presentations. Score _____

_____

_____

_____

_____

CHAPTER **31** Branding, Packaging, and Labeling

Software Activity (Optional)

Spreadsheet Application

OBJECTIVE: *To analyze the results of a survey on brand recognition.*

ACTIVITY: A fruit drink manufacturer recently conducted a survey asking consumers which brands they recognized. The results of the survey are shown in the spreadsheet below. The manufacturer has been test marketing a new brand for this market. The marketing manager wants to determine whether the advertising and product promotion have resulted in significant gains in brand recognition. The name of the product is Fruition.

	A	B	C	D	E
1	Chapter 31 Branding, Packaging, and Labeling				
2					
3					
4		Number of	Percentage		
5		Customers	of Total		
6	Brand	Recognizing Brand	(Sample = 3,980)		
7					
8	Fruitbreak	1,020			
9	A Taste of Fruit	950			
10	Mountain Springs	3,790			
11	Fruit Spa	3,810			
12	Fruition	250			
13	Juicer	1,780			

Spreadsheet Directions

1. Turn on your computer and open your spreadsheet software program.

2. Create a spreadsheet like the one above using your spreadsheet application.

3. Enter a formula to calculate the percentage of the total for each brand. The total number of consumers in the survey was 3,980.

4. Use the percentages calculated to create a bar chart showing the percentage of brand recognition for each brand.

5. Save your work. Print out a copy of your work if your teacher has instructed you to do so. Then answer the questions that follow.

Continued on next page

Interpreting Results

1. Which brand has the highest percentage of brand recognition?

   _____

   _____

2. Which brand has the lowest percentage of brand recognition?

   _____

   _____

Drawing Conclusions

3. What do you think the low brand recognition for Fruition means in terms of advertising and market promotion? Explain the reasons for your conclusions.

   _____

   _____

   _____

   _____

   _____

   _____

   _____

   _____

   _____

   _____

   _____

   _____

   _____

   _____

   _____

   _____

   _____

   _____

CHAPTER 32 Extended Product Features

Vocabulary Review

DIRECTIONS: *Complete each sentence with the correct term.*

credit	implied warranty	warranty
budget accounts	installment accounts	warranty of fitness for a particular purpose
disclaimer	limited warranty	warranty of merchantability
express warranty	regular, or 30-day, accounts	
full warranty	revolving accounts	

1. A promise from a seller that a product which is sold is fit for its intended purpose is an example of a(n) _____.

2. A(n) _____ is one that is explicitly stated in writing or spoken word, to induce a customer to buy.

3. A warranty that exists automatically by state law whenever a purchase takes place is called a(n) _____.

4. Under a(n) _____, if a product is found to be defective within the warranty period, it will be repaired or replaced at no cost to the purchaser.

5. A(n) _____ arises when a seller advises a customer that a product is suitable for a particular use.

6. A guarantee is another word for _____.

7. Under _____ there is no credit charge if the bill is paid on time.

8. A(n) _____ is often used to limit damages that can be recovered by a customer.

9. It is not uncommon for a(n) _____ to specify that the manufacturer will pay for replacement parts but charge the customer for labor or shipping.

10. _____ is an arrangement whereby businesses or individuals can obtain products or money in exchange for a promise to pay later.

11. _____ are normally used for large purchases and require a down payment and a separate contract for each purchase.

12. With _____, a minimum payment is usually a certain percentage of the balance owed or a minimum dollar amount.

13. Under _____, the customer is not required to pay an interest charge as long as the amount owed is paid within the interest-free time period.

CHAPTER 32 Extended Product Features

Fact and Idea Review

DIRECTIONS: *Test your ability to identify the key concepts about warranties by answering the following questions.*

1. How does an express warranty differ from an implied warranty?

   _____

   _____

2. How does a full warranty differ from a limited warranty?

   _____

   _____

   _____

3. Why are warranty disclaimers used by businesses?

   _____

4. How does a warranty differ from a guarantee?

   _____

   _____

5. How does a warranty of merchantability differ from a warranty of fitness for a particular purpose?

   _____

   _____

   _____

6. How is a warranty different from an extended service contract?

   _____

   _____

   _____

7. Who pays for an extended service contract, and how long does it last?

   _____

   _____

CHAPTER 32 Extended Product Features

Marketing Application 1

DIRECTIONS: *Read the warranty below. Then use it to answer the questions that follow.*

Bush's Written Warranty To You

In order to provide you with timely assistance, please thoroughly inspect your furniture for missing or defective parts immediately after opening the carton. To receive a replacement or missing part under this warranty, call our Consumer Service Department. Please have your model, part, and lot numbers found in the instruction booklet available for your reference. You will also need your sales receipt or other proof of purchase. Replacement part(s) will be shipped to you at no charge with Bush Industries assuming all shipping and handling expense.

All Bush, Eric Morgan by Bush, and Case Casard by Bush furniture is warranted to the original purchaser at the time of purchase and for a period of six years thereafter.

We warrant to you, the original purchaser, that our furniture and all its parts and components are free of defects in material or workmanship. "Defects," as used in this warranty, is defined as any imperfections which impair the use of the furniture product.

Our warranty is expressly limited to the replacement of furniture parts and components. For six years after the date of purchase, Bush Industries will replace any part described on the enclosed Furniture Parts List that is defective in material or workmanship.

This warranty applies under conditions of normal use. Our furniture products are not intended for outdoor use. The warranty does not cover: 1) defects caused by improper assembly or disassembly; 2) defects occurring after purchase due to product modification, intentional damage, accident, misuse, abuse, negligence, or exposure to the elements; and, 3) labor or assembly costs.

IMPLIED WARRANTIES, INCLUDING THE WARRANTY OF MERCHANTABILITY, SHALL NOT EXTEND BEYOND THE DURATION OF THE WRITTEN WARRANTY STATED ABOVE, AND IN NO EVENT SHALL BUSH INDUSTRIES BE LIABLE FOR INCIDENTAL OR CONSEQUENTIAL DAMAGES RESULTING FROM USE OF THE PRODUCT. Some states do not allow a limitation on how long an implied warranty lasts or the exclusion or limitation of incidental or consequential damages, so the above limitation and exclusion may not apply to you.

IMPORTANT REMINDER: Please fill out and return your Product Registration Card promptly. Although not required, it will help us serve you even better in the future.

THIS WARRANTY GIVES YOU SPECIFIC LEGAL RIGHTS. YOU MAY ALSO HAVE OTHER RIGHTS WHICH MAY VARY FROM STATE TO STATE.

Part No. A45351
1/97–1.5MM

- -

Please retain this portion of the card for your records. You may need to refer to this information in case of warranty claim or for insurance purposes.

Date Purchased _____

Dealer Name _____

Model # _____

Product Purchased _____

BUSH INDUSTRIES, INC.
One Madison Drive
Jamestown, NY 14702

Continued on next page

1. Would you classify this warranty to be a full or limited warranty? Provide your rationale.

_____

_____

_____

_____

2. What procedures must the customer follow to make a claim under this warranty?

_____

_____

_____

_____

3. If the warranty conditions are met, what is the length of time that the company will warrant the product?

_____

_____

_____

_____

4. Are there any limitations to the implied warranty period?

_____

_____

_____

_____

5. The warranty applies under conditions of normal use. What conditions does the warranty not cover?

_____

_____

_____

_____

CHAPTER 32 Extended Product Features

Marketing Application 2

DIRECTIONS: *Read the following chart and then answer the questions that follow.*

Institution Credit Card Plan	Annual Type of Percentage Rate (APR)	Pricing (V/F)	Grace Period	Annual Fee
Security Bank Visa	13.74	Variable	30 days	$18
Simmons First Visa	8.50	Fixed	25 days	$35
Travelers Bank MasterCard/ Visa	16.00	Variable	25 days	$0
Union Bank MasterCard	19.80	Fixed	25 days	$15

1. Which of the banks has the best grace period and why?

_____

_____

_____

_____

_____

2. Why is having a grace period important to consumers?

_____

_____

_____

_____

Continued on next page

3. Which of the banks has the most favorable annual fee arrangement and why?

_____

_____

_____

_____

4. Which bank has the least favorable interest rate and why?

_____

_____

_____

_____

_____

5. How do banks receive their income from credit cards?

_____

_____

_____

_____

6. Why is credit important to our economy?

_____

_____

_____

_____

7. Why does the government pass legislation regulating credit?

_____

_____

_____

_____

CHAPTER 32 Extended Product Features

The DECA Connection

Role Play: Sales Associate

Situation: You are to assume the role of a sales associate in an appliance store. The store sells nationally known and advertised appliances. Management encourages employees to sell extended service contracts with every appliance purchase. An extended service contract has the following features: 1) all parts and repairs provided (minus a $20 deductible) for every operating problem; 2) fast, convenient service scheduling; 3) factory-trained service experts; and 4) unlimited repairs for the entire term of the contract. Management believes that the top quality service available through their extended service contract maximizes years of enjoyment on appliances, is very affordable, and offers great protection in the event of needed repairs. The store charges $25 per hour for repairs that are not covered by warranty or an extended service contract.

Activity: A customer (judge) has just purchased a $300 nationally branded microwave oven. The oven comes with a limited manufacturer's warranty on parts and repairs for one year. The store's extended service contract rates for parts and repairs when purchased at time of sale are as follows: one year $29.95; two years $59.90; and three years $89.85. The customer seems unwilling to spend additional money for an extended service contract. Your task is to convince the customer of the need, value, and importance of obtaining an extended service policy for a new appliance. You must convince the customer to purchase the policy even though the microwave oven just purchased is of high quality.

Evaluation: You will be evaluated on how well you meet the following performance indicators:
- Explain warranties and guarantees.
- Handle customer inquiries.
- Sell a good/service/idea to individuals.
- Facilitate the customer buying decision.
- Explain the role of customer service as a component of selling relationships.

DIRECTIONS: *Organize your thoughts around the performance indicators noted above. Use these performance indicators to jot down your ideas during the preparation period. Time your preparation period to last 15 minutes and your role play presentation to last a maximum of ten minutes. After your role play, use the performance indicators to evaluate your efforts.*

_____

_____

_____

_____

_____

Continued on next page

Assessment: Assume each performance indicator is worth 20 points (20 × 5 = 100 points). Use the evaluation levels listed below for judging consistency.

Excellent (16–20) Participant demonstrated the performance indicator in a professional manner, exceeds business standards.

Good (10–15) Participant demonstrated the performance indicator in an acceptable manner; meets minimal business standards; there would be no need for additional formalized training at this time.

Fair (4–9) Participant demonstrated the performance indicator with limited effectiveness; performance generally fell below minimal business standards; additional training would be required to improve knowledge, attitude, and/or skills.

Poor (0–3) Participant demonstrated the performance indicator with little effectiveness or not at all; a great deal of formal training would be needed.

Explain warranties and guarantees.   Score _____

_____

_____

_____

Handle customer inquiries.   Score _____

_____

_____

_____

Sell a good/service/idea to individuals.   Score _____

_____

_____

_____

Facilitate the customer buying decision.   Score _____

_____

_____

_____

Explain the role of customer service.   Score _____

_____

_____

_____

_____

_____

CHAPTER 32 Extended Product Features

Software Activity (Optional)

Spreadsheet Application

OBJECTIVE: *To analyze the cost to a business of selling on credit.*

ACTIVITY: The Ticket Broker serves as a sales agent for concert promoters and community organizations. The company earns its revenue from a percentage of the price of each ticket sold. It also charges a handling fee of $1.50 per ticket, which is five percent of the average ticket price of $30. The majority of tickets sold by the Ticket Broker are sold on credit. The company accepts Visa and MasterCard and pays a service fee of 2.5 percent. It also accepts American Express and Discover, paying service fees of 2.8 percent for those transactions. Both cash and credit ticket sales are shown in the spreadsheet below.

	A	B	C	D	E	F	G
1	Chapter 32 Extended Product Features						
2							
3			Visa and	Am. Exp. and			
4		Cash	MasterCard	Discover			
5	Event	Sales	Sales	Sales	Total		
6							
7	Pop music concerts	$1,500,000	$5,670,000	$1,250,000			
8	Touring Broadway plays	$200,000	$5,700,000	$2,885,000			
9	Ballet/opera	$300,000	$600,000	$900,000			
10	Classical music concerts	$400,000	$800,000	$1,240,000			
11	Sports events	$890,000	$6,490,000	$2,080,000			
12							
13	Total						
14							
15	Credit Service Fees						

Continued on next page

Spreadsheet Directions

1. Turn on your computer and open your spreadsheet software program.

2. Create a spreadsheet like the one on page 285 using your spreadsheet application.

3. Enter a formula to calculate total sales for each type of event.

4. Enter a formula to calculate total cash sales for all events, total Visa and MasterCard sales, total American Express and Discover sales, and total sales.

5. Enter a formula to calculate the servicing cost of the Visa and MasterCard sales.

6. Enter a formula to calculate the servicing cost of the American Express and Discover sales.

7. After completing all calculations, save your work. Print out a copy of your work if your teacher has instructed you to do so, then answer the questions that follow.

Interpreting Results

1. What is the amount of total cash sales?

_____

2. What is the amount of total sales for pop music concerts?

_____

Drawing Conclusions

3. Explain why you think retailers and other companies accept credit cards for customer purchases when their use costs them money.

_____
_____
_____
_____
_____
_____
_____
_____
_____
_____
_____
_____

CHAPTER 33 Entrepreneurial Concepts

Vocabulary Review

DIRECTIONS: *Match each definition with the correct term.*

Articles of Incorporation	foreign corporation	partnership
corporation	franchise	sole proprietorship
DBA	general partnership	stockholders
entrepreneurs	limited liability company	unlimited liability
entrepreneurship	limited partnership	

_____ 1. People who organize, manage, and take the risks of owning and operating a business.

_____ 2. This identifies the name and address of your corporation, its purpose, the names of initial directors, and the amount of stock that will be issued to each director.

_____ 3. A legal agreement between two or more people to be jointly responsible for the success or failure of a business.

_____ 4. The people who own a publicly held corporation.

_____ 5. A corporation incorporated under the laws of a different state than the one in which it does business.

_____ 6. Each limited partner is liable for any debts only up to the limit of his or her involvement in the company.

_____ 7. The process of starting and managing your own business.

_____ 8. A legal agreement to operate a business in the name of a recognized company.

_____ 9. A business owned and operated by one person.

_____ 10. Financial responsibility is not limited to your investment in the business, but extends to your total ability to make payments.

_____ 11. A state-chartered business that legally operates apart from the owners.

_____ 12. Each partner shares in the profits and losses and has unlimited liability for the company's debts.

_____ 13. A blend of a partnership and a corporation.

_____ 14. Filing a statement for this part of the registration process for a sole proprietorship or a partnership.

CHAPTER **33** Entrepreneurial Concepts

Fact and Idea Review

DIRECTIONS: *Decide whether each characteristic listed below describes a* **sole proprietorship,** **partnership, corporation,** *or* **limited liability company** *and label it accordingly.*

_____ 1. The most common form of business ownership.

_____ 2. The skills of the owners are combined in this type of business.

_____ 3. This type of business can own assets and borrow money without directly involving the shareholders.

_____ 4. There are two types of this business organization: general and limited.

_____ 5. The value of this type of business is divided into shares of stock.

_____ 6. This allows the greatest freedom in making decisions.

_____ 7. This is the easiest form of business organization to start.

_____ 8. This type of business is generally taxed less than other forms of business.

_____ 9. Actions of one owner are legally binding on the other owners in this type of business organization.

_____ 10. Each owner has limited liability in this type of business organization.

_____ 11. This type of business is a blend of characteristics of other types of businesses.

_____ 12. Each owner has a voice in this type of business organization.

_____ 13. This is the most complicated form of business ownership.

_____ 14. In this type of business, governing bodies or boards hire directors to manage the affairs of the business.

_____ 15. Raising outside capital is the most difficult in this type of business.

_____ 16. Government regulations are the most complicated with this form of business organization.

_____ 17. Death of one of the owners dissolves this type of business.

_____ 18. The owner is personally liable for the debts of the business.

_____ 19. Raising money for expansion of the business is easiest in this type of business.

_____ 20. Growth is limited by the personal motivation of the owner in this type of business organization.

_____ 21. In this type of business, the owners are called members.

CHAPTER 33 Entrepreneurial Concepts

Marketing Application 1

DIRECTIONS: *Are you the kind of person who can get a business started and make it run? The self-assessment questionnaire below was taken from U.S. Small Business Administration training materials. It is designed to determine whether you have the necessary entrepreneurial qualities. Under each question, check the letter that says what you feel or comes closest to it. Use the scoring key that follows the questions to complete your self-assessment.*

1. **Are you a self-starter?**

   a. I do things on my own. Nobody has to tell me to get going.

   b. If someone gets me started, I keep going all right.

   c. Easy does it. I don't put myself out until I have to.

2. **How do you feel about other people?**

   a. I like people. I can get along with just about anybody.

   b. I have plenty of friends—I don't need anyone else.

   c. Most people irritate me.

3. **Can you take responsibility?**

   a. I like to take charge of things and see them through.

   b. I'll take over if I have to, but I'd rather let someone else be responsible.

   c. There's always some eager person around wanting to show how smart they are. I say let them.

4. **How good an organizer are you?**

   a. I like to have a plan before I start. I'm usually the one to get things lined up when the group wants to do something.

   b. I do all right unless things get too confused. Then I quit.

   c. You get all set and then something comes along and presents too many problems. So I just take things as they come.

5. **Can you lead others?**

   a. I can get most people to go along when I start something.

   b. I can give the orders if someone tells me what we should do.

   c. I let someone else get things moving. Then I go along if I feel like it.

Continued on next page

6. **How good a worker are you?**

   a. I can keep going as long as I need to. I don't mind working hard for something I want.

   b. I'll work hard for a while, but when I've had enough, that's it.

   c. I can't see that hard work gets you anywhere.

7. **Can you make decisions?**

   a. I can make up my mind in a hurry if I have to. It usually turns out O.K., too.

   b. I can if I have plenty of time. If I have to make up my mind fast, I think later I should have decided the other way.

   c. I don't like to be the one who has to decide things.

8. **Can people trust what you say?**

   a. You bet they can. I don't say things I don't mean.

   b. I try to be on the level most of the time, but sometimes I just say what's easiest.

   c. Why bother if the other person doesn't know the difference?

9. **Can you stick with it?**

   a. If I make up my mind to do something, I don't let anything stop me.

   b. I usually finish what I start—if it goes well.

   c. If it doesn't go well right away, I quit. Why beat your brains out?

10. **How good is your health?**

   a. I never run down!

   b. I have enough energy for most things I want to do.

   c. I run out of energy sooner than most of my friends seem to.

Scoring Key

Count the number of checks by each letter for each question.

How many checks were placed next to the letter a?   _____

How many checks were placed next to the letter b?   _____

How many checks were placed next to the letter c?   _____

If six or more of your checks were placed beside the letter a, you probably have what it takes to run a business.

If six or more of your checks were placed beside the letter b, you are likely to have more trouble than you can handle by yourself. It would be better to find a partner who is strong on the points where you are weak.

If six or more of your checks were placed beside the letter c, not even a good partner will be able to help you successfully run a business.

If you do not have a majority of checks by any letter, you probably should start working for someone to gain valuable experience before you consider starting your own business.

(Source: SBA, Office of Management Assistance, Small Business Management Training Instructors' Guide, *Home-Based Business: The Basics of Doing Business from Your Home.* Washington, D.C., September 1984.)

CHAPTER 33 Entrepreneurial Concepts

Marketing Application 2

A Profile of an Entrepreneur

Using books, autobiographies, biographies, periodicals, or the Internet, select an individual (living or not) who has been nationally successful in operating his or her own business and develop a profile about the person. There are literally thousands of individuals you may use for this marketing application. A few examples are Henry Ford, Calvin Klein, Orville Redenbacher, Oprah Winfrey, Bill Gates, and Levi Strauss. Then answer the questions that follow. After your profile is completed, be prepared to present a two to three minute oral report about the entrepreneur you investigated.

1. Who is the entrepreneur you investigated?

   _____

   _____

2. What is the name and nature of the business he/she started?

   _____

   _____

   _____

   _____

   _____

   _____

   _____

3. What is the history of the entrepreneur (i.e. place of birth, education, job history, family background, etc)?

   _____

   _____

   _____

   _____

   _____

   _____

   _____

Continued on next page

4. What skills, special abilities, and interests did this individual possess that helped to make her/him a successful entrepreneur?

_____

_____

_____

_____

_____

_____

_____

_____

_____

_____

5. In your opinion, what personal traits did this person possess that made him/her so successful as an entrepreneur?

_____

_____

_____

_____

_____

_____

_____

_____

_____

_____

_____

_____

CHAPTER 33 Entrepreneurial Concepts

The DECA Connection

Role Play: Marketing Student

Situation: You are to assume the role of student in a high school marketing class. You are very interested in using the skills you have developed in your marketing class to help you get a job with a company with entrepreneurial drive and spirit. A new online business has opened in your community and is seeking new employees with excellent personal skills, such as responsibility, initiative, good time management behavior, and the abilities to problem-solve and work well with others. The company uses a job interviewing technique called targeted selection. Targeted selection defines a job on certain important dimensions and asks applicants to reflect on past performance and experiences to predict future effectiveness as an employee.

Activity: You have decided to apply for the job and will interview with the entrepreneur (judge) who started the new business. The owner is asking the same questions of all applicants to measure their personal and interpersonal skills. You are to prepare answers for your interview with the entrepreneur.

The questions are as follows:

1. When have you had the opportunity to work as a member of a team? How did you take initiative as a member of the team?
2. When have you had to solve a problem? What was the result?
3. When have you been responsible for the success or failure of a project? What was the result?
4. What would your previous coworkers say about your willingness to work well with them? Can you give me an example to support your answer?
5. How do you manage your time? Can you give me some examples from your past activities?

Evaluation: You will be evaluated on how well you meet the following performance indicators:

- Assess personal interests and skills needed for success in business.
- Analyze employer expectations in the business environment.
- Identify personality traits important to business.
- Participate as a team member.
- Demonstrate problem-solving skills.

DIRECTIONS: *Organize your thoughts around the performance indicators noted above. Use these performance indicators to jot down your ideas during the preparation period. Time your preparation period to last 15 minutes and your role play presentation to last a maximum of ten minutes. After your role play, use the performance indicators to evaluate your efforts.*

_____

_____

_____

Continued on next page

Assessment: Assume each performance indicator is worth 20 points ($20 \times 5 = 100$ points). Use the evaluation levels listed below for judging consistency.

Excellent (16–20) Participant demonstrated the performance indicator in a professional manner, exceeds business standards.

Good (10–15) Participant demonstrated the performance indicator in an acceptable manner; meets minimal business standards; there would be no need for additional formalized training at this time.

Fair (4–9) Participant demonstrated the performance indicator with limited effectiveness; performance generally fell below minimal business standards; additional training would be required to improve knowledge, attitude, and/or skills.

Poor (0–3) Participant demonstrated the performance indicator with little effectiveness or not at all; a great deal of formal training would be needed.

Assess personal interests and skills needed for success. Score _____

_____

_____

_____

Analyze employer expectations in the business environment. Score _____

_____

_____

_____

Identify personality traits important to business. Score _____

_____

_____

_____

Participate as a team member. Score _____

_____

_____

_____

Demonstrate problem-solving skills. Score _____

_____

_____

_____

_____

CHAPTER **33** Entrepreneurial Concepts

Software Activity (Optional)

Presentation Application

OBJECTIVE: *Examine different ways of becoming an entrepreneur and the advantages and disadvantages of the different methods.*

ACTIVITY: Lots of businesses in your neighborhood are operated by entrepreneurs—from the flower shop to your local McDonald's—but those entrepreneurs did not all take the same path to owning their own businesses. Some started their businesses from scratch, while others purchased a business from someone else or took over a family business. Still others purchased a franchise.

Identify a successful entrepreneur and find out everything you can about the path he or she took to success. If possible, interview a business owner in your neighborhood. Otherwise, read up on an entrepreneur in newspapers, magazines, or on the Internet. Answer the following questions:

- Did this person start the business from scratch, buy an existing business, purchase a franchise, or take over a family business?

- How is the business organized: sole proprietorship, partnership, or corporation? Why did the entrepreneur choose that form of organization?

- What is the entrepreneur's background, and what does this person feel best prepared him or her for owning a business?

- What does the entrepreneur feel are the best and worst things about owning a business?

Now, develop a slide presentation that describes the entrepreneur's path to success. Prepare one slide for each of the following topics: title; entrepreneur's name; entrepreneur's education; entrepreneur's career path; type of business organization; pros of entrepreneurship; cons of entrepreneurship; and keys to success. Be sure to include clip art or other art and graphics when appropriate to illustrate your point.

Presentation Directions

1. Start your presentation software program.

2. Follow your software's instructions to create a title slide. Save your file as **CH33PROB**.

3. Based on your interview or research, develop at least seven more slides to profile this entrepreneur.

4. Print out a copy of your slides if your teacher has instructed you to do so.

5. Answer the following questions.

Continued on next page

Interpreting Results

1. What are the advantages and disadvantages of buying an existing business versus starting your own?

_____

_____

_____

_____

_____

2. Present your slide presentation to your class. What similarities do you see in the way different businesses were organized? How does the organization of a business affect the business's future?

_____

_____

_____

_____

_____

_____

Drawing Conclusions

3. Why is it important for potential entrepreneurs to understand the background and experience of other entrepreneurs?

_____

_____

_____

_____

_____

_____

_____

_____

CHAPTER 34 Risk Management

Vocabulary Review

DIRECTIONS: *Fill in the puzzle blanks by using terms from the chapter. Then read down the column of boxed entries to discover the Mystery Phrase.*

1. The possibility of financial loss.
2. A type of bond that protects a business from employee dishonesty.
3. There are three kinds of _____ risks—economic, natural, and human.
4. When it is impossible to prevent or transfer risks, businesses must assume responsibility for them. This is called _____ _____.
5. A type of insurance paid by employers to cover employees who suffer job-related injuries and illness and to protect employers from being sued by an employee who is injured on the job.
6. Floods, tornadoes, and hurricanes are examples of this type of risk.
7. This type of risk is often caused by employees or customers.

8. One way to transfer risk is through limiting _____.
9. The stealing of merchandise from a business.
10. This kind of risk results from changes in overall business conditions.
11. These insure against losses that might occur when work or a contract is not finished on time or as agreed.
12. Product _____ is another type of economic risk for businesses that depend on fashion or the latest trends to market goods and services.
13. A(n) _____ policy is a contract between a business and an insurance company to cover a certain business risk.
14. Optional coverage on a basic insurance policy.

1. ◯ __ __ __
2. __ __ __ __ ◯ __ __ __ __ __
3. __ __ __ __ __ ◯ __ __
4. __ __ ◯ __ __ __ __ __ __ __
5. __ __ __ __ ◯ __ __ __ __ __ __ __
6. __ __ __ __ __ ◯ __ __
7. __ __ __ ◯ __ __
8. __ __ __ ◯ __ __ __ __ __ __ __ __
9. __ __ __ __ __ __ __ ◯ __ __
10. ◯ __ __ __ __ __ __ __ __
11. __ __ __ __ ◯ __ __ __ __ __
12. __ __ __ __ __ ◯ __ __ __
13. __ __ __ ◯ __ __ __ __
14. __ __ ◯ __ __ __ __ __ __ __ __ __ __ __

Mystery Phrase: _____

CHAPTER 34 Risk Management

Fact and Idea Review

DIRECTIONS: *Classify each of the following situations according to the risk it represents—*
economic, human, or natural.

_____ 1. A major employer moves its headquarters to another state,
resulting in a loss of jobs.

_____ 2. An earthquake in California leads to increased losses for an
insurance company.

_____ 3. Basketball shoes endorsed by professional players are no
longer trendy among teenagers.

_____ 4. Employees at a local restaurant improperly cook hamburgers,
leading to customers being hospitalized.

_____ 5. An inventory shortage occurs due to employee theft in the
warehouse.

_____ 6. A reduction in snowfall over the past winter leads to fewer
skiers and lost sales for Colorado ski resorts.

_____ 7. Poor employee cash register training causes some customers to
leave the stores because of long lines.

_____ 8. A high unemployment rate causes a downturn in the retail
sales sector for the year.

_____ 9. An improperly designed tire breaks apart in certain situations
and results in customer lawsuits against the corporation for
deaths and injuries.

_____ 10. A surplus of apartments causes apartment owners to lower
rents.

_____ 11. The Americans with Disabilities Act requires a local restaurant
to modify its entranceways.

_____ 12. A local manufacturer has to pay higher wages because there is
a lack of skilled apprentices in the community.

_____ 13. A building contractor must pay employees a higher wage
because the city has passed a "living wage" ordinance.

_____ 14. Because of discriminatory promotional practices, a company
must pay an award to some current employees.

_____ 15. Higher than expected interest rates lead to a slowdown in sales
of manufactured housing units.

_____ 16. High gasoline prices result in lower attendance at Florida
amusement parks.

_____ 17. Faulty wiring installation leads to an apartment fire.

CHAPTER 34 Risk Management

Marketing Application 1

DIRECTIONS: *Read the following story. Then answer the questions that follow.*

Jacquelyn West reported early to her first day of work for Quick Print Graphics. The human resources manager, Jim Sinclair, summarized the company's extensive employee handbook, focusing on employment practices, employee benefits, and job expectations. The orientation ended with a tour of the production facilities. During the tour, Sinclair told West how the company—through its published policy—uses a four-step procedure to train new workers on job tasks:

Step 1: The immediate supervisor should be prepared to teach and should prepare a new employee to learn.

Step 2: The immediate supervisor should demonstrate and explain the tasks to be learned to a new employee.

Step 3: The new employee should demonstrate and explain each new task.

Step 4: The new employee should perform the new tasks on the job with supervision.

After explaining the steps involved with new worker training, Sinclair introduced West to Larry Ahleman, her immediate supervisor, and left for other duties. Ahleman told West that the company had just received a shipment of paper and that the truck had to be unloaded. "Just lift the cartons one at a time and place them in their designated bins," Ahleman said. Ahleman then excused himself to attend a meeting with a supplier. West began unloading the truck and, within an hour, injured her back and had to leave work. Because of her injury, West had to take sick leave for the rest of the week.

1. What type of risk is illustrated by this case? What is your rationale?

_____

_____

_____

_____

_____

_____

2. In your opinion what was the basic reason for West's injury?

_____

_____

_____

_____

_____

Continued on next page

3. Speculate on what aspects of employee training should be covered in company training to reduce company risk.

_____

_____

_____

_____

_____

_____

_____

4. Why is it important for supervisors to demonstrate and explain new tasks to employees?

_____

_____

_____

_____

_____

_____

_____

5. What other ways can companies prevent and control human risks?

_____

_____

_____

_____

_____

_____

_____

_____

CHAPTER *34* Risk Management

Marketing Application 2

DIRECTIONS: *Workers' compensation insurance is a type of insurance paid by employers to help employees who suffer job-related injuries and illnesses. The federal government requires businesses to carry workers' compensation insurance, but each state sets its own policies and procedures for administration. All occupations carry a specific industry code and the insurance rates are based on every $100 of wages. Premiums are calculated on the estimated yearly payroll. Employers with small payrolls have to pay the minimum premium. One of your duties as an independent insurance agent is to write workers' compensation policies for advertising businesses in your community. Use the table below to calculate the premiums for three types of businesses:*

Basic Manual for Workers' Compensation and Employers' Liability Insurance
Michigan Version

Code No.	Rate	Min. Prem.	Code No.	Rate	Min. Prem.	Code No.	Rate	Min. Prem.
8803	0.29	229	9051	0.44	244	9156	2.45	445
8810	0.44	244	9052	3.60	560	9220	6.06	750
8820	0.27	227	9053	4.79	679	9402	11.04	750
8829	6.33	750	9058	2.79	479	9403	21.04	750
8831	2.17	417	9059	2.06	406	9410	1.88	388
8832	0.60	260	9060	3.02	502	9501	7.39	750
8833	2.53	453	9061	3.78	578	9519	4.31	631
8835	4.81	681	9063	1.59	359	9521	8.71	750
8837	5.55	750	9065	1.43	343	9522	5.31	731
8868	0.60	260	9093	2.89	489	9530	38.56	750
8869	0.27	227	9101	4.21	621	9558	18.77	750
8870	0.30	230	9102	3.03	503	9559	3.15	515
8901	0.51	251	9104	3.94	594	9586	0.98	298
9015	5.95	750	9108 P	97.85	-	9620	1.03	303
9040	4.33	633	9145	3.09	509			

Code	Type of Business
9501	Advertising Display—installation or removal of advertising cards in or on vehicles
9521	Advertising Display Service—for stores
9558	Advertising Company—Outdoor

Continued on next page

1. Which of these types of businesses has the highest workers' compensation rate? What is the rate charged per $100 of employee wages?

_____

2. Use the table to calculate annual premiums for companies listed below.

_____

_____

_____

_____

Company	Code	Annual Payroll	Premium
Best Outdoor Signage	9558	$25,000	
John's Display Service	9521	$10,000	
Anderson's Advertising	9501	$55,000	
Design Team	9521	$6,600	
Model Printing Service	9558	$100,000	
The Place, Inc.	9521	$115,000	

3. Looking at the rate tables and your calculations, what can you surmise about the relationship of the type of business and the rate charged per hundred?

_____

_____

_____

4. Suppose The Place, Inc. underestimated its yearly payroll by $36,000. After a payroll audit by the insurance company, what would be the additional premium owed?

_____

5. Suppose Model Printing Service overestimated its yearly payroll by $8,000. What amount of credit would be owed to them from the insurance company?

_____

6. Why do you think the government mandated the provision of workers' compensation insurance?

_____

_____

_____

_____

_____

CHAPTER 34 Risk Management

The DECA Connection

Role Play: Marketing Manager

Situation: You are to assume the role of marketing manager for an independent manufactured housing company that has several sales outlets, a mobile home park, two installation companies, and a corporate home office. A young and resourceful entrepreneur originally established the company as a single sales outlet. Because of the booming economy and low interest rates, sales of manufactured housing units have grown among first-time homebuyers and retirees building second homes on vacation properties. The company's sales staff has also grown from five employees to more than fifty employees in multiple locations. You have noticed that managers at the sales outlets have been spending large amounts of time answering questions from new sales employees about company policies related to company practices, rules, and regulations. At the present time, there is no organized training and orientation program for the company. You have suggested to the owner (judge) a new program to provide a general orientation to the company, its policies, job expectations, employment practices, and general rules and regulations related to both customers and employees. Even though the owner believes that many duties are learned on the job, he has agreed to your suggestion and has asked for your input on what should be included in an orientation and training program.

Activity: The owner (judge) wants you to identify in outline form the items that should be included in an orientation program that would be of interest to new employees and of benefit to the company. You are to present your ideas to the owner. Your presentation should also include how the company could benefit from an effective orientation and training program.

Evaluation: You will be evaluated on how well you meet the following performance indicators:

- Orient new employees.
- Explain the role of training and human resource development.
- Explain the nature of risk management.
- Explain the types of business risk.
- Prepare simple written reports.

DIRECTIONS: *Organize your thoughts around the performance indicators noted above. Use these performance indicators to jot down your ideas during the preparation period. Time your preparation period to last 15 minutes and your role play presentation to last a maximum of ten minutes. After your role play, use the performance indicators to evaluate your efforts.*

_____

_____

_____

_____

_____

Continued on next page

Assessment: Assume each performance indicator is worth 20 points (20 × 5 = 100 points). Use the evaluation levels listed below for judging consistency.

Excellent (16–20) Participant demonstrated the performance indicator in a professional manner, exceeds business standards.

Good (10–15) Participant demonstrated the performance indicator in an acceptable manner; meets minimal business standards; there would be no need for additional formalized training at this time.

Fair (4–9) Participant demonstrated the performance indicator with limited effectiveness; performance generally fell below minimal business standards; additional training would be required to improve knowledge, attitude, and/or skills.

Poor (0–3) Participant demonstrated the performance indicator with little effectiveness or not at all; a great deal of formal training would be needed.

Orient new employees. Score _____

_____

_____

Explain the role of training and human resource development. Score _____

_____

_____

Explain the nature of risk management. Score _____

_____

_____

Explain the types of business risk. Score _____

_____

_____

Prepare simple written reports. Score _____

_____

_____

_____

_____

CHAPTER **34** Risk Management

Presentation Application

OBJECTIVE: *Identify risks faced by a business and present a risk management program.*

ACTIVITY: As a business owner, one of your primary goals will be to make a profit. However, there is no guarantee that this will happen. Every business faces risks, from economic risks such as poor sales to unavoidable natural risks such as earthquakes or tornadoes.

While a business cannot totally eliminate all the risks of doing business, marketers can reduce and manage risks through careful planning. Risks are managed by using the best available marketing information, analyzing opportunities, and making decisions to balance risks with adequate monetary returns.

Practice Situation

Imagine a business that you would like to start in the future. List at least three risks to the success of that business. Include economic risks, natural risks, and human risks. Then develop a plan for dealing with each of these risks. Will you prevent and control the risk by carefully training and screening employees? Will you transfer the risk by purchasing insurance? Or will you accept the risk as a part of doing business? Be ready to explain your reasoning.

Create a slide presentation describing the risks faced by your imaginary business and your plan for managing them. Each slide should list a risk, followed by the plan for dealing with it. Be specific. If you plan to add security to your store to prevent shoplifting, describe the types of security measures you will use. Include clip art or other art and graphics when appropriate to illustrate your risk management plan.

Risk Management Plan for (Name of Business)

Type of Risk

Risk management strategy
- Detail 1
- Detail 2
- Detail 3

Type of Risk

Risk management strategy
- Detail 1
- Detail 2
- Detail 3

Type of Risk

Risk management strategy
- Detail 1
- Detail 2
- Detail 3

Continued on next page

Presentation Directions

1. Start your presentation software program.

2. Follow the instructions for your software to create a title page. Save your file as **CH34PROB**.

3. Based on the information you have collected, create at least three more slides identifying risks to that business and your plan for managing them.

4. Save your work and print out a copy of your slides if your teacher has instructed you to do so.

5. Answer the following questions.

Interpreting Results

1. Why is it important for entrepreneurs to identify risks and develop risk management programs?

_____

_____

_____

_____

2. Pay attention to your classmates' slide presentations. What risks were shared by businesses that seemed unrelated? What businesses had unique risks and what were they?

_____

_____

_____

Drawing Conclusions

3. Why is it important for a marketing professional to have a risk management program in place?

_____

_____

_____

_____

CHAPTER 35 Developing a Business Plan

Vocabulary Review

DIRECTIONS: *Complete the crossword puzzle using key terms from the chapter.*

Across

4. How a person thinks a business should be run.
5. Cooperative association formed by labor unions or groups of employees for the benefit of their members. (2 words)
7. Money needed to finance a new business.
8. A process used to evaluate your likelihood to succeed at running a business. (2 words)

9. Geographical area from which a business draws its customers. (2 words)
10. Identifiable population statistics.
11. Proposal that describes every part of a new business. (2 words)
12. One of the 6 Cs of credit—a distinctive quality or trait.

Down

1. Written statements about the requirements of a job. (2 words)
2. Another term for buying income.
3. Something of value pledged to a lender to ensure repayment of a loan.
6. Chart showing reporting relationships.
10. Capital raised by borrowing money.

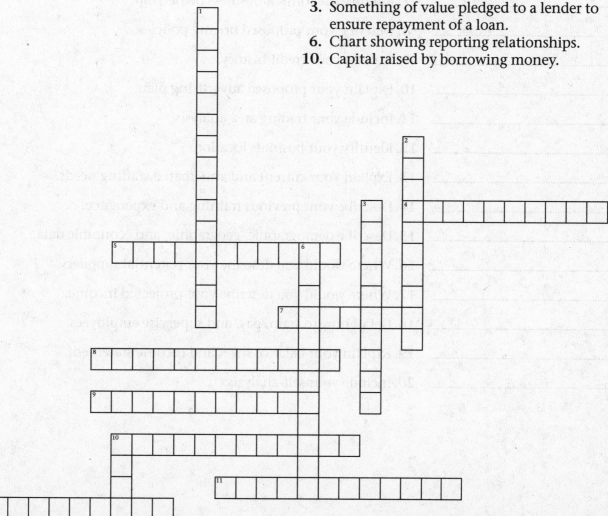

CHAPTER 35 Developing a Business Plan

Fact and Idea Review

DIRECTIONS: *For each of the activities identified below, indicate in which section of the business plan—**description and analysis (DA), organization and marketing plan (OMP)**, or **financial plan (FP)**—you would discuss the activity.*

_____ 1. Describe your plan and the products you will sell.

_____ 2. Detail promotional activities for the new business.

_____ 3. Describe sources of capital?

_____ 4. Describe a loan repayment plan.

_____ 5. Identify your business philosophy.

_____ 6. Describe your business's organization chart.

_____ 7. Identify the form of business ownership.

_____ 8. Describe your proposed pricing policies.

_____ 9. Explain your credit history.

_____ 10. Explain your proposed advertising plan.

_____ 11. Include your trading area analysis.

_____ 12. Identify your business location.

_____ 13. Explain your current and anticipated staffing needs.

_____ 14. Describe your previous training and experience.

_____ 15. Describe demographic, geographic, and economic data.

_____ 16. Where would you describe your potential suppliers.

_____ 17. Where would you describe your projected income.

_____ 18. Detail how to train, pay, and supervise employees.

_____ 19. Explain your balance sheet and income statement.

_____ 20. Include your self-analysis.

CHAPTER 35   Developing a Business Plan

Marketing Application 1

DIRECTIONS: *Select a proposed or existing business in your community, and do a trading area analysis on it. Use the checklist that follows as a guide. For each numbered item, circle or highlight one of the options in parentheses. Then, provide a rationale based on geographic, demographic, or economic data available for the area.*

Trading Area Analysis Checklist

A. Location

_____

B. Economic Considerations

   1. Economic base (primarily farming, manufacturing, retail, or mixed)

_____

_____

_____

   2. Economic trends (highly satisfactory, growing, stable, declining)

_____

_____

_____

   3. Permanency of neighborhood (old and well-established, old and reviving, new and promising, uncertain)

_____

_____

_____

   4. Seasonality (little or no seasonal change, mild seasonal change, major seasonal change)

_____

_____

_____

   5. Future of geographical area (most promising, satisfactory, uncertain, poor outlook)

_____

_____

_____

Continued on next page

C. Population

1. Income distribution (mostly wealthy, well-distributed, mostly middle income, poor)

   _____

   _____

2. Income trends (growing, large and stable, small and stable, declining)

   _____

   _____

3. Residential status (majority of people in area own homes, pay substantial rent, pay moderate rent, pay low rent)

   _____

D. Competition

1. Number of competing stores (few, average, many, too many)

   _____

   _____

2. Presence of chain stores in area (none, few, average number, many)

   _____

   _____

3. Quality of competing stores (poor quality, average quality, good quality, excellent quality)

   _____

   _____

4. Customer base (majority of customers shop in the area, out of the area)

   _____

   _____

E. General Attractiveness of Area

1. General character of city or geographical area (homes neat and clean, mixed, shabby)

   _____

2. General appearance of lawns, parks, streets, etc. (neat and attractive, needs some attention, run-down)

   _____

3. Availability of facilities (near banks, transportation, and utilities; far from facilities)

   _____

4. Quality of facilities (good schools and churches, average, poor)

   _____

CHAPTER 35 Developing a Business Plan

Marketing Application 2

DIRECTIONS: *Consider the following case study about an aspiring entrepreneur. You are to assume the role of a professional business consultant and advise this new entrepreneur about how to develop organization and marketing plans for his business. Use the information below and your knowledge of marketing to answer the questions that follow.*

Web Site Design Service

Satish Dulam has been working part-time as a cooperative education student during his senior year. He works for a small commercial art and design agency in a fast-growing suburban area. Since he has taken computer applications courses and is very familiar with Web page editing software, his employer allows him to design Web sites for existing clients. He has noticed that increasing numbers of local businesses are asking the agency for help in designing Web sites or for updating and improving their existing ones.

Satish feels that he can design Web pages with text, photos, graphics, and hyperlinks faster and more creatively than many of his coworkers at his place of business. So, he plans to begin a Web site design service after graduation, working out of his parents' residence. In this way he plans to keep his expenses down and work full-time as a Web site designer.

Satish has completed a self-analysis of his skills, knowledge, and abilities and is convinced that he could be successful in operating his own business. In addition, he has checked and received the necessary zoning, licensing, and permit approvals for a home-based business. Because his parents were excited about his idea, they provided him with the capital to buy the necessary computer equipment and software, set up a portion of their home as an office, and began promoting his service.

Satish believes his service has great sales potential because of the increasing number of small businesses moving into the area. He is sure that he can provide a quality Web site design service at competitive prices. However, he needs additional assistance with the development of his organization and marketing plans and has employed you as a professional business consultant to advise him.

1. Based upon the details in the case, what type of business organization should Satish initially establish and why?

   _____

   _____

   _____

   _____

   _____

   _____

Continued on next page

2. Why is it important for Satish to prepare a job description for himself?

_____

_____

_____

_____

3. What would you suggest that he include in his business plan regarding his proposed good or service?

_____

_____

_____

_____

4. What suggestions do you have relating to pricing policies?

_____

_____

_____

_____

5. What suggestions would you give to him regarding promotional activities?

_____

_____

_____

_____

_____

_____

Student _____ Date _____

Class _____ Teacher _____

CHAPTER 35 Developing a Business Plan

The DECA Connection

Role Play: Small Business Owner

Situation: You have catered a few parties for family and friends. After receiving accolades on each occasion, you have decided that you could create a profitable catering business in your local area. You have decided to open your own business with a friend who shares your enthusiasm for cooking and entertaining. From your marketing class in high school, you know that starting your own business requires a business plan, complete with company objectives, suggested personnel, and planned financing.

Activity: A family friend (judge) who works as a loan officer for a local bank has agreed to review your business plan with you. She has requested that you put your plan in writing and present it to her orally, as well.

Evaluation: You will be evaluated on how well you meet the following performance indicators:

- Develop a business plan.
- Develop company objectives.
- Develop a personnel organization plan.
- Describe sources of financing for businesses.
- Determine the financing needed to start a business.

DIRECTIONS: *Organize your thoughts around the performance indicators noted above. Use these performance indicators to jot down your ideas during the preparation period. Time your preparation period to last 15 minutes and your role play presentation to last a maximum of ten minutes. After your role play, use the performance indicators to evaluate your efforts.*

_____

_____

_____

_____

_____

_____

_____

_____

_____

_____

Continued on next page

Assessment: Assume each performance indicator is worth 20 points (20 × 5 = 100 points). Use the evaluation levels listed below for judging consistency.

Excellent (16–20) Participant demonstrated the performance indicator in a professional manner, exceeds business standards.

Good (10–15) Participant demonstrated the performance indicator in an acceptable manner; meets minimal business standards; there would be no need for additional formalized training at this time.

Fair (4–9) Participant demonstrated the performance indicator with limited effectiveness; performance generally fell below minimal business standards; additional training would be required to improve knowledge, attitude, and/or skills.

Poor (0–3) Participant demonstrated the performance indicator with little effectiveness or not at all; a great deal of formal training would be needed.

Develop a business plan.   Score _____

_____

_____

_____

Develop company objectives.   Score _____

_____

_____

_____

Develop a personnel organization plan.   Score _____

_____

_____

_____

Describe sources of financing for businesses.   Score _____

_____

_____

_____

Determine the financing needed to start a business.   Score _____

_____

_____

_____

_____

CHAPTER **35** Developing a Business Plan

Software Activity (Optional)

Presentation Application

OBJECTIVE: *To create a marketing plan for a new business.*

ACTIVITY: A business plan is a vital component of any new business because it will help you obtain financing, open your business, and successfully manage your business. An important part of any business plan is a marketing plan—a plan for pricing and promoting your products.

Imagine a business you would like to open and create a marketing plan for that business. Create a pricing policy that will produce a profit and be low enough to attract customers. Decide what promotional activities you will undertake to attract customers to your business. Be specific: What is your advertising budget? What type of advertising will you utilize?

Develop a slide presentation to explain your marketing plan. Your slide presentation should include a title slide and at least three more slides explaining your pricing policy and promotional activities.

Marketing Plan for
(Name of Business)

Promotional Activities
Advertising Budget
Target Media

Promotional Activities
Advertising
Other promotions
Seasonal promotions

Pricing Policy
- Price of product
- Other expenses
- Desired profit
- Competitors' prices

Continued on next page

Presentation Directions

1. Start your presentation software program.

2. Follow the directions for your software to create a title slide. Save the file as **CH35PROB**.

3. Based on the marketing plan you have developed, create at least three more slides to describe and justify the marketing plan.

4. Save your work.

5. Print out a copy of your slides if your teacher has instructed you to do so.

6. Answer the following questions.

Interpreting Results

1. How will your competitors' prices affect your pricing policy? When would a business be able to charge more or less than its competitors?

_____

_____

_____

_____

_____

2. Compare your slide presentation with those of your classmates. Examine the presentations to see if their marketing plans were clearly explained. Describe the similarities and differences between the plans and presentations.

_____

_____

_____

_____

_____

Drawing Conclusions

3. Why is it important to create a marketing plan as part of a business plan before you open your business?

_____

_____

_____

_____

_____

_____

CHAPTER **36** Financing the Business

Vocabulary Review

DIRECTIONS: *Match each definition with the correct term.*

asset	interest	net worth
balance sheet	liability	personal financial statement
cash flow statement	net income	principal
gross sales	net sales	start-up costs
income statement		

_____ 1. The amount left after operating expenses are subtracted from gross profit.

_____ 2. This financial statement is often called a profit and loss statement.

_____ 3. A summary of your current financial condition.

_____ 4. A projection of how much money you will need for your business's first year of operation.

_____ 5. The total of all sales returns and allowances is subtracted from gross sales to get this result.

_____ 6. Anything of monetary value that you own.

_____ 7. A monthly plan that shows when you anticipate cash coming into the business and when you expect to pay out cash.

_____ 8. A summary of a business's assets, liabilities, and owner's equity.

_____ 9. The difference between the assets of a business and its liabilities.

_____ 10. An amount you pay for the use of money that you borrowed.

_____ 11. The total of all sales for any period of time.

_____ 12. A debt that you owe.

_____ 13. The amount that you borrow.

CHAPTER **36** Financing the Business

Fact and Idea Review

DIRECTIONS: *Complete each sentence using the correct term.*

cost of goods sold	interest	operating expenses
fixed expenses	net income from operations	rate of interest
gross pay	net pay	total expenses
gross sales	net profit (or loss) after taxes	variable expenses
income statement		

1. If your company sells only on a cash basis, then your _____ will be the total of your cash sales.

2. _____ are divided into variable and fixed expenses.

3. The total amount spent to produce or buy the merchandise to be sold is called the _____.

4. The _____ is a summary of business income and expenses during a specific period, such as a month, quarter, or a year.

5. _____ change from one month to the next based upon the needs of the business.

6. The amount earned by an employee is that person's _____.

7. Costs which stay the same for a certain period of time such as rent or insurance are called _____.

8. _____ is found by subtracting total expenses from gross profit.

9. _____ is what an employee receives after deductions for taxes, insurance, and voluntary deductions.

10. Total variable expenses added to total fixed expenses equal your _____.

11. The amount of money left over after federal, state, and local taxes are subtracted represents a business's _____.

12. If you borrow money to start a business, you will also have to pay _____.

13. Interest expressed as a percentage of the principal is called the _____.

CHAPTER **36** Financing the Business

Marketing Application 1

DIRECTIONS: *Alanzo Martinez and Edgar Ruiz own a recreational vehicle dealership and repair facility called Sports Unlimited. Study the following information on the business. Then use it and the form on the following page to prepare balance sheets for the partnership for two consecutive years.*

Year 1

As of July 31, 20—, the business had these assets: $65,000 in the bank, $800 in the till, and $50 in petty cash. Accounts receivable came to $26,300 and inventory to $1,950,000. The firm had prepaid a six-month insurance policy and license fees—a total of $11,000. The business site, three acres owned by the partners, was valued at $525,000. The dealership's building, also owned by the partnership, was appraised at $650,000. Equipment used in the business totaled $55,775; furniture and fixtures were worth $12,425. The business owned one delivery van valued at $28,000.

As of the same date, the business had these liabilities: accounts payable of $620,000; notes totaling $480,000 (one short-term note for $130,000 and another long-term note on the building for $350,000); and taxes payable of $32,800. Accrued payroll was $15,000. The partners owed $225,000 on the property.

Year 2

As of July 31, 20— the business had the following assets: $68,000 in the bank, $1,500 in the till, and $100 in petty cash. Accounts receivable came to $27,700 and inventory to $2,125,000. The business had prepaid insurance and licenses of $12,500. The business site was appraised at $538,000 and the building at $664,000. Equipment used in the business totaled $62,500; furniture and fixtures were worth $13,000. The business's delivery van depreciated to $20,000. It had added a pick-up truck worth $18,000.

As of the same date, the business had these liabilities: accounts payable of $630,000, notes totaling $330,000 (a new short-term note for $90,000 and the old long-term note on the building, now worth $340,000), and taxes payable of $40,500. Accrued payroll was $17,100. The partners owed $200,000 on the property.

Continued on next page

Sports Unlimited
Balance Sheet

	20—	20—
Current Assets		
Cash	_____	_____
Accounts receivable	_____	_____
Inventory	_____	_____
Fixed Assets		
Real estate and building	_____	_____
Fixtures and equipment	_____	_____
Vehicles	_____	_____
Other Assets		
Licenses and insurance	_____	_____
Goodwill	_____	_____
TOTAL ASSETS	_____	_____
Current Liabilities		
Notes payable (due within one year)	_____	_____
Accounts payable	_____	_____
Accrued expenses (payroll)	_____	_____
Taxes owed	_____	_____
Long-Term Liabilities		
Notes payable (due after one year)	_____	_____
Other (property mortgage)	_____	_____
TOTAL LIABILITIES	_____	_____
NET WORTH (ASSETS minus LIABILITIES)	_____	_____

TOTAL LIABILITIES plus NET WORTH should equal ASSETS

CHAPTER 36 Financing the Business

Marketing Application 2

DIRECTIONS: *Hanna Lukasik, a new entrepreneur, has owned Renata European Hair Studio & Spa for six months. She is completing a cash flow statement for the remaining six months of her first year of operation. Study the following information on the business provided below. Use it and the cash flow form she has developed to prepare a cash flow statement for the last six months of Year 1 for the business.*

Year 1

Hanna entered her seventh month of business in July with a beginning balance of $4,200 in the bank. She is projecting $5,000 in sales for the month of July and an increase of $500 in sales receipts for each month thereafter. For the first three months, her supply costs (chemicals, styling products, etc.) will total $500 each month. Beginning in October her supply costs will increase to $600 for each of the remaining months. Part-time labor costs are $1,500 for the first three months and will then rise to $1,800 per month. Overhead (electricity, gas, etc.) is projected to be $300 for each month. The owner will pay herself a salary of $2,500 for the first month and a $100 increase for each month thereafter. Because she owns the building, there are no rent expenses. Insurance of $500 is paid in July and again in October. She will purchase a $2,500 computer during October. Advertising in the Yellow Pages will cost $200 each month. Telephone costs will be $150 for each of the first three months and then $175 for each of the remaining months. Her personal income taxes are projected to be $350 for each of the first three months and then total $400 for each of the remaining months.

Continued on next page

Renata European Hair Studio & Spa
Projected Cash Flow Statement

Statement for the six months ending December 31, 20—

MONTH	July	Aug.	Sep.	Oct.	Nov.	Dec.
Total Cash Income						
Sales Receipts						
Expenses						
Materials						
Labor						
Overhead						
Salaries						
Rent						
Insurance						
Office Equipment						
Advertising						
Telephone						
Income tax						
Total Expenses						
NET CASH FLOW						
Beginning balance						
CASH SURPLUS						
Cash deeds						

CHAPTER 36 Financing the Business

The DECA Connection

Role Play: School Store Manager

Situation: You are to assume the role of assistant manager for your DECA school store. Your DECA Chapter has just voted to use some of the school store's profits to subsidize DECA members who become eligible to compete at this year's National DECA Conference. At this point in the year, it is important to see just how well the school store is doing. This is especially important because you instituted a special school credit card for students with a "B" or better grade average. They have 30 days to pay for their credit charges. Therefore, the school store manager has asked that you prepare a profit and loss statement and analyze its operations to date.

Activity: The school store manager (judge) wants you to prepare a profit and loss statement for the first three months of operation. Use the following figures in your calculations: Sales $15,600; sales returns $100; cost of goods sold $9,300; depreciation on the sales register $45 and on the fixtures $30; employee salaries $2,880; payroll taxes $432; promotion $775; and miscellaneous expenses $210. To analyze the profit and loss statement, calculate the operating ratios for cost of goods sold, gross profit, promotion, total expenses, and net profit from operations. Also be prepared to explain why the net profit does not reflect the actual cash available at any given time, especially when considering the money needed for the National DECA Conference competitors.

Evaluation: You will be evaluated on how well you meet the following performance indicators:

- Describe the nature of business records.
- Prepare profit and loss statements.
- Calculate financial ratios.
- Describe the nature of profit and loss statements.
- Describe the nature of cash flow statements.

DIRECTIONS: *Organize your thoughts around the performance indicators noted above. Use these performance indicators to jot down your ideas during the preparation period. Time your preparation period to last 15 minutes and your role play presentation to last a maximum of ten minutes. After your role play, use the performance indicators to evaluate your efforts.*

_____

_____

_____

_____

_____

_____

Continued on next page

Assessment: Assume each performance indicator is worth 20 points (20 × 5 = 100 points). Use the evaluation levels listed below for judging consistency.

Excellent (16–20) Participant demonstrated the performance indicator in a professional manner, exceeds business standards.

Good (10–15) Participant demonstrated the performance indicator in an acceptable manner; meets minimal business standards; there would be no need for additional formalized training at this time.

Fair (4–9) Participant demonstrated the performance indicator with limited effectiveness; performance generally fell below minimal business standards; additional training would be required to improve knowledge, attitude, and/or skills.

Poor (0–3) Participant demonstrated the performance indicator with little effectiveness or not at all; a great deal of formal training would be needed.

Describe the nature of business records.   Score _____

_____

_____

_____

Prepare profit and loss statements.   Score _____

_____

_____

_____

Calculate financial ratios.   Score _____

_____

_____

_____

Describe the nature of profit and loss statements.   Score _____

_____

_____

_____

Describe the nature of cash flow statements.   Score _____

_____

_____

_____

CHAPTER 36 Financing the Business

Spreadsheet Application

OBJECTIVE: *Calculate startup costs.*

ACTIVITY: Startup costs are the expenses that entrepreneurs have when they first set up their businesses. To identify startup costs, entrepreneurs review every aspect of their business plan and list everything that requires a cash outlay before the business even opens. A dollar estimate should be made for each item. The startup expenses for a new business are listed and estimated on the printout shown below. Use a spreadsheet program to calculate a subtotal for each category as well as a total for all expenses.

	A	B	C
1	**Chapter 36 Financing the Business**		
2			
3			
4		**Total Funds Required**	**Subtotals/Totals**
5	FIXED ASSETS		
6	Equipment	$11,500	
7	Fixtures	$25,400	
8	Furniture	$5,450	
9	Outdoor Signs	$560	
10	(Subtotal)		
11	PRE-PAID ITEMS AND DEPOSITS		
12	Rent Deposit	$500	
13	Utilities Deposit	$100	
14	Telephone Deposit	$200	
15	Insurance Payments	$850	
16	Taxes, Licenses, and Fees	$150	
17	(Subtotal)		
18	PRE-OPENING EXPENSES		
19	Advertising and Promotion	$1,500	
20	Training	$800	
21	Legal and Accounting Services	$2,000	
22	(Subtotal)		
23	INVENTORY AND SUPPLIES		
24	Goods Purchased	$80,000	
25	Supplies	$2,600	
26	(Subtotal)		
27	WORKING CAPITAL		
28	Petty Cash	$200	
29	Projected Cash Deficits	$5,000	
30	3-Months Operating Expenses	$28,500	
31	(Subtotal)		
32	TOTAL		

Continued on next page

Spreadsheet Directions

1. Start your spreadsheet software program.

2. Create a spreadsheet like the one on page 325.

3. In column C, enter a formula to calculate the subtotal for each of the categories listed. After calculating each subtotal, enter a formula for a total of all startup expenses.

4. After completing your calculations, save your work to a new file.

5. Print out a copy of your work if your teacher has instructed you to do so.

6. Answer the following questions.

Interpreting Results

1. Examine the data for each of the subtotals. Which category has the highest expenses? Which has the lowest?

_____

_____

_____

2. What is the total startup expenses required for this business?

_____

_____

_____

Drawing Conclusions

3. Many of these expenses are based on estimates. What will be the impact of underestimating specific expenses?

_____

_____

_____

_____

_____

4. Will an entrepreneur be able to borrow funds to cover all these startup expenses?

_____

_____

_____

_____

CHAPTER 37 Identifying Career Opportunities

Vocabulary Review

DIRECTIONS: *Match each definition with the correct term.*

aptitude	*Occupational Outlook Handbook (OOH)*
career outlook	planning goals
internship	specific goal
lifestyle goals	realistic goal
*O*NET*	values
occupational area	

_____ 1. The number and types of jobs available in any field.

_____ 2. Paid or nonpaid position that provides direct work experience and exposure to aspects of a career.

_____ 3. Steps you take to get from where you are now to where you want to be.

_____ 4. An ability, natural talent, or a potential for learning a certain skill.

_____ 5. Reference that gives detailed information on educational requirements, salaries, working conditions, and job prospects in a wide range of occupations.

_____ 6. A goal stated in exact terms and with some detail.

_____ 7. Your ambitions for the way you hope to live your life.

_____ 8. A database with information on skills, abilities, knowledge, work activities, and interests associated with occupations.

_____ 9. Beliefs that are important to you and help determine how you live your life.

_____ 10. A goal that you have a reasonable chance of attaining.

_____ 11. A category of jobs that involvs similar interests and skills.

CHAPTER 37 Identifying Career Opportunities

Fact and Idea Review

DIRECTIONS: *Complete the following statements by filling in the blanks using words or phrases from the chapter. Note: In some cases, there may be more than one correct answer.*

1. Deciding whether you'd prefer to live in the city or the country, or if you value leisure time over work, is part of setting _____.

2. When you make a survey of your values, interests, skills and aptitudes, personality, preferred work environment, and relationship preferences, you are doing a form of _____.

3. At the center of most people's lifestyle goals will probably be their _____.

4. In deciding which career is ideal for you, you should assess whether you relate best to data, _____, or _____.

5. Learning about a particular career by talking to someone who works in that career is known as an _____.

6. As you look at a career, it is important to ask whether it will provide the _____ support for the lifestyle you want.

7. More than anything else, jobs are distinguished by their _____ and _____.

8. Trying a job to help you learn about it is called _____.

9. A personal career profile allows you to compare your self-assessment side by side with a particular _____.

10. In order to avoid being locked into an unsuitable career, you should make your decisions _____.

11. When you set your planning goals, you should start with your _____ career goal.

12. Writing down your long-range goals, your medium-range goals, and your short-range goals will produce a personal _____.

CHAPTER 37 Identifying Career Opportunities

Marketing Application 1

DIRECTIONS: *Study the lifestyle patterns below. On the lines following each diagram on this and the next page, describe a real or fictional person whose lifestyle fits that pattern.*

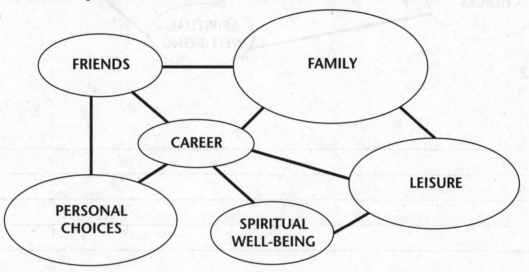

Pattern 1

_____

_____

_____

_____

_____

_____

_____

_____

_____

_____

_____

_____

_____

_____

Continued on next page

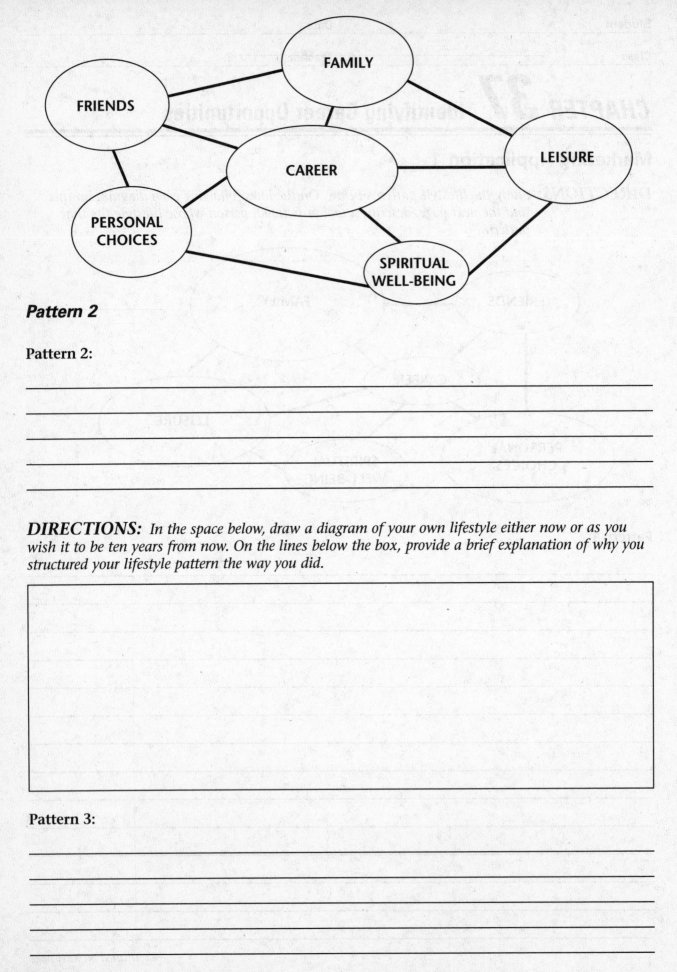

Pattern 2

Pattern 2:

_____

_____

_____

_____

_____

DIRECTIONS: _In the space below, draw a diagram of your own lifestyle either now or as you wish it to be ten years from now. On the lines below the box, provide a brief explanation of why you structured your lifestyle pattern the way you did._

Pattern 3:

_____

_____

_____

_____

_____

CHAPTER **37** Identifying Career Opportunities

Marketing Application 2

DIRECTIONS: *Select a career that interests you, and fill out the following questionnaire regarding it. Then based on what you learn, decide if it might be a suitable career choice for you.*

Career: _____

A. Values

Does this career match my values? Explain.

_____

B. Salaries and Benefits

1. What is the salary range from beginning to highest level in this career?

   _____

2. Would my salary be adequate to support my lifestyle in 5, 10, or 20 years? Explain.

   _____

3. Will this career provide the benefits I need? Explain.

   _____

C. Education/Training Required

1. What requirements for pursuing this career have I already completed?

   _____

2. What requirements must I complete before I can enter this career?

   _____

3. What additional training will help me advance in this career?

   _____

4. Considering my school record, are these requirements realistic for me?

   _____

5. How will I pay for this?

   _____

Continued on next page

D. Career Duties and Responsibilities

Do the duties and responsibilities sound interesting? Why?

_____

_____

E. Skills and Aptitudes Required

Do I have the skills and aptitudes needed to succeed in this career? Specify.

_____

_____

F. Type of Personality Needed

Do I have the type of personality needed in this career? Explain.

_____

_____

_____

G. Work Environment and Relationships

1. Is the working environment satisfactory? Explain.

_____

_____

2. Are the working hours compatible with my future lifestyle? Explain.

_____

_____

3. Do the data, people, and things relationships match my own preferences? Explain.

_____

_____

H. Career Outlook

1. Will there be a demand for this career when I am ready?

_____

2. Am I willing to relocate to have this career? Qualify your answer.

_____

3. Is this a possible career choice? Explain.

_____

_____

_____

_____

CHAPTER 37 Identifying Career Opportunities

The DECA Connection

Role Play: Intern Coordinator

Situation: You are to assume the role of employee of a large advertising agency. Your agency has formed a partnership with a local high school to provide unpaid internships for high school students interested in advertising careers.

Activity: Your supervisor (judge) has asked you to develop plans for four internships for presentation to the rest of the management team and the high school counselors. You are to present your ideas to your supervisor.

Evaluation: You will be evaluated on how well you meet the following performance indicators:

- Assess personal interests and skills needed for success in business.
- Describe techniques for obtaining work experience.
- Analyze employer expectations in the business environment.
- Explain employment opportunities in marketing.
- Make oral presentations.

DIRECTIONS: *Organize your thoughts around the performance indicators noted above. Use these performance indicators to jot down your ideas during the preparation period. Time your preparation period to last 15 minutes and your role play presentation to last a maximum of ten minutes. After your role play, use the performance indicators to evaluate your efforts.*

_____

_____

_____

_____

_____

_____

_____

_____

_____

_____

Continued on next page

Assessment: Assume each performance indicator is worth 20 points (20 × 5 = 100 points). Use the evaluation levels listed below for judging consistency.

Excellent (16–20) Participant demonstrated the performance indicator in a professional manner, exceeds business standards.

Good (10–15) Participant demonstrated the performance indicator in an acceptable manner; meets minimal business standards; there would be no need for additional formalized training at this time.

Fair (4–9) Participant demonstrated the performance indicator with limited effectiveness; performance generally fell below minimal business standards; additional training would be required to improve knowledge, attitude, and/or skills.

Poor (0–3) Participant demonstrated the performance indicator with little effectiveness or not at all; a great deal of formal training would be needed.

Assess personal interests and skills needed for success. Score _____

_____

_____

_____

Describe techniques for obtaining work experience. Score _____

_____

_____

_____

Analyze employer expectations in the business environment. Score _____

_____

_____

_____

Explain employment opportunities in marketing. Score _____

_____

_____

_____

Make oral presentations. Score _____

_____

_____

_____

_____

CHAPTER 37 Identifying Career Opportunities

Software Activity (Optional)

Spreadsheet Application

OBJECTIVE: *Calculate growth trends for marketing occupations.*

ACTIVITY: When planning a career in marketing, you should research employment trends. A key trend is whether the number of jobs in a particular field is rising or falling. Research can provide you with information about current and projected employment figures for thousands of occupations. The more you know, the easier it will be to decide what is right for you.

The printout below shows employment figures in 1996 for all occupations, all executive and managerial occupations, and selected managerial occupations. In addition, projected employment figures for 2006 are shown for these three categories:

	A	B	C	D
1	Chapter 37 Identifying Career Opportunities			
2				
3				
4			Projected	Projected
5		Employment	Employment	Percentage
6	OCCUPATIONAL AREAS	in 2002	in 2012	Increase/Decrease
7				
8	TOTAL, All Occupations	132,353,000	150,927,000	
9	All Executive and Managerial Occupations	13,542,000	15,866,000	
10	Advertising Services	291,000	324,000	
11	Travel and Tourism Marketing	156,000	179,000	
12	Food Marketing	249,000	294,000	
13	Restaurant Management	386,000	430,000	
14	Financial Services Marketing	343,000	498,000	
15	Business Services Marketing	800,000	946,000	
16	Fashion Merchandising	589,000	757,000	
17	Sports and Entertainment Marketing	207,000	202,000	
18	Retail Merchandising	482,000	620,000	
19	Apparel and Accessories Marketing	271,000	315,000	
20	Vehicles and Petroleum Marketing	232,000	251,000	

Spreadsheet Directions

1. Turn on your computer and open your spreadsheet software program.

2. Create a spreadsheet like the one above using your spreadsheet software.

3. Enter a formula for All Occupations to calculate the projected percentage increase or decrease in the number of jobs between 1996 and 2006.

4. Copy the formula to appropriate cells in all remaining rows. After completing your calculations, save your work to a new file.   *Continued on next page*

5. Print out a copy of your work if your teacher has instructed you to do so, and answer the questions that follow.

Interpreting Results

1. What is the projected percentage increase/decrease for All Occupations between 2002 and 2012?

_____

_____

2. Between 2002 and 2012, which marketing occupations are projected or expected to increase more than All Occupations?

_____

_____

_____

Drawing Conclusions

3. Why is it important to know the projected number of new jobs that will be created, as well as the percentage increase that is projected?

_____

_____

4. In planning for a future managerial career, which of the following occupations would offer you the greatest potential based on job growth: fashion merchandisers or financial services marketers?

_____

_____

_____

_____

5. Should you choose a career based on high growth projections for jobs in the field?

_____

_____

_____

_____

_____

CHAPTER 38 Finding and Applying for a Job

Vocabulary Review

DIRECTIONS: *Study the lists below and the Magic Square puzzle block. (Notice that each lettered vocabulary term has a matching lettered cell in the square.) To solve the puzzle, select a definition for each term from the numbered list. Then write each definition's number in the appropriately labeled puzzle cell. If you have correctly matched all the terms and definitions, the total of the numbers will be the same across each row and down each column.*

A. public employment agencies

B. standard English

C. cover letter

D. job lead

E. private employment agencies

F. staffing/temporary agencies

G. résumé

H. references

I. networking

1. Document that summarizes your personal information, education, and experience.

2. The formal style of writing and speaking you have learned in school.

3. Staffing services that hire you and assign you to a company.

4. These charge a fee to help you find a job.

5. The art of building alliances.

6. Tax supported places where you can find job hunting help and leads.

7. A letter of application without information on education and experience.

8. Information about a job opening.

9. People who know your work habits and will recommend you.

A	B	C
D	E	F
G	H	I

Magic number: all rows and columns add up to _____.

CHAPTER 38 Finding and Applying for a Job

Fact and Idea Review

DIRECTIONS: *Complete the following statements by filling in the blanks using words or phrases from the chapter.*

1. Before you can legally begin working, a document you will likely need is a _____.

2. When obvious sources of job leads have dried up, _____ is a way of finding more leads on your own.

3. _____ is finding and using contacts among all the people you know.

4. When speaking with prospective employers, it is expected that you will use _____.

5. In the employment history section of a job application form, you should list your employment in _____.

6. Frank thought of several adults who would vouch for his honesty and willingness to work and who could be _____ for him.

7. When you write a _____ to a prospective employer, you are essentially writing a sales pitch.

8. A _____ helps an employer during an interview by organizing all the facts about you that relate to the job you want.

9. The decision to hire an applicant is usually made on the basis of his or her _____.

10. During an interview, grooming, body language, and speech all combine to make a _____.

11. Finding out information about a company is an important thing to do _____ you schedule an interview.

12. Short phone calls, thank-you letters, or personal visits are all ways of _____ an interview.

Student		Date	

Class		Teacher	

CHAPTER 38 Finding and Applying for a Job

Marketing Application 1

DIRECTIONS: *The classified ads below describe two jobs in marketing. In each ad, the information about the job is incomplete. Answer the questions below to help you develop a plan to follow up on these job leads. If the information is not given, state that it is not given.*

A. ABC Marketing
Part-time customer help. Contact Bonnie 555-8617. Call for appointment 8–10am.

B. Marketing
CAREER MINDED?
Ecologically sound product brokerage seeks career oriented individuals to help fill entry-level positions with potential for management. Attitude more important than experience. 818/555-0331

---

1. What is the name of the company that is advertising?

   A. _____

   B. _____

2. How would knowing the name of the company help you in preparing to submit an application for the job?

   _____

   _____

3. Does the job involve dealing with a product or a service?

   A. _____

   B. _____

4. Both of the ads list telephone numbers for contact. Make a list of four or more questions that you would ask over the phone to help you in preparing to apply for these positions.

   _____

   _____

   _____

   _____

   _____

CHAPTER 38 Finding and Applying for a Job

Marketing Application 2

DIRECTIONS: *Preparing for an interview is an important step in the interview process. In many interviews, the interviewer will say something like "Tell me about yourself." This can present an awkward moment unless you are prepared to answer in a way that will make the interviewer want to hire you. Think about how you would respond to such a request and write your response on the lines below.*

_____

_____

_____

_____

_____

_____

_____

_____

_____

_____

_____

_____

_____

_____

_____

_____

_____

_____

_____

_____

_____

_____

_____

_____

CHAPTER **38** Finding and Applying for a Job

The DECA Connection

Role Play: Career Counselor

Situation: You are to assume the role of employee for a career-counseling firm. Your supervisor (judge) has asked you to prepare an oral presentation on using the Internet for gathering career information as well as for job searching.

Activity: Your presentation should include an explanation of how to use online government career resources as well as how to search for specific jobs using search engines and online career sites.

Evaluation: You will be evaluated on how well you meet the following performance indicators:

- Utilize job-search strategies.
- Demonstrate basic search skills on the Web.
- Explain employment opportunities in business.
- Identify sources of career information.
- Make oral presentations.

DIRECTIONS: *Organize your thoughts around the performance indicators noted above. Use these performance indicators to jot down your ideas during the preparation period. Time your preparation period to last 15 minutes and your role play presentation to last a maximum of ten minutes. After your role play, use the performance indicators to evaluate your efforts.*

_____

_____

_____

_____

_____

_____

_____

_____

_____

_____

_____

_____

Continued on next page

Assessment: Assume each performance indicator is worth 20 points (20 × 5 = 100 points). Use the evaluation levels listed below for judging consistency.

Excellent (16–20) Participant demonstrated the performance indicator in a professional manner, exceeds business standards.

Good (10–15) Participant demonstrated the performance indicator in an acceptable manner; meets minimal business standards; there would be no need for additional formalized training at this time.

Fair (4–9) Participant demonstrated the performance indicator with limited effectiveness; performance generally fell below minimal business standards; additional training would be required to improve knowledge, attitude, and/or skills.

Poor (0–3) Participant demonstrated the performance indicator with little effectiveness or not at all; a great deal of formal training would be needed.

Utilize job-search strategies. Score _____

_____

_____

_____

Demonstrate basic search skills on the Web. Score _____

_____

_____

_____

Explain employment opportunities in business. Score _____

_____

_____

_____

Identify sources of career information. Score _____

_____

_____

_____

Make oral presentations. Score _____

_____

_____

_____

_____

CHAPTER **38** Finding and Applying for a Job

Software Activity (Optional)

Word Processing Application

OBJECTIVE: *To write a letter of application in response to a job advertisement.*

ACTIVITY: Assume that you have just completed high school and are looking for a job. You see the following help wanted ad in the local newspaper.

Marketing/Sales Trainee

Advertising specialty and promotional products company seeks a motivated, customer-minded person for inside sales trainee position. Must be outgoing, organized, a team player, and have good communication skills. Salary, full benefits, and a sales territory position in 1–3 years. Send resume to: Karen Salo, Director of Human Resources, The Daily News, 28 N. First Street, Springfield, IL 60702.

To help you get started, the correct form to use in addressing your letter is shown below.

Month Day, Year

Ms. Karen Salo
Director of Human Resources
The Daily News
28 N. First Street
Springfield, IL 60702

Dear Ms. Salo:

Word Processing Directions

1. Turn on your computer and open your word processing software program.

2. Write a letter expressing interest in this position and describing why your skills fit the needs of the job. When you are finished, proofread your work and make any corrections.

3. Save your letter. Print out a copy of your work if your teacher has instructed you to do so, then answer the questions that follow.

Continued on next page

Interpreting Results

1. Compare the skills mentioned in your finished letter with the skills described in the ad. How does your letter highlight the skills that are needed for the job?

_____

_____

_____

_____

_____

_____

_____

2. Does your opening paragraph grab the attention of a reader? Is your letter accurate in spelling and grammar? Could your letter actually be sent to a prospective employer? Why or why not?

_____

_____

_____

_____

_____

_____

_____

Drawing Conclusions

3. Some newspaper ads give only a post office box number for replies. In such a case, whom should you address in the salutation?

_____

_____

_____

_____

_____

_____

_____

_____